Pot-Luck

Or, The British home cookery book; over a
thousand recipes from old family Ms. Books

Editor

May Byron

Alpha Editions

This edition published in 2019

ISBN : 9789353975524

Design and Setting By
Alpha Editions
email - alphaedis@gmail.com

POT-LUCK
OR THE BRITISH HOME
· · COOKERY BOOK · ·
OVER A THOUSAND RECIPES
FROM OLD FAMILY MS. BOOKS

COLLECTED & EDITED
BY MAY BYRON

"Old fashioned···but choicely good." IZAAK WALTON
"To be chronicled, and chronicled, and cut and
chronicled, and all to be praised" FULLER.

HODDER AND STOUGHTON
LONDON · NEW YORK · TORONTO

FIRST EDITION *in 1914*
SECOND EDITION *March 1915*

PREFACE

THIS is not the ordinary conventional cookery book, affording instructions how to dress, cook, and serve every variety of joint, fish, vegetable, etc., etc., etc. I take for granted that the reader is already acquainted with ordinary means and methods, and is versed in the preparation of simple food. To be a " good plain " cook always appears to me a contradiction in terms : because, if a person's treatment of *plain* dishes is *good*, she should be equally good at more elaborate ones. The same amount of application will serve for both. To make "plain" dishes palatable is, indeed, the highest test to which a woman can be put. The culinary skill demanded in these pages is of an everyday, common-sense character, such as any housewife, old or young, may exercise with pleasure. For these are chiefly specimens of the " good plain cooking " which was done by our mothers, and grandmothers, and great-grandmothers—the old home cookery before tinned things and preservatives were invented. This book is, in its way, unique.

In almost every family, at one time (before the present multiplication of printed cookery books) there existed a manuscript recipe book, or collection of old recipes tied together : passed on from one neighbour to another, or handed down from one generation to another as something really worth knowing. Some of these books and papers have been so frequently made use of, that they are almost worn out. The neat Italian handwriting is nearly obliterated, the yellow edges of the paper are stained and discoloured with wear : it is difficult to decipher the often shaky spelling and quaint phraseology of the MSS. To collect and select such recipes, therefore, is no easy task, and one very seldom attempted. They are often so jealously guarded and treasured by their owners, that the mere permission to copy them has to be besought as a special favour. I have, however, attempted to bring together a fairly representative collection, and I am sure that among the nearly eleven hundred formulas here set forth, many a reader will recognise with delight some little bit of cookery characteristic of her own old home, or will welcome with much satisfaction some long-lost method after whose ingredients she has frequently made search in vain.

It will be seen that these are chiefly country dishes, dating back to the good old days when cities had not claimed the multitudes of the shires. Some, indeed, go back to the seventeenth century, when the disparity between town and country was not so great—when hardly a Londoner but had his garden, and cornfields separated the City from the present West End. Where possible, I have indicated the origin of the recipe, or at least the county from which its possessor came. Should any reader care to perpetuate some cherished recipe not included here, I shall be most happy, if it be forwarded, to insert it in a future edition.

The country meals are not as those of the town. A good hearty breakfast, about eight : a good hearty dinner about one : and that never-sufficiently-to-be-praised evening meal entitled " high tea," about six : this is the usual farmhouse routine. Sometimes, indeed,—as on Sunday, for instance,—a light supper about eight-thirty is substituted for high tea : but for the most part, people who go to rest early need no more than a cup of cocoa or some other hot beverage at bedtime.

There is little doubt that " high tea " is a much more wholesome affair than late dinner. But, beyond this, it affords the opportunity for a vast variety of dishes, both salted and sweet, which do not easily come into the scope of any other meal : and, for this reason if no other, it is devoutly to be encouraged. A Guildhall banquet can hardly vary the accepted and monotonous sequence of its courses : but " high tea " provides you with continual surprises, unexpected tit-bits, appetising old-ashioned affairs. It obviates the use of alcoholic liquors : and is of all meals the most sociable, friendly, and satisfactory. I wish some able author would arise and devote his talents to the offering of *A Plea for High Tea.* A large number of these recipes would conduce to aid his eloquence. If only out of the hundred and fifty cakes here presented, he might vary the bill of fare perpetually: out of all the various cheese, egg, fish, and savoury made-dishes, it would be an interesting trial of skill to select the evening's bill of fare. But the latter are equally useful to the town-dweller, inasmuch that they are of large avail for luncheon or for Sunday supper. A glance at the list of contents will acquaint the reader with the very wide range here proffered for choice: and "right so," as the old authors would have expressed themselves, I commend this little book to all and sundry.

M. B.

CONTENTS

CHAPTER I

BEEF AND MUTTON RECIPES

FRESH MEAT

MUTTON

COLD MEAT

CHAPTER II

PORK AND VEAL RECIPES

PORK

VEAL

CHAPTER III

FOWL AND GAME

CHAPTER IV

SOUP RECIPES

CHAPTER V

FISH RECIPES

CONTENTS   XV

CHAPTER VI

VEGETABLES AND VEGETARIAN DISHES

b

CONTENTS

CHAPTER VII

SALADS

CHAPTER VIII

CHEESE DISHES

CHAPTER IX

EGG DISHES

CHAPTER X

SAVOURIES

CHAPTER XI

SAUCES

SAUCES FOR MEAT

CHAPTER XII

PICKLES

CHAPTER XIII

PUDDINGS

CHAPTER XIV

PASTRY AND SWEET DISHES

PASTRY

FRUIT DISHES

VARIOUS

CHAPTER XV

CREAMS, CUSTARDS, JUNKETS, SYLLABUBS, ETC.

CONTENTS

CUSTARDS

JUNKETS

SYLLABUBS

TRIFLES

CHAPTER XVI

JAMS, JELLIES, PRESERVES, FRUIT PASTES, ETC.

JAMS, JELLIES, MARMALADES

CHAPTER XVII

SWEETMEATS AND CANDIES

CHAPTER XVIII

CAKES

c

CONTENTS

CHAPTER XIX

BREAD, ROLLS, BUNS, MUFFINS, ETC.

CONTENTS

CHAPTER XX

BEVERAGES

HOME-MADE WINES (ALCOHOLIC)

BEERS (NON-ALCOHOLIC)

LEMONADE, SYRUPS, FRUIT VINEGARS, ETC.

VARIOUS MIXED BEVERAGES (ALCOHOLIC)

CONTENTS

CHAPTER XXI

INVALID AND CONVALESCENT COOKERY

INVALID AND CONVALESCENT COOKERY

INVALID BEVERAGES

CONTENTS

CHAPTER XXII

VARIOUS

SOME PRELIMINARY REMARKS

PLEASE read these attentively. They are most important to the successful carrying-out of the recipes. Practised and expert cooks may regard them as " coals to Newcastle," but to less experienced women they will be of value : there is a moment in everybody's life when a thing is learned for the first time, and indeed, some of the following points are unknown to, or neglected by, cooks who profess themselves quite proficient.

1. *Let all hot foods be served upon hot dishes, with hot plates,* and *kept hot* under a warmed cover. This rule is frequently ignored by people who consider they are good cooks, with the result that the most carefully prepared dish is spoiled. The simplest food served " hot-and-hot " is better than the most *recherché* one upon cold plates and dishes. If you can't heat your dishes, etc., in the oven or on the rack, put them in the fender, or dip them in hot water, or stand them on top of a boiling pan. But, by hook or crook, heat them.

2. *Vice-versa.* Never serve cold foods upon lukewarm or just-washed plates and dishes. Be sure

that a cold preparation *is* cold : and if not, take means to make it so. Stand it out-of-doors, or in a bowl of cold water, or in a basin of wet silver-sand : but get it cold, not horridly tepid.

3. *Always allow a little more than the time allotted in a recipe*, in arranging for the hour of a meal. Punctuality in serving a plain dish is better than a costly dish served late. As a rule, it is safe to allow *at least* a quarter of an hour per lb. for baking (plus a quarter of an hour extra " for the oven," *i.e.* before the meat starts cooking), and twenty minutes per lb. for boiling meat, with rather more for steaming ; it being remembered, in the former case, that no two range ovens are alike, and that it is very difficult to maintain the same degree of uniform heat for hours at a time (especially as certain ovens are affected by certain winds) : and in the second case, that *boiling*, as regards meat, is not *boiling* but quiet simmering. Meat *boiled* is meat spoiled. All this must be taken into consideration in arranging a meal. Where a gas-stove is employed, the heat can, of course, be maintained at a more uniform temperature. Steaming is, in almost every case of meat and vegetables, superior to boiling.

4. Always go by weight and measure : it is safer than " rule of thumb." The accurate balance of ingredients, especially as regards flavourings and seasonings, is one of the secrets of success : any deviation from it upsets the recipe. Lots of people

will not take the trouble to follow out the exact proportions defined, and then are astonished at the failure of their attempts. Occasionally, however, a recipe may be actually altered ; as, for instance, the next paragraph will show.

5. In boiled suet puddings, the best rule (whatever the recipe may say) is to use flour and breadcrumbs in equal quantities, or even in a larger proportion of crumbs than flour : never *all* flour. This ensures lightness. Suet should be grated rather than chopped : bread passed through a fine sieve, rather than grated. The cloth, if any, should be rinsed and wrung out in *boiling* water and well floured. Where a pudding is steamed, no cloth is required.

6. Dried fruits should be quickly washed, and dried in a clean cloth, before using. It is surprising how they accumulate dust and grit. All whole Valencia raisins should be *well* stoned, and sultanas *well* picked. Bought " stoned " raisins are never so fresh and nice as whole ones. Currants should be scalded and then dried as above. Many persons are too lazy to do this properly.

7. Never omit salt from the making of any so-called salted dish. Pepper is a matter of discretion—but salt is a matter of necessity. This applies especially to vegetables, sauces, and gravies, where folks too often forget it. But also remember to put a small pinch of salt into the making of every *sweet* dish—puddings, pies, cakes, custards,

etc. This is most important. It enhances and brings out the flavour in a marvellous manner.

8. It is better to keep jams and all dry stores against an inside wall. They will gather mould or mildew much sooner against an outer one.

9. Never, if possible, omit that trifling touch of decoration which makes the simplest dish look appetising, and the homeliest table attractive. A few sprigs of parsley, with cold dishes, or with fish : a little cut lemon, and so forth, are an immense addition to the look of a dish. And a jar of flowers upon the table—the cheapest, the commonest flowers and leaves—makes all the difference in the world. A meal then appears—without one's know_ing why—something more than merely eating to satisfy the wants of the body. It becomes a pleasant and attractive affair, beneficial and tonic to the mind.

10. *Use up* and make the best of what you have, before proceeding to purchase fresh material. But do not be penny-wise in the utilising of any scraps or remainders when they are evidently on the down-grade. Never let mere motives of economy tempt you to risk using anything which is in the least sour, stale, or tainted, especially as regards fish, stock, meat, or vegetables. Health is the first consideration of all.

Further practical hints will be found appended to the various sections.

POSTSCRIPT

The terms " spoonful," " cupful," etc., have been very loosely used by the original transcribers of these recipes. I have cleared up any doubt, to the best of my ability, by interpolating the (probable) correct amount. As a general rule it will be found that " spoonful " means *tablespoonful*, and " cupful," *breakfastcupful* ; but the reader must exercise her own discretion in two or three cases.

Several local, provincial, or obsolete words seem to require interpretation.

Barm and *yeast* are identical.

To *Cree* (North-country) is to expand by slow cooking in water. To *Plim* is the South-country equivalent.

To *Coddle* is to parboil.

Earning is curdling-liquid, such as rennet.

Farce is forcemeat or stuffing.

Peeps are flower-petals.

Pot may mean jar, pan, " crock," or " mug " (North-country), or gallipot : according to the context.

Sack may be modernised as very sweet white wine,—Sherry, Marsala, Madeira, etc.

French wine usually indicates claret, and *Lisbon wine*, port.

A *Tossing-pan* is a frying-pan.

CHAPTER I

BEEF AND MUTTON RECIPES

NOTE.—To the housewife pretty nearly at the end of her resources, no less than to the hungry folk for whom she caters, several of the following suggestions will come with all the force of novelty. I have divided them, for purposes of the cook's convenience, into methods of treating hot meat and cold. We are only too apt to become stale and monotonous in our repetition, month by month and year by year, of certain too-familiar joints and *réchauffés*. But anything which can obliterate the memory of the horrid word "hash," should be as desirable as it is rare. Where stews are concerned (whether of fresh or cooked meat), I would like to remind the reader that anything baked in earthenware is infinitely better cooked and better flavoured than it can ever be in a metal vessel. The earthenware retains and imparts heat and flavour in a most marvellous manner. And indeed, speaking generally, I would say, steer clear of metal whenever and wherever you can, making use of wood and earthenware alone. Also, it is to be observed, that careful basting (too frequently ignored) is an essential point, not only in the cooking, but in the appearance of any baked or roasted meat.

1

FRESH MEAT

1. BEEF COLLOP MINCED (Kent, 1809)

Chop two pounds of beef very fine, taking from it every particle of fat and string; put an onion shred small into a stewpan with pepper and salt and a piece of butter. Let them boil about a minute; put in the meat and move it about with a spoon till it looks a little white; then add a little good gravy and spice to your taste. Let it come to a boil, when it will be quite done enough.

2. GALANTINE OF BEEF (Hertfordshire)

Mince a quarter of a pound of beef and half a pound of bacon. Put both in a basin with six ounces of breadcrumbs, and pepper and salt. Beat two eggs and a gill of stock together and add to the other ingredients, and mix all well. Shape this into a nice roll, tie in a buttered pudding cloth, and boil for two hours; turn out, let it set, and glaze it.

3. ROLLED BEEF (Hertfordshire)

A pound and a half of steak or gravy beef, four ounces of breadcrumbs, an ounce and a half of chopped suet, one egg, seasoning to taste of parsley, thyme, salt, and pepper. The meat should be in one piece, and about half an inch thick. Put the meat on a board and flatten it with a rolling-pin. Mix all the dry ingredients after having chopped the parsley finely. Then add the beaten egg, or, if you wish to be very economical, a little milk. Spread the forcemeat over the beef, roll up,

and tie into shape with tape or string. Put into a
deep pie-dish. Pour over it three-quarters of a pint
of boiling water, cover and stew in a slow oven for
one and a half or two hours. Take out the meat, and
put it on a dish. Mix smooth a tablespoonful of flour
with cold water, add this to the gravy, place in a
saucepan, and stir over the fire till the gravy is
thick. Colour it with a little browning, pour over
the meat, and serve.

4. BEEF KIDNEYS À LA RUSSE (Hertfordshire)

Soak some beef kidney in cold water for an hour,
change the water once or twice as it colours. Then
set it in a saucepan, cover it with cold water and
bring to the boil; drain off the water and add more,
then simmer the kidney gently for fifteen minutes.
Pour off the liquor and cut out the sinew, etc., from
the kidney. Slice the meat thinly, dredge with
seasoned flour, and fry in hot butter until brown.
Take out the meat, stir in a tablespoonful of flour in
the butter and brown thoroughly; add a tablespoonful of tomato juice, and a little lemon juice, pepper
and salt, and sufficient gravy to make enough
sauce to cover the kidney. Place the meat in the
sauce and cook all slowly for one hour, adding some
gravy if necessary. Serve with fried croûtons of
bread, and tiny rolls of fried bacon.

5. BEEF OLIVES (Cheshire)

Take one and a half pounds of beef (steak for
preference) and cut it into pieces four inches long,
about the same in width, and half an inch thick.
Mince up the trimmings and odds and ends of the
beef, along with two ounces of suet, and one tea-

spoonful each of parsley, thyme, and marjoram.
Add three ounces of breadcrumbs, a grated lemon-
rind, a little grated nutmeg, one beaten egg, and
a pint of brown gravy, half a teaspoonful of salt,
and a little pepper. When these ingredients are
thoroughly united, beat out each piece of beef as
flat as possible, and spread each piece with the
above mixture : roll it up and tie it tightly. Place
the rolls in a stew-pan with one pint seasoned brown
gravy, and stew gently for three-quarters of an
hour. Dish with a border of mashed potato or
rice, and pour gravy round the olives.

6. FOR SPICED BEEF (Lancashire)
(This is a very good and old recipe)

To one gallon of boiling water add as much salt
as will swim an egg, half an ounce saltpetre, half
an ounce salt prunelle, half an ounce mustard seed,
ditto of cloves, cayenne pods, cinnamon, mace ;
one ounce of ginger, half a pound of sugar (Demerara) ; all to be boiled together. The spices to be
boiled in the water, and then the salt and sugar to be
added when cold. The meat to be put in this pickle
for several weeks. Keep turning. Silver side of
beef or any part of round.

7. STEWED RUMP OF BEEF (Eighteenth Century)

Half roast your beef, then put it in a large saucepan or cauldron, with two quarts of water, and one
of red wine, two or three blades of mace, a shalot,
a spoonful of lemon pickle, two of walnut ketchup,
the same of browning, cayenne pepper and salt to
your taste ; let it stew over a gentle fire, close covered
for two hours ; then take up your beef, and lay it on

a deep dish, skim off the fat, and strain the gravy, and put in half a pint of mushrooms; thicken your gravy, and pour it over your beef, lay round it forcemeat balls : garnish with horse radish, and serve it up.

8. BROILED BEEF STEAKS (Eighteenth Century)

Cut your steaks off a rump of beef about half an inch thick, let your fire be clear, rub your gridiron well with beef suet, when it is hot lay them on ; let them broil until they begin to brown, turn them, and, when the other side is brown, lay them on a hot dish, with a slice of butter betwixt every steak ; sprinkle a little pepper and salt over them, let them stand two or three minutes, then slice a shalot as thin as possible into a tablespoonful of water ; lay on your steaks again, keep turning them till they are done enough, put them on your dish, pour the shalot and water amongst them, and send them to the table.

9. TO DRESS BEEF STEAKS THE COMMON WAY (Eighteenth Century)

Fry your steaks in butter a good brown, then put in half a pint of water, an onion sliced, a spoonful of walnut ketchup, a little caper liquor, pepper and salt, cover them close with a dish and let them stew gently ; when they are done enough, thicken the gravy with flour and butter, and serve them up.

10. MADRAS STEAK (Hertfordshire)

Procure a good beef steak, dip it in flour, and place it in a baking tin, letting it lie flat, placing on the top slices of onions ; put greased paper over. Put in an oven and cook for twenty minutes ; mix together a teaspoonful of curry powder, a table-spoonful of vinegar in a cup of hot water, and add it to beef ; replace the lid and let stew gently for an hour and a half ; serve very hot with onion on top and gravy poured round.

11. STEWED STEAK (Sussex)

Fry first with one shalot, then put it into a pan, with a little good gravy, a teaspoonful of made mustard, a very little cayenne pepper, and a little salt. Cover closely and let it cook gently for two and a half hours. Then add a little browning, a little mushroom ketchup—or any other sauce—ladle the gravy over it and turn it once.

12. BRAZILIAN STEW (Sussex)

Take one pound of shin of beef, cut it into dice, dip the pieces into about two tablespoonfuls of vinegar. Stick one clove in an onion, take one carrot, one strip of celery, and add half a pint of water. Put the whole in a jar and cook slowly in a cool oven, or stand the jar in a saucepan of water.

13. FRENCH STEW (Surrey)

Cut into pieces two or three pounds of the lean of fresh, tender beef, veal, or pork ; peel and slice a quarter of a peck of ripe tomatoes : season the whole with a little pepper and salt. Put all into a stewpot, and cover it close, opening it only occa-sionally to see how it is cooking. Put no water to the stew, the tomato-juice is enough liquid. When the tomatoes are all dissolved, stir in a piece of fresh butter dredged with flour, and the stew remains about a quarter of an hour longer. When the meat is done through, have ready some bits of very dry toast, cut in three-corner shape, having the crust off. Dip the toast for a moment in some hot water, butter it, and stand it up round the inside of a deep dish. Fill in the stew and serve hot.

14. LANCASTER STEW (Hertfordshire)

Fry two large onions light brown; mix a tablespoon of flour and fry it; add a quart of thin stock or water, and a tablespoonful of vinegar. Cut two pounds of gravy beef or skirting into pieces, add them, let simmer for three hours; an hour before serving drop in some savoury balls, made with half a pound of flour, teaspoonful of baking powder, the same of salt, half of pepper, parsley, thyme, half an onion chopped, three tablespoonfuls of suet, mixed with water. Dish the meat in centre with balls around.

15. BOILED TONGUE (Eighteenth Century)

If your tongue be a dry one, steep it in water all night, then boil it three hours; if you would have it to eat hot, stick it with cloves, rub it over with the yolk of an egg, strew over it bread crumbs, baste it with butter, set it before the fire till it is a light brown; when you dish it up, pour a little brown gravy, or red wine sauce, mixed the same way as for venison; lay slices of currant jelly round it. N.B.—If it be a pickled one, only wash the water out of it.

VARIOUS

16. CORNISH PASTY (West-country)

Into half a pound of flour rub three ounces of lard or dripping, and a salt-spoonful of salt. Slice up finely about half a pound of uncooked potatoes, about half a pound of tender beefsteak cut into small pieces about two inches in length : add about two ounces of chopped onions. Make a paste with the flour and dripping, roll to about three-quarters of an inch thick, and cut it the size and shape of a dinner-plate. Lay the potatoes and meat on one half, and fold over the other half as for a jam "turn-over," moistening the edges with a little water, and pinch them in all round. Bake in a moderate oven from half to three-quarters of an hour.

17. MOCK GAME (Warwickshire)

Required : beef steak, rashers of bacon, red currant jelly, lemon, vinegar, salt. Cut steak into strips, roll up each strip with a slice of bacon inside, tie each roll. Fry these lightly, put rolls into a saucepan containing one tablespoonful of vinegar, one teaspoonful of grated lemon rind, two tablespoonfuls of red currant jelly, three or four pepper-corns, and cloves and salt to taste. Stew until tender, place the rolls on a hot dish, thicken the liquid, add some good stock, pour this over the steak and serve, garnished with toast sippets and red currant jelly and parsley.

18. STEWED OX TAILS (Devonshire)

Cut two ox-tails into joints and fry them in butter. Place them in a quart of cold water, with

a little onion, cloves, mace, lemon-peel, one tablespoonful of lemon-juice, and three sprigs of parsley ;
let all simmer gently for three hours, then take the
tails out and thicken the gravy with two or three
tablespoonfuls of flour. Strain it through a sieve,
season with pepper and salt ; place the tails in the
gravy, and gently simmer for one hour more. Dish
and serve with chopped parsley and toast.

19. TRIPE (Surrey)

Take two pounds of fresh tripe, well cleaned and
dressed. Cut the coarse fat away, and boil it for
about half an hour in equal parts of milk and water.
The water should have been on the fire for half an
hour previously, with four large, sliced (English)
onions in. When the tripe is cooked, make the
liquid into a rich onion sauce, and serve it very
hot over the tripe.

20. CURRIED TRIPE (Hertfordshire)

Take two or three large onions, and fry them in
dripping till tender. Chop them very fine, or, if
preferred, pass through a sieve, and put them with
a dessertspoonful of curry powder and peaflour
mixed. When quite smooth, add gradually one
pint of stock, and stir till it boils. Now take
one and a half pounds of boiled tripe, cut
it into pieces about one inch square, and put it
into the sauce. Let all stew together for one and
a half hours. Have ready some well boiled rice,
make a ball of it on the dish, pour the tripe into
the centre and serve. Squeeze a little lemon juice
over the whole. This dish is both economical and
nutritious.

21. FRICASSEE OF TRIPE (Yorkshire, 1769)

I

Take the whitest seam tripes you can get, and cut them in long pieces, put them into a stewpan with a little good gravy, a few breadcrumbs, a lump of butter, a little vinegar to your taste, and a little mustard if you like it. Shake it up all together with a little shredded parsley; let it stew slowly till done. Garnish your dish with sippets.

22. ANOTHER WAY

II

Take the whitest and thickest seam tripe, cut the white part in thin slices, put it into a stewpan with a little white gravy, lemon-juice, shredded lemon-peel, and a tablespoonful of white wine. Take the yolks of two or three eggs and beat them very well; put to them a little thick cream, shredded parsley, and two or three (minced) chives if you have any. Shake it all together over the fire till it be as thick as cream, but don't let it boil for fear it curdle. Garnish with sippets, sliced lemon, or mushrooms. This will eat like chicken.

MUTTON

23. BASQUE OF MUTTON (Eighteenth Century)

Take the caul of a leg of veal, lay it in a copper dish the size of a small punch bowl, take the lean of a leg of mutton that has been kept a week, chop it exceedingly small, take half its weight in beef marrow, the crumbs of a penny loaf, the yolks of four eggs, half a pint of red wine, the rind of half a lemon grated; mix it like sausage meat, and lay it in your caul in the inside of your dish, close up the caul, and bake it in a quick oven; when it comes out, lay your dish upside down, and turn the whole out; pour over it brown gravy and send it up with venison sauce in a boat. Garnish with pickles.

24. ROLLED BREAST OF MUTTON (Hertfordshire)

Take a breast of mutton, lay it on a board, and remove the bones. Trim it neatly, and remove some of the fat. Cover the side from which the bones have been removed with slices of ham, and then with a layer of meat stuffing, which has a flavouring of lemon grated. Quarter some pickled walnuts, and place them here and there on the forcemeat. Now roll the meat neatly and tightly, screwing the flap over. Bind it round with tape and roast it. The meat should be wrapped in caul or greased paper for the first hour it is in the roaster, and afterwards basted in the ordinary way. Place the mutton on a hot dish, remove the tape, and make a little good gravy. Strain it well, and stir it into a tablespoonful of red currant jelly, and pour it over and round the meat. Then take two tablespoonfuls of lightly browned breadcrumbs, a teaspoonful of mixed herbs, a quarter of a teaspoonful of pepper, half a teaspoonful of salt, and mix thoroughly. Sprinkle this over the meat and serve.

25. THE BEST WAY TO COOK A CHOP (Essex)

Place the chop in a colander and pour over it some boiling water. This seals up the tissues and does not allow any nutritious juices to be wasted.

Now place it on a gridiron over a hot, clear fire, and
cook in the usual manner. Turn with a knife, and
do not prick in any way. Serve with a small piece
of butter and a dust of pepper and salt.

26. NAPLES CHOPS (Warwickshire)

Take as many nice loin chops as you require for
a dish ; trim away nearly all the fat, fry them
lightly and place in a stewpan, dredging them
quickly with browned flour. Cut in slices two or three
large onions, season highly with black pepper, and
fry to a golden brown ; scatter the onions over the
chops, and pour in enough stock or water just to
cover the meat. Have a pint of chestnuts boiled
and peeled, lay them on the onions, place a cover
on the stewpan, and cook the contents slowly for
two hours. The onions and chestnuts will be cooked
by the time the meat is tender.

27. DEVILLED CUTLETS (Essex)

One and a half pounds of nicely trimmed cutlets,
two ounces of butter, quarter of a pint of cream,
one teaspoonful of cornflour, one small teaspoonful
of mustard, a good pinch of cayenne, two dessertspoonfuls of Worcester sauce. Melt the butter in
a frying pan, lay in the cutlets, which should be
smartly trimmed, and fry lightly till cooked. Take
up the cutlets on a plate and keep hot. Put the
cornflour, mustard, and cayenne into a basin, mix
in the Worcester sauce gradually until smooth. Put
the frying pan on the fire again, with the butter still
in it in which the cutlets were fried. Add the
cream and stir well together. Let it boil up ; now

put in the Worcester sauce mixture. Stir well
until it boils up and is quite smooth. Lay in the
cutlets and let them stand at the side of the fire
for two or three minutes until *very hot* through.
Dish in two rows and pour the sauce over. If it be
too thick before dishing, half a cup of milk with a
small scrap of butter may be stirred in to thin it.

28. HAGGIS (Scotland)

Having washed a sheep's heart and lights, parboil
and mince them small, with a pound of suet and
two large onions : add rather less than two handfuls
of oatmeal, and season thoroughly with pepper
and salt : mix all these articles well together, sew
them up tightly in a bag, and boil for about three
hours : serve with some good gravy, seasoned and
thickened, or with sharp sauce. This is a cheap,
but not a very delicate dish.

29. A HARICOT OF MUTTON OR LAMB
(Eighteenth Century)

Cut a neck or loin of mutton or lamb in nice cutlets, and fry them a light brown ; have ready some
very good gravy made of the scrag of the mutton
and some veal, with a piece of lean bacon and a few
capers ; season to your taste with pepper, salt, thyme,
onions, which must be strained off, and added to
the cutlets, just an hour before you send them to
the table. Cook them on a slow fire, dish them up
handsomely with turnips and carrots cut in small
dice, with a good deal of gravy, thickened with a
piece of butter rolled in flour ; if they are not tender
they will not be good. Send them up very hot.

30. ANOTHER WAY

Take a neck of mutton and cut it into chops,
flour them and put them into a stewpan, set them
over the fire, and keep turning them till brown,
then take them out, and put a little water into the
same pan, and keep it stirring until brown over the
fire, with a bunch of sweet herbs, a bay leaf, an
onion, and what other spice you please ; boil them
well together, and then strain the broth through a
sieve into an earthen pot by itself, and skim the
fat off, which done, it is good gravy; then add
turnips and carrots, with two small onions, a little
celery and other roots, then put the gravy to them,
and as much water as will cover them ; keep it
over a gentle fire till ready to serve up.

31. HARICOT OF A LEG OF MUTTON
(Eighteenth Century)

Cut the best end of a leg of mutton into chops in
single ribs, flatten them, and fry a light brown ; then
put them in a large saucepan, with two quarts of
water, a large carrot cut in slices, cut at the edge
like wheels ; when they have stewed for a quarter
of an hour, put in two turnips cut in square slices,
the white part of a head of celery, two heads of
cabbage lettuces fried, and cayenne to your taste;
boil them all together till they are tender. The
gravy is not to be thickened. Put into a tureen or
soup dish.

32. HARICOT MUTTON (Yorkshire)

Two pounds of best end neck of mutton, one pint
of warm water or stock, one ounce of dripping,
one carrot, one turnip, one onion, half a table-

spoonful flour, salt, and pepper. Cut the meat into small joints, remove all gristle and most of the fat, make the dripping quite hot and fry the meat quickly in it, and then place in another pan. Fry the sliced onion, add to the meat also the carrot and turnip cut in small squares. Simmer gently one and a half to two hours, skim off any fat. Mix the flour with a little cold water, stir into the gravy, allow it to boil for a few minutes— then serve.

33. POTTED HEAD (Scotland)

Take half a sheep's head, removing the brains ; wash the head thoroughly and soak it for an hour or two in warm water ; then break it up and lay it in a pan with just sufficient water to cover it well ; bring to the boil, skim well, and simmer steadily, closely covered, till the bones will slip from the flesh. Now lift the meat out, remove the bones, cut into dice, seasoning it as you do so with the following mixture : two teaspoonfuls of salt, one of freshly ground black pepper, one of powdered allspice, and if liked, a saltspoonful of cayenne. Return the meat to the pan, allow it to simmer uncovered for a few minutes, then pour it, with its liquor strained, into a wetted basin or mould, putting in with it the tongue, which should have been cooked separately, and leave till set. If liked, the liquor may be sharply boiled up to reduce it while the meat is being cut up.

34. HODGE PODGE OF MUTTON
(Eighteenth Century)

Cut a neck or loin of mutton into steaks (i.e. chops or cutlets), take off all the fat, then put the

steaks into a pitcher or jar, with lettuce, turnips,
carrots, two cucumbers cut in quarters, four or five
onions, and pepper and salt; you must not put any
water to it; stop the pitcher very close, then set
it in a pan of boiling water; let it boil four hours.
Keep the pan supplied with fresh boiling water
as it wastes.

35. HODGE PODGE (Kent, 1809)

Take a quantity of shelled green peas, with onions,
carrots, and turnips, and a sprinkling of salt and
pepper. Put them into a pot *with a lid*, with a
quantity of water corresponding to the quantity of
soup wanted, containing a few mutton or lamb
chops. Let the mess boil slowly, or simmer for
five or six hours.

36. HOT-POT (Essex)

This should be made in a round deep pie-dish.
Take two pounds of mutton chops, four sheep's
kidneys, and one pound or more of peeled potatoes.
Place alternate layers of the sliced potatoes, chops,
and kidneys, with sliced onions, pepper, and salt,
till the dish is full. If liked, oysters and anchovies
may be added, and are a great improvement to the
flavour of the hot-pot. Cover the top of the dish
with whole potatoes, and pour over it a little water
for gravy. Bake in a moderate oven for full three
hours, and let the potatoes on the top be nicely
browned. Fasten a serviette round the dish and
serve very hot.

37. KIDNEYS ON TOAST (Cheshire)

Mince up some mutton kidneys very fine ; season
with salt, pepper, and grated lemon-peel. Place

in a saucepan and toss the mixture in a little butter
until very hot, then beat up an egg, stir well into
the kidneys, and serve on thin slices of toast.

38. LAMBS' TAIL PIE (Kent)

This is a very old Kentish pie. In spring, when
the lambs' tails are cut, these are collected. About
half the tail, the thicker end, is used. It is flayed
and jointed : generally about two dozen tails are
used in making an ordinary-sized pie. Of course
the crust is made in the usual way.

(I have been told that the soft bones in the tails
when cooked are like gelatine.)

39. FORCED LEG OF MUTTON (Eighteenth Century)

Raise the skin and take out the lean part of the
mutton, chop it exceedingly fine, shred a bundle of
sweet herbs, grate a penny loaf, and half a lemon, take
nutmeg, pepper and salt to taste, make them into a
forcemeat, but leave the bone and shank in their
places, and it will appear like a whole leg ; lay it on
an earthen dish, with a pint of red wine under it, and
send it to the oven ; it will take two hours and a
half ; when it comes out, take off all the fat, strain
the gravy over the mutton, lay round it hard yolks
of eggs, and pickled mushrooms. Garnish with
pickles and serve up.

40. NAVARINE OF MUTTON (Hertfordshire)

Take three pounds of neck or breast of mutton,
trim it in neat pieces, sprinkle with flour, and fry
in three ounces of butter ; pour off the liquid fat,
and add a pint and a half of water, eight button
onions previously fried, three sprigs of parsley, six

2

small turnips cut into olive shapes, a tablespoonful
of tomato sauce, pepper, salt ; gradually bring to
boiling point and take off the scum ; gently simmer
an hour and a half.   Pile on a dish with the vegetables
round.

41. MUTTON OLIVES (Hertfordshire)

Take as many slices of cold mutton as required,
have ready some good veal forcemeat, put a piece on
one end of the mutton, roll it up securely, and tie
with cotton.   Place the rolls in a baking dish, pour
good gravy over, cover tin with greased paper, and
cook for half an hour ; serve with mashed potatoes
and red currant jelly.

42. MUTTON PATTIES WITH FINE HERBS
(Eighteenth Century)

Take part of the fillet from a loin or neck of
mutton, and cut it in dice, with half the quantity
of calves' udder, previously dressed.   Put two
ounces of butter in a stewpan, with a chopped
shalot, parsley, six chopped mushrooms, salt, and
pepper : let that heat over the fire a few minutes.
Then mix the meat with it, and set the whole to cool.
Line a dozen or more patty-pans with puff-paste ;
fill them with the meat, and put on the cover, from
the centre of which cut out a small piece the size
of a wafer.   Pinch the borders all round.   Egg the
patties, cut out another cover, with a still smaller
hole : place this lightly on the top : egg and bake
them.   When done, take them from the moulds,
and fill them with an Italian sauce.   Dish on a
napkin and serve.

43. TO MAKE FRENCH STEAKS OF NECK OF MUTTON (Eighteenth Century)

Let your mutton be very good and large, and cut off most part of the fat of the neck; then cut the steaks two inches thick, make a large hole through the middle of the fleshy part of the steak with a penknife, and stuff it with a little nutmeg, pepper, and salt, mixed with the yolk of an egg : when they are stuffed, wrap them in writing-paper, and put them in a Dutch oven; set them before the fire to broil, they will take near an hour; put a little brown gravy in your dish, and serve them up in the papers.

44. NECK OF MUTTON TO EAT LIKE VENISON (Eighteenth Century)

Cut a large neck, before the shoulder is taken off, broader than usual, and the flap of the shoulder with it ; to make it look handsomer, stick your neck all over in little holes with a sharp penknife, and pour a bottle of red wine over it, and let it lie in the wine four or five days ; turn and rub it three or four times a day, then take it out, and hang it up for three days in the open air, out of the sun, and dry it often with a cloth, to keep it from musting; when you roast it, baste it with the wine it was steeped in, if any left ; if not, fresh wine ; put white paper, three or four folds, to keep in the fat; roast it thoroughly, and take off the skin, and baste it nicely ; serve it up.

45. SHOULDER OF MUTTON SURPRISED (Eighteenth Century)

Half broil a shoulder, then put it in a tossing pan, with two quarts of veal gravy, four ounces of rice, a teaspoonful of mushroom powder, a little

beaten mace, and stew it an hour, or till the rice is
cooked enough, then take up your mutton and keep
it hot; put to the rice half a pint of good cream, and
a lump of butter rolled in flour, shake it well, and
boil it a few minutes : garnish with barberries or
pickles, and send it up.

46. RAISED PIES (Yorkshire)

Put two pounds of flour on the pasteboard, and
put on the fire in a saucepan three-quarters of a
pint of water and half a pound of good lard. When
the water boils, make a hole in the middle of the
flour, pour in the water by degrees, gently mixing
the flour with it with a spoon. When it is well
mixed, knead it with your hands till it becomes
stiff. Dredge a little flour to prevent it sticking to
the board, or you cannot make it look smooth.
Do not roll with the rolling-pin, but roll it with
your hands, about the thickness of a quart-pot :
cut it into six pieces, leaving a little for the covers.
Put one hand in the middle and keep the other close
on the outside, till you have worked it either in an
oval or a round shape. Have your meat ready cut
and seasoned with pepper and salt : if pork, cut it
in small slices, the griskin is the best for pasties.
If you use mutton, cut it in very neat cutlets, and
put them in the pies as you make them. Roll out
the cover with the rolling-pin, just the size of the
pie, wet it round the edge, put it on the pie and
press together with your thumb and finger, and
then cut all round with a pair of scissors quite
even, and pinch them inside and out, and bake them
an hour and a half.

47. SQUAB PIE (Devonshire)

Take a pie-dish, put at the bottom a layer of
sliced apples, strew over them a little sugar, then
a layer of fresh mutton (well seasoned with salt and
pepper). Then another layer of apples. Peel
some onions and slice them, lay them on the apples,
then a layer of mutton, then apples and onions.
Pour in a pint of water, cover all over with a good
crust, and bake.

48. SQUAB PIE (Kent)

Take two pounds of the best end of the neck of
mutton, cut it into small pieces, flavour with salt
and pepper, and put a layer of it at the bottom of
a pie-dish, next add a layer of sliced apples and
onions, with about a dessertspoonful of brown sugar,
then another layer of mutton. Cover with a good
pie-crust, and bake as an ordinary meat pie.

49. OXFORD JOHN (Eighteenth Century)

Take a stale leg of mutton, cut it in as thin collops
as you possibly can, taking out all the fat sinews.
Season them with mace, pepper, and salt, strew
among them a little shred parsley, thyme, and two or
three shalots. Put a good lump of butter in a stewpan ; when it is hot put in all the collops, keep
stirring them with a wooden spoon till they are
three parts done, then add half a pint of gravy and
a little juice of lemon, thicken it with a little flour
and butter, let them simmer four or five minutes and
they will be quite done enough. If you let them boil,
or have them ready before you want them, they
will grow hard. Serve them up hot, with fried
bread cut in slices over and around.

50. BROILED MUTTON STEAKS (Eighteenth Century)

Cut your steaks half an inch thick. When your gridiron is hot, rub it with fresh suet, lay on your steaks, keep turning them as quickly as possible. If you do not take care, the fat that drops from the steaks will smoke them. When they are done enough, put them into a hot dish, rub them well with butter, slice a shalot very thin into a spoonful of water, pour it on them with a spoonful of mushroom ketchup and salt; serve them up hot.

51. SHEEP'S HEAD (Cheshire)

Steep two or three hours. Split the head; take out the brains and tongue to boil separately. Boil the head gently for three hours with a carrot, onions, celery, sweet herbs, a few cloves, and pepper and salt; egg and crumb and brown before the fire. Mince the lights, and serve the liver in slices, well fried. Boil the brains in muslin, and arrange all together on one dish.

COLD MEAT

52. BEEF-CAKES (Cheshire)

To each pound of cold roast beef, add a quarter of a pound of ham or bacon. Mince very finely, season with pepper, salt, and sweet herbs : add one or two eggs well whisked. Make into small square cakes about half an inch thick ; fry them in boiling dripping, drain, and serve with good gravy.

53. BUBBLE AND SQUEAK (Essex)

Either slices of cold boiled beef or cold roast beef can be used. Fry the slices of meat gently in a little fat, and arrange them nicely round a centre of fried greens : these should be boiled till tender, well drained, minced, and then placed in a frying pan with a little butter, a finely sliced onion, and seasoned with pepper and salt. When the onion is done, the greens are ready to serve.

54. CURRY (Kent)

Fry the meat in plenty of butter or fat, and plenty of onions—but do not let it be fried hard, then put it in a saucepan with a dessert-spoonful of curry-powder, some cayenne, a little vinegar, a little milk, some butter about the size of an egg, and thicken it with flour. Let it stew gently for several hours. This is very good.

55. HUNTERS' PIE (Kent)

Have a deep dish, and mince up very fine some underdone beef or mutton—a little fat must be put with it, but no skin, nor anything not to be eaten ; fill the dish three-parts full. Put some good stock made from bones and also any gravy from the beef that is to be had—season with pepper, salt, and a tablespoonful of ketchup. Put this into the oven to get warm, and then lay over a nice thick crust of moist mashed potatoes, or else finely grated bread-crumbs, and put little bits of butter on the top here and there. Bake slowly for an hour.

56. SOUFFLÉ OF LAMB (Essex)

Half a pound of cold cooked mutton or lamb,
one ounce of butter, one ounce of flour, half a pint
of stock, one teaspoonful of chopped parsley, one
tablespoonful of tomato sauce, two eggs. Trim
away all skin, fat, and gristle, and pass the meat
twice through a mincer to mince it finely. Melt the
butter in a saucepan. Stir in the flour smoothly,
add the stock, and stir until it boils. Put in the
meat, parsley, tomato sauce, and season to taste.
Take off the fire, and let it cool a little. Thoroughly
stir in the yolks of eggs, and lightly stir the stiffly
whipped white of egg through the mixture. Put
into a buttered pie dish, or else divide the mixture
into buttered pattypans. Shake a few crumbs over
the top, and bake in the oven for ten to fifteen
minutes. Serve at once.

57. MACARONI WITH MEAT (Essex)

Throw the macaroni in boiling water, and when
it is soft strain it and put it into a pan with butter,
turning it all the time, and not allowing it to get
brown. Have ready some finely chopped onions
and meat well seasoned and browned, then place a
layer of macaroni and a layer of parmesan and a
layer of minced meat till the tray or dish is full.
Well beat up four eggs and add to the other ingredients. Make a sauce by placing a lump of butter
on the fire and throwing a spoonful of flour over it,
and then adding gradually a pint of milk. Pour this
sauce over the macaroni, not forgetting to mix
with it pepper and salt, nutmeg and cinnamon.
Bake it in a dish that can come to table. It will

take about forty minutes, and must not be too brown, or it will be hard. Before sending it to table, cut the mixture into diamonds about two inches long.

58. MEAT CAKE (Sussex)

Mince half a pound of cold underdone meat, add two ounces of breadcrumbs, and the same of cooked rice—or macaroni cut small. Beat an egg into a cupful of gravy mixed with half an ounce of flour. Add salt, pepper, fried onions, a teaspoonful of celery sauce, a few tinned mushrooms, or anchovy sauce, or mixed pickles. Grease a cake tin, coat it well with bread crumbs, pack in close, cover with bread crumbs, and bake about an hour.

59. MEAT SALADS (Essex)

Any small scraps of meat or poultry, etc., should be cut up neatly and mixed with some cold cooked vegetables or salad ; place this mixture in small shells or cases, cover with mayonnaise sauce, and garnish with strips of boned and filleted anchovies.

60. SCALLOPED MEAT (Hertfordshire)

Take any remains of cold meat or sausages, mince all together, butter a flat dish, sprinkle it thickly with brown-bread crumbs ; lay the meat over them, and cover with crumbs ; put pieces of butter over it, and brown in the oven.

61. COLD MEAT STEW (Sussex)

Two pounds of cold meat in slices, one teaspoonful of red currant jelly, one mustard-spoonful of

made mustard, one tablespoonful of ketchup, one
dessertspoonful Worcester sauce, one small dessertspoonful Harvey's, one glass of claret, to be all
stewed together with some good stock, the meat put
in, and all mixed well, and served very hot.

62. MUTTON OLIVES (Devonshire)

Required : Slices of cold roast mutton, veal stuffing, mashed potatoes, gravy. Take slices of mutton,
trim neatly ; dust one side of each with pepper, salt,
and a little allspice. Put a small piece of stuffing
on each and roll up, tying firmly with cotton. Place
the rolls in a baking tin, pour some good gravy
over, cover with greased paper, bake for half an
hour. Make a mound of mashed potatoes on a
dish, arrange the olives round, thicken the gravy
and pour round.

63. PILAFF (Hertfordshire)

Take three ounces of Patna rice, and pour over it
half a pint of water and a tablespoonful of tomato
purée ; season to taste. Melt a piece of butter the
size of an egg, stir in the rice gradually, and
place on the stove to simmer for fifteen minutes ;
cut up any cold meat in squares, fry them lightly
in butter, put into a saucepan with a spoonful of
tomato purée, and simmer for three hours. Place the
rice in the centre of the dish and the meat round it.

64. POTATO PIE (Derbyshire)

Put layers of meat, either cooked or uncooked,
with alternate layers of potato and onion *uncooked*,
in a deep bowl ; season with plenty of pepper and

salt ; and fill up with water. Cover the whole with a good short crust, and bake in a slow oven. This is a very nice winter dish, and is much improved by adding oysters between the meat and vegetables.

65. FORCEMEAT FOR PATTIES (Cheshire)

Shred, or very finely mince, a little ham, cold veal, or fowl, beef-suet, and a little onion, parsley, and lemon-peel. Add salt, nutmeg, pepper, mace, and breadcrumbs. (The respective quantities of all these will depend upon your requirements, your discretion, and the material in hand.) Pound all well together, add a little finely chopped thyme or marjoram, bind with a well-beaten egg, or two eggs if necessary.

66. FORCEMEAT FOR PIES (Eighteenth Century)

Take one and a half pounds of wild rabbits' flesh, and two pounds four ounces of fat bacon ; chop the whole, and pound it, with half an ounce herbaceous mixture, a little salt, an egg, and two extra yolks.

67. OBSERVATIONS ON MADE DISHES, ETC.
(Eighteenth Century)

Be careful the tossing-pan is well tinned, quite clean, and not gritty, and put every ingredient into your white sauce, and have it of a proper thickness and well boiled before you put in eggs and cream, for they will not add much to the thickness. Do not stir them with a spoon after they are in, nor set your pan on the fire, for the stuff will gather at the bottom, and be in lumps, but hold your pan a good height from the fire, and keep shaking the pan round one way, it will keep the sauce from curdling, and be sure you do not let it boil.   It is the best way to take up your meat, collops, or hash, or any other kind of dish you are making, with a fish slice, and strain your sauce upon it ; for it is almost impossible to prevent little bits of meat from mixing with the sauce. By this method the sauce will look clear.

In the brown made dishes, take special care no fat is on the top of the gravy, but skim it clean off, that it may be of a fine brown, and taste of no one thing in particular. If you use any wine, put it in some time before your dish is ready, to take off the rawness, for nothing can give a made dish a more disagreeable taste than raw wine or fresh anchovy. When you use fried forcemeat balls, put them on a sieve to drain the fat from them, and never let them boil in your sauce, or it will give it a greasy look, and soften the balls ; the best way is to put them in after your meat is dished up.

CHAPTER II

PORK AND VEAL RECIPES

NOTE.—These are mainly occupied with that most useful subject, cold meat cookery. Both pork and veal, unless carefully prepared, are apt to be even less digestible the second day of their appearance than the first. By skilful treatment, however, and a little extra trouble, they may be *réchauffés* in most attractive and innocuous ways. Those who are fortunate enough to possess their own pigs are acquainted with that vast variety of dishes which accrues upon the preparation of pork, etc., and to those I hardly need offer any reminder. As to the pigless person, he or she is *prima facie* debarred from the enjoyment of "lardy cake" and other such savoury foods. So I do not set down recipes for these : in either case they would be needless. The German "Roast Pork in Vinegar" and the Lancashire "Veal Cake" should specially be singled out for trial, but all the recipes are good.

PORK

68. BACON AND EGG PIE TO EAT COLD
(Eighteenth Century)

Steep a few thin slices of bacon in water to take out the salt, lay your bacon in the dish, beat eight

eggs with a pint of thick cream, put in it a little
pepper and salt, and pour it on the bacon, lay over
it a good cold paste, bake it in a moderate oven a
day before you want it.

69. TO MAKE BRAWN (Surrey)

Having divided the head down the middle, remove the brains, and cut off the ears, then let the
head lie in cold water for twelve hours : boil it
until the bones can be readily taken out, and when
done, take off the skin as entire as possible : while
the meat and the tongue are hot, chop them rather
fine, and season with pepper, salt, a little nutmeg,
two or three cloves, and some cayenne : then place
part of the skin at the bottom of a pan, lay on it
the chopped meat, and put the rest of the skin over
the top, place it under a heavy weight, and let it
remain until quite cold ; part of the liquor in which
the head has been dressed must be boiled up with
vinegar and salt, and thrown over the head. It is
eaten with vinegar and mustard. (A little brown
sugar added to these is an improvement.   Ed).

70. BRAWN (Essex)

Procure a pig's head which has been in salt not
more than three or four days, wash it and put it on
in sufficient water to cover it well. Let it cook
gently for about three hours, until quite tender,
then take it out, remove the bones (which should
come away easily) and cut up all the meat in small
pieces, putting it into a basin, which should be
kept hot over boiling water, or the brawn will set
too soon.   Season with pepper (no salt) and a little
powdered mace and sage if liked ; put into a press-

ing tin if one is at hand, and pour over the meat about half a pint of the liquor in which it has boiled. If a brawn tin is not to be had, use an ordinary large cake tin, put a plate closely fitting on top, and set on that the heaviest weights you have—either scale-weights or flat-irons.

71. BRAWN (Staffordshire)

Take half a pig's head, with the tongue and two feet. Rub it all with salt and pepper and let it lie a few days, rubbing well and turning every day. Then boil very gently until the meat comes easily off the bones. Take it out of the saucepan, put it on a board, and cut it all up into rather small pieces, then season with pepper and salt, and press it into a mould or proper brawn tin with holes at the bottom to let the gravy escape, and put a heavy weight on the top. Turn it out when cold, and send to table cold.

72. TO BOIL A HAM (Eighteenth Century)

Steep your ham all night in water, then boil it. If it be of a middle size it will take three hours boiling, and a small one two hours and a half; when you take it up, pull off the skin, and smear it all over with beaten egg; strew on bread crumbs, baste it with butter, set it to the fire till it be a light brown ; if it be to eat hot, garnish with carrots and serve it up.

73. HAM CAKE (Essex)

Mince finely one and a half pounds of cooked ham ; boil a slice of bread in half a pint of milk, and mix this with the ham, beating them well together and binding them with a well-beaten egg. Have ready a wetted mould, pack the mixture into this, and bake for an hour in a very hot oven, by which time it should be nicely coloured ; then turn out, and serve either hot or cold. Rabbit or veal may be used in the same way.

74. MINCED HAM (Isle of Wight)

Mix half a pound of cracker crumbs with an equal quantity of finely minced lean boiled ham : moisten this mixture with stock, or water, and butter, adding salt to taste. Put the mixture in a baking tin, make depressions in it the size of an egg, and break an egg into each hollow. Bake a delicate brown in a good oven.

75. PEPPER HAMS (Kent, 1809)

One pound of bay salt, half a pound of common salt, two ounces of saltpetre and pepper pounded all together very small ; rub the hams well all over. Let them lie four days, rubbing them once a day then pour over them a pound of treacle, turn and rub them with the pickle three or four times a week for a month, then lay them in cold water twenty-four hours and hang them up to dry, after which they need not be steeped but put into cold water to boil. For hams from twelve to sixteen pounds each, three hours will be enough to boil them.

76. TO POT HAM (Ireland)

From the remains of a cold ham take a pound of the lean to half a pound of the fat, or a quarter of fat is enough. Mince it very fine, or run it through a machine. Add a small teaspoonful of pounded mace, a quarter of a nutmeg, and salt, and, if possible a little dry powdered bay leaf. Press this mixture down well in the pot or dish. Bake for about twenty-five minutes, taking care the top does not brown, and cover with melted lard, first pressing the ham.

77. PIG'S CHEEK COLLARED (Surrey)

Lay two pig's cheeks, with the tongue, in a dish, and strew it well over with salt and saltpetre; let them stand for six days, and then boil them till the bones can be readily separated from the meat. Have ready a long strip of strong linen cloth, on which place the cheek, with the skin outwards, and on it the tongue, seasoning the whole highly with cayenne pepper, cloves, a very little mace, and salt; roll it up firmly and boil it for two hours; when done, set it under a heavy weight until cold, when the cloth must be removed. A cow-heel may be boiled, boned, and rolled up with it.

78. PIG'S SHIN AND SAUSAGES (Sussex)

Take a pig's shin, spread it all over with sausage-meat, roll up, tie tight, and boil.

79. PORK CHEESE (French)

Take out the bones from a pig's head without cutting the skin, remove the flesh, separate the fat from the lean, and cut the whole in strips; do the same with the ears, and season the whole with salt, pepper, powdered nutmeg, and other spices, thyme, bay leaves, sage, and parsley, all chopped fine, the grated rind of a lemon, and its juice. Put the skin of the head into a salad bowl, and arrange

3

in it the lean and the fat of the meat in alternate layers, as also two or three pigs' tongues cut up in the same way, with a little of the inner fat of the pig and some sliced truffles, if you have any : when all the meat is used, fold over the skin and sew it up, removing any superfluous part. Put this preparation into a stewpan of little more than its own size, with carrots, sweet herbs, salt, and pepper, and moisten with a little white (French) wine ; simmer very gently for six or seven hours ; take it off the fire, and when merely warm put the head into a mould of the shape of a cheese, and so that a part of the head may be above the mould, and put a board over it covered with weights. This cheese is always eaten cold with mustard and vinegar. Pork cheese is also made with the ears and tongues alone, one layer of the ears cut into strips, and one layer of the tongues, seasoned as above, and piled together into a mould, to be pressed down in the same way as the head. The mode of proceeding is altogether the same as for the head, with the exception of enclosing it in a skin.

80. PORK CHEESE (Italian)

Mince and pound a pig's liver ; do the same, but separately, with a quantity of the inner fat of pork, equal in weight to that of the liver. Mix them together and season with salt, pepper, nutmeg, coriander, chopped parsley, thyme, and sage : cover the bottom and line the sides of a tin saucepan or shape with thin slices of larding, fill the mould and cover with larding : bake in an oven.

When quite cold, dip the mould in boiling water and shake out the cheese.

81. LEICESTERSHIRE PORK PIE

Cut the pork in square pieces, fat and lean, about the size of a cobnut; season with pepper and salt, and a small quantity of sage and thyme chopped fine, and set it aside in a dish in a cool place. Next make some hot paste, using for this purpose fresh-made, heated hog's lard instead of butter, in the proportion of eight ounces to the pound of flour. These pies must be raised by hand in the following manner : First mould the paste into a round ball upon the slab, then roll it out to the thickness of half-an-inch, and with the back of the right hand indent the centre in a circle, reaching to within three inches of the edge of the paste ; next, gather up the edges all round, pressing it closely with the fingers and thumbs, so as to give it the form of a purse ; then continue to work upwards until the sides are raised sufficiently high ; the pie should now be placed on a baking sheet, with a round of buttered paper under it, and, after it has been filled with the pork previously prepared for the purpose, covered in with some of the paste in the usual manner. Trim the edges and pinch it round with the pincers, decorate it, egg it over, and bake till done, calculating the time it should remain in the oven according to the quantity of meat it contains.

82. ROAST PORK IN VINEGAR (German)

Take off the shin from your leg of pork, and do not leave too much fat either. Pour some vinegar,

with cloves and onions, into a large earthen vessel;
rub your pork well with a handful of salt, and place
it in the vinegar, where it must remain three or
four days and be frequently turned. If you like
you can also stick a few cloves into it. Put your
pork in the oven in the same vessel it has lain in,
with all the vinegar about it. (This is extremely
tasty and delicious. Ed.)

83. BROILED PORK STEAKS (Eighteenth Century)

Observe the same directions as for mutton steaks
(see No. 50), only pork requires more broiling; when
they are done enough, put in a little good gravy;
a little sage rubbed very fine, strewed over them,
gives them a fine taste.

84. STUFFED PORK (Isle of Wight)

Take two pounds of streaky green pork (the
thinner the better), and one pound of sausage meat.
Spread the sausage meat on the under side of the
pork, covering one half; now fold the other half over,
bind with strips of calico, and boil. When cooked,
press between two plates. This makes a good
breakfast dish.

85. SAVOURY GOOSE (Sussex)

Take half a pound of pig's liver, two onions, one
pound of potatoes. Take a spoonful of flour mixed in
water with salt, pepper, and a teaspoonful of minced
sage. Cut the liver in thin slices and lay in a pie
dish. Then put the potatoes partly cooked on top.
Bake.

86. EPPING SAUSAGES (Kent)

Six pounds of young pork, quite free from skin, gristle, or fat. Cut it small, and beat it fine in a mortar. Chop six pounds beef suet very fine, with a handful of sage leaves. Spread the meat on a clean dresser, and shake the sage over it. Shred the rind of a lemon fine, and throw it with sweet herbs on the meat, two nutmegs grated, a spoonful of pepper, with a large spoonful of salt. Throw the suet over, and mix all well together. Put it down close in a pot, and when it is to be used, roll it up with as much egg as will make it smooth.

87. OXFORD SAUSAGES

One pound young pork, fat and lean, one pound beef suet, chopped fine together ; half a pound of grated bread, half the peel of a lemon grated, a nutmeg grated, six sage leaves chopped fine, one teaspoonful of pepper, and two of salt, and a little thyme, savory, and marjoram shred fine. Mix well together, and put it close down in a pan till used. Roll out the sausages, and fry in fresh butter, or broil over a clear fire, and serve up hot.

VEAL

88. BRAIN CAKES (Essex)

Well wash and clean the brains, then put them into a pan of boiling salted water slightly acidulated with lemon juice, and let them cook over a slow fire for an hour ; lift them out, drain well, and leave till cold ; then cut into rounds, egg and bread-crumb them, and fry in hot fat.

89. BOILED BREAST OF VEAL
(Eighteenth Century)

Skewer your breast of veal, so that it will lie flat
in the dish, boil it an hour (if a large one an hour
and a quarter), make white sauce, pour it over, and
garnish with pickles.

90 CALF'S HEAD BOILED (Middlesex)

Split the head, and carefully take out the brains
and tongue ; wash it well, and let it lie two hours
in cold water ; boil it with the tongue and brains
gently in plenty of water until it is quite tender ;
pour over the head parsley-butter made very thick ;
rub the brains through a sieve, add to them some
chopped parsley, pepper, salt, and a bit of butter ;
mix the whole well together, and put it round the
tongue.

91. CALF'S HEAD PIE (Eighteenth Century)

Parboil a calf's head. When cold, cut it in pieces,
season it well with pepper and salt, put it in a
raised crust, with half a pint of strong gravy ; bake
it an hour and a half. When it comes out of the
oven, cut off the lid, chop the yolks of three hard-
boiled eggs small, strew them over the top of the pie,
with three or four slices of lemon and pour on some
good melted butter. Send it to the table without
a lid.

92. A GOOD WAY TO DRESS A CALF'S HEART
(Eighteenth Century)

Take a calf's heart, stuff it with good forcemeat.
and send to the oven in an earthen dish, with a

little water under it; lay butter over it, dredge it with flour. Boil half the liver and all the lights together half an hour, then chop them small and put them in a tossing pan, with a pint of gravy, one spoonful of lemon pickle, and one of ketchup; squeeze in half a lemon; pepper and salt; thicken it with a good piece of butter rolled in flour. When you dish it up, pour the minced meat at the bottom, and have ready, fried a fine brown, the other half of the liver cut in thin slices, and little bits of bacon. Set the heart in the middle, and lay the liver and bacon over the mincemeat, and set them before the fire; baste them with butter, and let them be a fine brown, then turn them on their other side, and baste and brown the same way; when they are thoroughly done, pour a good brown gravy with the yolks of hard-boiled eggs, over them; garnish with crisp parsley and lemon.

93. VEAL CUTLETS (Yorkshire, 1769)

Take a neck of veal, cut it in joints, flatten them with a rolling-pin, and cut off the ends of the long bones. Season them with a little pepper, salt, and nutmeg, broil them on a gridiron over a slow fire. When they are done enough, serve them up with brown gravy and forcemeat balls. Garnish the dish with lemon.

94. ANOTHER WAY

Take a neck of veal and proceed as above; season the cutlets with pepper and salt, and dredge some flour over them. Fry them in butter over a quick fire, then put from them the fat they were fried in,

and put to them a little gravy, a tablespoonful of
ketchup, the same of white wine or lemon-juice,
and grate in some nutmeg. Thicken them with
flour and butter, and serve up. Garnish with
lemon.

95. NECK-OF-VEAL CUTLETS
(Eighteenth Century)

Cut a neck of veal into cutlets, fry them a light
brown, then put them in a tossing pan, and stew
them till tender in a quart of good gravy, then add
one spoonful of gravy, the same of ketchup, a few
pickled mushrooms, a little salt, and cayenne
pepper; thicken your gravy with flour and butter,
let it boil a few minutes, lay your cutlets in a dish,
with the top of the ribs in the middle, pour your
sauce over them, lay your mushrooms over the
cutlets, and send them up.

96. CALVES' FEET (Cambridgeshire)

Two calves' feet, the rind of a lemon, mace,
cloves, mignonette, and pepper to taste. Boil till
bones drop out, then place pieces of meat on the
dish it is to be served in. Boil the liquor till it
clarifies, and reduce to just sufficient to serve each
piece. Last of all sprinkle with chopped parsley.
Sufficient for four persons.

97. CALVES' TONGUES (Seventeenth Century)

Boil them tender and peel them, then lard them
with lemon-peel and fat bacon. Then lay them
to the fire and half roast them. Then put them into
a pipkin or earthen dish with claret, whole spice,
and sliced lemon, a few caraway seeds, a little

rosemary, and a little salt. Heat up all together and serve them upon toast. Thus you may do with sheep's tongues also.

98. VEAL CAKE (Lancashire)

Boil six or eight eggs hard, cut the yolks in two, lay some of the pieces at the bottom of a mould, shake in a little chopped parsley, put some slices of veal and ham, add the eggs again, with white pepper and salt, and so on till the dish is full ; then put in enough water to cover the meat, lay on about one ounce of butter, tie it over with a double paper, and bake about one hour. Then press it down together with a spoon, and let it stand till cold.

99. SCOTCH COLLOPS (Kent, 1809)

Take part of a leg of veal, cut it in thin pieces, take off all the skin from every piece, chop it with the back of a knife to make it tender. Fry it, not very brown, in sweet butter. As it comes out of the pan, season it with lemon peel, thyme, pepper, salt, a little nutmeg, and mace. Make rich gravy with beef and veal. Toss up the collops with gravy thickened with sweet butter and flour, and squeeze in some juice of lemons, and mushrooms. If white, add cream ; garnish with forcemeat balls, bacon, and lemons.

100. SCOTCH COLLOPS THE FRENCH WAY
(Eighteenth Century)

Take a leg of veal, cut your collops pretty thick, five or six inches long, and three inches broad ; rub them over with the yolk of an egg, put pepper and

salt, and grate a little nutmeg on them, and a little
shred parsley ; lay them on an earthen dish, and
serve.

101. VEAL KIDNEY PIE (Hertfordshire)

Mince two veal kidneys with some of the fat that
surrounds them, season with herbs, cloves, nutmeg,
pepper and salt, and a little chopped celery. Put
in a pie-dish with four hard-boiled eggs in slices,
half a cupful of breadcrumbs, a wineglassful of
white wine and a little stock. Cover with a good
crust, and bake for two hours.

102. VEAL LOAF (Surrey)

Take a cold fillet of veal, omit the fat, and mince
as fine as possible. Mix with a quarter of a pound
of fat ham, chopped : one teacupful grated bread
crumbs, one grated nutmeg, one saltspoonful of salt,
two beaten eggs, half a saltspoonful of cayenne. Mix
well together in the form of a loaf. Glaze over
with yolk of egg, and strew pounded cracker over.
Set the dish in an oven, and bake half an hour.
Make a gravy of veal trimmings, or any gravy left
over from the previous day, when the meat was
served. Heat it up, thickened by the yolk of an egg
dropped in just before taken up, and serve the loaf
with the gravy poured round it.

103. MINCED VEAL (Eighteenth Century)

Cut your veal in slices, then cut it in little square
bits, but do not chop it. Put it in a saucepan, with
two or three spoonfuls of gravy, a slice of lemon, a
little pepper and salt, a good lump of butter rolled

in flour, a teaspoonful of lemon pickle, and a large
spoonful of cream ; keep shaking it over the fire
till it boils, but do not let it boil above a minute,
if you do it will make your veal eat hard ; put
sippets round your dish, and serve it up.

104. VEAL OLIVE PIE (Eighteenth Century)

Cut a fillet of veal in thin slices, rub them over
with the yolks of eggs, strew them over with a few
crumbs of bread ; shred a little lemon peel very fine,
and put on them, with a little grated nutmeg, pepper,
and salt; roll them up very tight, tie or skewer
them, and lay them in a pewter dish; pour over
them half a pint of good gravy made of bones,
make a light paste, and lay it round the dish;
roll the lid half an inch thick and lay it on. Make
a beef olive pie the same way.

105. VEAL OLIVES (Eighteenth Century)

Cut the thick part of a leg of veal in thin slices,
flatten them with the broad side of a cleaver, rub
them over with the yolk of an egg, strew over every
piece a very thin slice of bacon, with a few breadcrumbs, a little lemon peel and parsley chopped
small, tie or skewer them, put them into a tin
dripping-pan to bake, or fry them ; then take a
pint of good gravy, add to it a spoonful of lemon
pickle, the same of walnut ketchup, and one of
browning, a little anchovy, and cayenne pepper,
thicken it with flour and butter, serve them up
with forcemeat balls, and strain the gravy hot upon
them ; garnish with pickles, and strew over them
a few pickled mushrooms. You may dress veal
cutlets the same way, but not roll them.

106.   SCOTCH OYSTERS (Yorkshire, 1769)

Take two pounds of the thick part of a leg of veal,
cut it in little bits clear from the skin, and put it in
a marble mortar, then shred one pound of beef-
suet and put to it, and beat them well together,
till they be firm as paste. Put to this a handful
of breadcrumbs and two or three eggs, season with
mace, nutmeg, pepper, and salt, and work it well
together. Take one part of this, about the size
of a pigeon, and wrap it in pieces of the veal caul;
make the rest into little flat cakes and fry them.
The rolls you may either broil in a dripping pan, or
set them in the oven. There is enough for a good-
sized dish ; lay them in the middle and set the
cakes round. Take some strong gravy, shred in a
few capers, and two or three mushrooms if you
have any ; thicken it up with a lump of butter,
and serve it up hot. Garnish your dish with pickles.

107. COMMON VEAL PATTIES (Eighteenth Century)

Take the kidney part of a very fat loin of veal,
chop the kidney, veal, and fat very small all together, season it with mace, pepper, and salt, to your
taste ; raise little patties the size of a teacup, fill
them with the meat, put thin lids on them, bake
them very crisp ; five are enough for a side dish.

108. SAVOURY VEAL PIE (Eighteenth Century)

Cut a loin of veal into steaks, season it with
beaten mace, nutmeg, pepper, and salt ; lay the
meat in your dish, with sweetbreads seasoned
with the meat, the yolks of six hard-boiled eggs,
and half a pint of good gravy ; lay round your

dish a good puff paste half an inch thick, and cover it with a lid the same thickness, bake it in a quick oven an hour and a quarter ; when you take it out of the oven, cut off the lid ; then cut the lid in eight or ten pieces, and stick it round the inside of the rim, cover the meat with slices of lemon, and serve it up.

109. STUFFED SHOULDER OF VEAL (Hertfordshire)

Take the bone out, and fill the cavity left by it with veal stuffing ; then roll up the veal neatly, and tie round firmly with string. Place in a stewpan, with just enough water to cover. Allow to simmer slowly for four hours. Prepare two carrots, two onions, and some herbs, and stew with the joint. To serve take out the veal, remove the string, strain the gravy, thicken with flour and pour over the whole. Chop the vegetables finely for a garnish.

VARIOUS

110. COLD CURRY (Surrey)

Four to six ounces of cold veal, chicken, or rabbit, one ounce butter, one sour apple, one large table-spoonful of curry powder, one good-sized onion, half a pint white stock (one that sets in a jelly), quarter of a pint of milk, quarter of a pint of cream, a little lemon juice, salt, and pepper. Put the butter, apple and onions finely chopped, and curry powder, into a saucepan, and cook for twenty minutes ; then add the stock and milk. Simmer until reduced to about a quarter of a pint, with saucepan uncovered. Put in the meat, cut into dice, and simmer

for twenty minutes ; then put aside to cool. When
cool, whip the cream and then stir in the mixture ;
add salt, pepper, and a few drops of lemon juice,
and put it in greased cases. Decorate with tomato,
hard-boiled eggs and parsley.

111. DRY CURRY (Hertfordshire)

Put into a stewpan a quarter of a pound of
butter, with two rather large onions cut small. Fry
till *light* brown, then add two tablespoonfuls curry
powder and a little salt. Have ready two pounds
of veal, chicken, or rabbit, cut into small pieces,
and add to the curry, and mix all well together.
Pour in one pint milk, and simmer slowly till the
mixture is absorbed. It should take about an hour.
Serve with rice.

112. STUFFED LIVER (Isle of Wight)

A calf's liver, and stuffing (sage and onions).
Make an incision through the centre of the liver to the
depth of half its thickness ; now put the knife into
the opening and by holding it flat, cut round on each
side. This will make a pocket to hold the stuffing.
Bake in a hot oven, well basting with good dripping.

113. MOCK SWEETBREADS (Cheshire)

Take three-quarters of a pound of veal, pass it
through a mincer two or three times till it is practically a pulp : add a little suet or bacon very finely
shredded or minced, the yolks of two eggs to bind,
and a few fine breadcrumbs to give it consistency.
Season with a little mace, pepper, and salt : add a
little cream or milk to moisten. Make up into the

shape of sweetbreads, and brown in good (but not fierce) oven. Serve with gravy.

114. THATCHED-HOUSE PIE
(Eighteenth Century)

Take an earthenware dish that is pretty deep, rub the inside with two ounces of butter, then spread over it two ounces of vermicelli. Make a good puff paste, roll it pretty thick, and lay it on the dish ; take three or four pigeons, season them very well with pepper and salt, put a good lump of butter in them and lay them in the dish with the breasts down, put a thick lid over them, and bake it in a moderate oven. When done enough, take the dish you intend for it and turn the pie into it, upside down, and the vermicelli will appear like thatch, which gives it the name of a thatched-house pie. It is a pretty side or corner dish, for a large dinner, or bottom dish for supper.

CHAPTER III

FOWL AND GAME

Note.—The manuscript-books of the last three centuries do not greatly trouble themselves over fowl and game : or, if they do, the recipes involve so lavish an expenditure of labour and material that they are out of place in these hard and hurried times. "Heron Pudding" is inserted as a culinary curiosity : for herons, like roast swans, roast peacocks, and other popular viands of the past, usually figure no longer upon our dinner-tables.

The recipes for cooking rabbits will be found extremely useful : especially that entitled "Jugged Rabbit." As a more elaborate but very tasty dish, "Roman Pie" may be instanced.

115. TO BOIL FOWLS (Eighteenth Century)

When you have plucked your fowls, draw them at the rump, cut off the head, neck, and legs, take the breast bone very carefully out, skewer them with the end of their legs in the body, tie them round with a string, singe and dust them well with flour ; put them into a kettle of cold water, cover it close, set it on the fire ; when the scum begins to rise, take it off, put on your cover, and let them cook very slowly for twenty minutes ; take them off, cover them

48

close, and the heat of the water will stew them enough in half an hour; it keeps the skin whole, and they will be both whiter and plumper than if they had boiled fast; when you take them up, drain them, pour over them white sauce, or melted butter.

116. TO DRESS AN OLD FOWL (Cheshire)

If for boiling, put it into lukewarm water with a piece of soda (bi-carbonate) about the size of a nut, and let it cook for the usual time.

If for roasting, pour boiling water on it, and leave it soaking for nearly two hours in a jar on the stove. Then dry it well, and do not flour it, but put a little lard over it before cooking.

117. FOWL SPATCHCOCKED WITH TARTARE SAUCE (Hertfordshire)

Roast a fowl, take it up, split it down the back, arrange it, well fastened up with skewers, spread-eagle fashion; grill over a good fire, place it on a hot dish with mushrooms round and serve with tartare sauce; or make some white sauce, stir in two yolks of eggs well beaten up; beat in some salad oil, then add tarragon, chervil, and enough vinegar to sharpen the sauce.

118. STUFFED FOWLS (Seventeenth Century)

Bone your fowls and fill them with the following forcemeat, and roast them. Take half a pound of beef suet, some finely minced mushrooms, a few sweet herbs and parsley shred fine, some grated lemon peel and nutmeg, pepper, and salt: six

4

ounces fine bread-crumbs, an egg well beaten (two,
if the egg be small). Have ready for sauce some
good gravy with mushrooms. You may lard the
fowls if you please.

119. SALMI OF GROUSE WITH CLARET (Surrey)

Cut up two roast grouse into members. Skin
them, and throw the trimmings and skin into a
stewpan, with two sliced shalots, a few mushroom
parings, a clove, half a blade of mace, a little
allspice, and a few peppercorns. Let the whole
sweat in a little consommé, at the corner of the
stove. Add a pint of brown sauce, having boiled
and clarified this, and two or three glasses of claret.
Let the whole boil down rather thick, and strain
it over the grouse. You may ornament the dish
with a few pieces of toast. Blackcock or ptarmigan
can be prepared the same way. These birds are
better for keeping till the feathers come readily
from the skin.

120. JUGGED HARE (Yorkshire, 1769)

Take a young hare, wash and wipe it well, cut the
egs into two or three pieces, and all the other parts
the same bigness. Beat them all flat with a paste-
pin, season with nutmeg and salt. Put them into
a pitcher or any other closed jar, with half a pound
of butter. Set the jar in a pot of boiling water,
cover it up close with a cloth or lid, and lay some
weight upon it for fear it should fall to one side.
It will take about two hours in stewing : mind your
pot be full of water and kept boiling all the time.
When the hare is done, take the gravy from it,
clear off the fat, and put the meat into the gravy

in a stewpan, with a tablespoonful or two of white
wine, or a little lemon-juice, shred lemon-peel, and
mace. You must thicken it up as you would a white
fricassee. Garnish your dish with sippets of toast
and lemon.

121. JUGGED HARE (Surrey)

Take a hare, skin it, draw it, cut it up, but do not
wash it. Flour the pieces and fry them a good
brown, in butter seasoned with salt and pepper.
Have ready about one and a half pints of gravy, made
from one and a half pounds of gravy beef. Put
the pieces of hare into an earthenware jar, add one
small onion stuck with five cloves, one lemon peeled
and cut, and the gravy. Cover the jar closely, set
it in a deep stewpan in cold water, and let the water
boil three to four hours, according to the age of the
hare. When it is done, take it out and set it over the
fire in a pan for a few minutes, and add one tablespoonful mushroom ketchup, two wine glasses of
port, a piece of butter well floured, and some forcemeat balls.

122. ROASTED HARE (Eighteenth Century)

Skewer your hare with the head upon one shoulder,
the fore legs stuck into the ribs, the hind legs doubled.
Make your pudding of the crumbs of a penny loaf,
a quarter of a pound of beef marrow or suet, and a
quarter of a pound of butter : shred the liver, a
sprig or two of winter savoury, a little lemon-peel,
a little cayenne pepper, half a nutmeg grated ; mix
them up in a light forcemeat, with a glass of red
wine and two eggs ; put it into the belly of your
hare, sew it up. Put a quart of good milk in your

dripping-pan, baste your hare with it till it is reduced
to half a gill, then dust and baste it well with butter.
If it be a large one it will require an hour and a half
roasting.

123. A HERON PUDDING (Kent)

Before cooking it must be ascertained that no
bones of the heron are broken. These bones are
filled with a fishy fluid, which, if allowed to come in
contact with the flesh, makes the whole bird taste of
fish. This fluid, however, should be always extracted
from the bones, and kept in the medicine cupboard,
for it is excellent applied to all sorts of cuts and
cracks. The heron is first picked and flayed. Then
slices are cut from the breast and legs to make the
pudding. The crust is made exactly like that of a
meat pudding, and the slices of heron put in and
seasoned exactly as meat would be. The pudding
is boiled for several hours, according to its size.
(I have been told that, as a matter of fact, it tastes
very much like a nice meat pudding.)

124. ROAST PARTRIDGES
The Italian way (Seventeenth Century)

Fill the partridges with butter worked with a
little salt : cover them with slices of bacon fat and
buttered paper : let them roast half or three-quarters
of an hour. Let them drain, and serve them
masked with an Italian sauce.

125. ROLLED PARTRIDGES (Eighteenth Century)

Having larded your partridges with ham or
bacon, strew over them some pepper and salt,

powdered mace, shredded lemon peel, and sweet
herbs cut small. Take some beefsteaks cut as thin
as possible, but without holes in them, and strew
some of the seasoning over them, then squeeze on
some lemon juice. Lay a partridge on each steak,
roll it up, and tie it round to keep it together. Set
on a stewpan with some slices of bacon and an
onion cut into pieces. Put the partridges carefully
in, put to them some rich gravy, and let them stew
gently till they are done. Then take them out of
the beef, lay them in a dish, and strain the gravy
over them.

126. PILLAU (Cheshire)

Spread a small baking-dish all over with rashers
of bacon ; stick an onion with a dozen cloves ; cut
a fowl in pieces, and rub it well with pepper and
salt ; put the onion in the middle of the dish, and
place the fowl over it. Have some rice boiled tender
to fill the dish. Fill up with gravy. Cover with a
water and flour paste ; bake about an hour ; take
off the crust, and garnish with hard-boiled eggs
cut in quarters, and sliced onions.

127. TO BOIL RABBITS (1815)

When you have cased (or drawn) your rabbits,
skewer them with their heads straight up, the fore
legs brought down, and their hind legs straight ;
boil them three-quarters of an hour at least, then
smother them with onion-sauce, made the same as
for boiled ducks. Put a sprig of myrtle or barberries in their mouths, and serve them up.

128. FIVE RECIPES FOR COOKING RABBITS
(Cheshire)

GIBELOTTE 1.—Take a quarter of a pound of lean
bacon, cut it in small dice, and fry it in a saucepan
with a little butter for a few minutes. Put the
bacon aside on a plate. Put the pieces of rabbit
in the saucepan with a little more butter, and toss
it about till the pieces are well set and begin to
colour. Dredge in a little flour, and stock, or wine
and water (white or red) enough to cover it; add
salt, pepper, powdered spice, and sweet herbs, and
let it simmer about a quarter of an hour. Meanwhile toss a dozen small pickling onions in a saucepan with a little butter and sugar, till they are well
coloured; add them to the gibelotte with the
bacon and a few button mushrooms. Let all
simmer twenty minutes or more; take out the
bundle of herbs, and serve.

GIBELOTTE 2.—Toss the pieces of rabbit in butter
till quite set; sprinkle with shalot, parsley, thyme,
and mushrooms, finely minced, pepper, and salt;
dredge a little flour over, and moisten with stock
(and white wine). Add the liver, and let all simmer
about twenty minutes or more. Take out the
liver and pound it; return it to the gibelotte, and
serve, garnished with sippets fried in butter.

GIBELOTTE 3.—Toss the pieces of rabbit with a
little olive oil and a shalot; pepper and salt; add
a little thyme, and fry till the pieces begin to
colour. Take them out one by one, and put them
into another saucepan, with five or six tablespoonfuls of tomato sauce. Keep shaking the pan

till the rabbit is quite done, adding a little chopped parsley. This is a dry stew.

GIBELOTTE 4. *Curried.*—Fry the pieces a light brown with sliced onion and strips of bacon. When they begin to colour, add curry powder and flour, with stock and salt. Let all simmer gently. Serve with a wall of plain boiled rice round. Some add slices of apple.

5. RABBIT AND ONION SAUCE.—Blanch the pieces of rabbit for ten minutes in boiling water. Put them into a saucepan with an onion stuck full of cloves, thyme, parsley, pepper, and salt. Cover with boiling water. Let them simmer about three-quarters of an hour. Serve on a dish, piled, with plenty of onion sauce poured over them.

129. TO FRICASSEE RABBITS BROWN
(Eighteenth Century

Cut up your rabbits, fry them in butter a light brown, put them in a tossing pan, with a pint of water, a teaspoonful of lemon pickle, a large teaspoonful of mushroom ketchup, the same of browning, a slice of lemon, cayenne pepper, and salt to your taste; stew them over a slow fire till they are done enough; thicken your gravy, and strain it; dish up your rabbits, and pour the gravy over them.

130. TO FRICASSEE RABBITS WHITE
(Eighteenth Century)

Cut up your rabbits as before, put them into a tossing pan, with a pint of veal gravy, a teaspoonful of lemon pickle, a slice of lemon, a little beaten mace, cayenne pepper, and salt, stew them over a slow fire; when they are done enough, thicken your gravy with flour and butter, strain it, then add the yolks of two eggs, mixed with a large teacupful of thick cream, and a little nutmeg grated in it; do not let it boil, and serve it up.

131. JUGGED RABBIT (Cheshire)

Take a rabbit of two to three pounds, and cut it up into joints. (An Ostend rabbit will be larger, but fatter: two wild rabbits will answer the same purpose, but will not have so much meat on.) Have an earthen stew-jar with a lid, and put the rabbit in, alternating each layer with a layer of thinly sliced onion. Season, as you go, with salt, pepper, and mace, mixed together with discretion. When the jar is nearly full, cover the meat with some five or six slices of thinly-cut bacon, and then add enough water to come nearly up to the bacon. Cover close with lid, and cook slowly in a good oven for two to three hours. Serve in the jar with a napkin round it. *N.B.*—This is extremely well-flavoured, but a trifle rich.

132. ROASTED RABBITS (Eighteenth Century)

When you have cased (or drawn) your rabbits, skewer their heads with their mouths upon their backs, stick their fore legs into their ribs, skewer the hind legs double, then make a pudding for them of the crumbs of a halfpenny loaf, a little parsley, sweet marjoram, thyme, a lemon peel, all shred fine, nutmeg, pepper, and salt to your taste, mix these up into a light stuffing, with a quarter of a

pound of butter, a little good cream, and two eggs ;
put it into the belly and sew up. Dredge and baste
the rabbits well with butter, roast them nearly an
hour, serve them up with parsley and butter for
sauce ; chop the livers, and lay them in heaps round
the edge of your dish.

133. A MADE DISH OF RABBITS' LIVERS
(Eighteenth Century)

Take six livers and chop them fine, with sweet
herbs and the yolks of two hard-boiled eggs. Season
with beaten spice and salt, and put in some plumped
currants, and a little melted butter. Mix very well
together and, having some paste ready rolled thin,
make the mixture into little patties, and fry
them.

134. ROMAN PIE (Sussex)

Half a pound of puff paste, two ounces of
macaroni, a small quantity of parmesan cheese,
according to taste, and a small chicken, boned.

Bone chicken, stew bones with gravy, make
rich white sauce, season to taste with salt and
mignonette. Cut white meat into small pieces, boil
macaroni till quite tender and cut into two-inch
lengths. Take a charlotte mould, first greasing
same, and sprinkle with vermicelli. Line with puff
paste, then add slices of white meat, then a sprinkling of cheese and salt, then macaroni, doing this
alternately. Then bake in a crisp oven one hour,
when it should be golden brown. Turn out and
serve with rich gravy and cheese. Rabbit or veal
may be used also.

135. ROOK PIE (Eighteenth Century)

Skin and draw six young rooks, and cut out the
back bones ; season them well with pepper and salt,
put them in a deep dish, with a quarter of a pint of
water ; lay over them half a pound of butter, make
a good puff paste, and cover the dish. Lay a paper
over it, for it requires a good deal of baking.

CHAPTER IV

SOUP RECIPES

NOTE.—We were never a soup-eating nation. The Englishman always desires to " get his teeth into " something solidly tangible ; and in nursery circles a damper is cast upon the dinner-table—a sense of being defrauded out of one's lawful dues—when soup, be it never so tasty, is produced. Even very thick soups—pea, and lentil, and those which are dense with rice, barley, sago, or macaroni—fail to restore equanimity. The common soups of our French neighbours—purely vegetable stock— economy of cabbage-water, and so forth, carried to its uttermost limit, would never appease the yearnings of those taught to reverence the Roast Beef of Old England.

So I have not included very many soups : and I have perforce omitted some which began with so prodigious a boiling down of beef and mutton, that they would have befitted a giant's cuisine. The ordinary cookery book will supply you with many excellent suggestions for soup : but the hints which follow are useful and occasionally quite novel.

It is advisable to keep a stock-pot in every house, if only for gravies : carefully straining off all vegetable matter after the boiling, and re-boiling (not merely *heating*) the stock every day should the

weather demand it. It is the falsest of false
economy to use stock which is in the tiniest degree
tainted. All bones should be well broken up before
being put in ; and salt should be invariably added.

136. ALMOND SOUP (Eighteenth Century)

Take a neck of veal and the scrag end of a neck
of mutton, chop them in small pieces, put them in a
large tossing-pan, cut in a turnip, with a blade or
two of mace, and five quarts of water ; set it over the
fire, and let it boil gently till it is reduced to two
quarts. Strain it through a hair sieve into a clear
pot, then put in six ounces of almonds, blanched and
beaten fine, half a pint of thick cream, and cayenne
pepper to your taste. Have ready three small French
rolls, the size of a small teacup ; if they are larger
they will not look well, and will drink up too much
of the soup ; blanch a few Jordan almonds, and
cut them lengthways, stick them round the edge
of the rolls, slantways, then stick them all over
the top of the rolls, and put them in the tureen.
When dished up, pour the soup upon the rolls ;
these rolls look like a hedgehog. Some French
cooks give this soup the name of Hedgehog Soup.

137. A VERY GOOD WHITE ALMOND SOUP
(Yorkshire, 1769)

Take veal, fowl, or any other white meat, boiled
down with a little mace (or other spice to your taste),
let it boil to a mash, then strain off the gravy. Take
some of the white fleshy part of the meat and rub
it through a fine colander. Have ready two ounces
of almonds, beaten fine, rub these through the
colander, then put all into the gravy, set it on the

fire to thicken a little, and stir into it two or three
tablespoonfuls of cream, and a little butter worked
into flour. Have ready a crisped French roll for
the middle, and slips of bread cut long like Savoy
biscuits. Serve up hot.

138. BARLEY BROTH (Kent, 1809)

Put a quantity of barley with onions (and, if they
can be got, carrots, and turnips), and a sprinkling
of salt and pepper, into a pot *having a lid*, with a
quantity of water equal to the quantity of broth
required, sufficient to boil a neck of mutton, which
should be put into it, and let the whole boil slowly
for five or six hours. During part of the time the
mutton should be taken out, otherwise it will be
over-boiled. In place of a neck, a flap of mutton
may be used, and grilled after it is boiled.

139. SHEEP'S HEAD BROTH (Kent, 1809)

In Scotland an excellent broth, similar to the
above is made of sheep's head, and sheep's feet.
The head and feet are not skinned as in England,
but the wool is singed off. It is a dish esteemed
even at the tables of the rich, as barley broth and
hodge-podge also are. The head, cold, eaten with
vinegar and mustard, is excellent eating, and is
used at breakfast in many parts of that country.

140. SPINACH BROTH (Seventeenth Century)

Take strong stock, boil a piece of neck of mutton
—four pounds or so, and a marrow bone in it. Then
put in half a pound of French barley, a bundle of
sweet herbs, two or three blades of large mace, and

let these boil well. Mince very small two large
onions and half a peck of spinach. Add it to the
broth, season to taste with salt, and let all boil an
hour or more. Serve the mutton and marrow bone
in a separate dish with pieces of toast or fried bread.

141. VEGETABLE BROTH (Kent, 1809)

Is composed of greens or cabbage, shorn or cut
into small pieces, onions, carrots, and turnips, or
one or more of them as can be got, also cut into
small pieces, with barley boiled slowly in a portion
of water corresponding to the quantity of broth
wanted, to which a sprinkling of salt and pepper is
added ; a small quantity of dripping is also added,
when that can be procured ; and vegetable broth,
if properly made, is a nourishing and palatable
food.

142. CHESTNUT SOUP (Sussex)

Boil the chestnuts till they burst open. Throw
them into cold water, peel them, crush them into
a paste (moistening with a little milk when desirable). Put them through a fine sieve. Set them
in an earthenware pan with an onion already cooking
in a little butter. Add a teaspoonful of sugar, a
saltspoonful of salt, a little pepper, a light hint of
spice, and as much milk as will make up the required
amount. Stir continually, and when it boils, add a
spoonful of rice-flour, made smooth in cold milk, and
a little cream if possible.

143. EGG SOUP (Seventeenth Century)

Having beaten the yolks of two eggs in a bowl,
along with a piece of butter the size of an egg,

take a pan or kettle of boiling stock in one hand and a spoon in the other, and pour in by degrees about a quart of stock, and keep stirring it well all the time. When the eggs are well mixed and the butter melted, pour it into a saucepan and keep stirring till it begins to simmer. Take it off the fire and pour it from one vessel into another till it is quite smooth and has a good froth. Then put it on the fire again, keep stirring it until it is quite hot, and then pour it into your soup-dish. (Salt and seasoning seem to have been forgotten here. Ed.)

144. FARINE BRÛLÉE (Surrey)

Fry some onions a light brown in dripping at the bottom of a saucepan. Then put in one small table-spoonful of flour to each person, and stir with a wooden spoon over the fire until the flour is a pale brown colour, then add the hot stock (half a pint for each person) and stir until it is quite smooth and thick. Cut up very thin slices of cheese, put them into the bottom of the tureen, and pour on the soup.

145. GRAVY SOUP THICKENED WITH YELLOW PEAS (Eighteenth Century)

Put a shin of beef to six quarts of water, with a pint of peas and six onions, set them over the fire and let them boil gently till all the juice be out of the meat, then strain it through a sieve, and add to the strained liquor one quart of strong gravy to make it brown; put in pepper and salt to your taste, then put in a little celery and beet leaves, and boil till they are tender.

146. HARE SOUP (Eighteenth Century)

Cut one large old hare in small pieces, and put it
in a jar, with three blades of mace, a little salt, two
large onions, half a pint of red wine, and three quarts
of water ; bake it in a quick oven three hours, then
strain it into a tossing-pan ; have ready boiled three
ounces of French barley, or sago water ; scald the
liver of the hare in boiling water two minutes ; run
it through a hair sieve, with the back of a wooden
spoon ; put it into the soup with the barley or sago
and a quarter of a pound of butter ; set it over the
fire, keep stirring it, but do not let it boil : if you
do not like liver, put in crisped bread steeped in
red wine. This is a rich soup, and proper for a
large entertainment ; and where two soups are
required, almond or onion soup may be used for
the top and the hare soup for the bottom.

147. LENTIL SOUP (Hertfordshire)

To a quart of strong stock put about a cup of
lentils, and seasoning to taste. Let it simmer till
the lentils are thoroughly mashed, then give it a
boil-up.

148. GERMAN LENTIL SOUP (VEGETARIAN)
(Kent)

Scald half a pound of lentils in boiling water, drain
and put on with quantity of boiling water required.
Fry some onions, celery and tomatoes in butter
till brown, and add. Simmer two hours.

149. MILK SOUP (Essex)

Take four large potatoes and one onion, peel and
cut them into quarters, and put them into two

quarts of boiling water or white stock. Boil till
done to a mash, strain through a colander, and rub
the vegetables through with a wooden spoon, return
the pulp and soup to the saucepan, with one pint
of milk, and bring to the boil ; when it boils, sprinkle
in three tablespoonfuls of crushed tapioca, stirring all the time. Boil fifteen minutes, and serve.

150. MULLIGATAWNY SOUP (Hertfordshire)

Fry some onion and carrot in butter till they become
a light brown, then add a small piece of apple, some
sultanas, coconut, chutney, Harvey's sauce, a pinch
of salt and pepper, a tablespoonful of curry powder,
a little curry paste, and about a quarter of a
pint of strong stock, and let simmer for about an
hour.

151. MULLIGATAWNY (Kent, 1809)

Take four onions sliced small and a head of garlic,
fry them a light brown, then put them into a stewpan
with the meat, which should be fowl or any white meat.
Three spoonfuls of curry powder and two of flour
mixed together, likewise a spoonful of lemon juice
and cayenne pepper to your taste. Pour over it a
pint of boiling water and let it simmer slowly for a
short time, then add a sufficient quantity of broth
made without vegetables to make a tureen of Mulli-
gatawny. The ingredients must then stew together
an hour. To be served up with a dish of rice as
for curry. Cold fowl will dress this way extremely
well.

5

152. ONION SOUP (Eighteenth Century)

Boil eight or ten large Spanish onions in milk and
water ; change it three times. When they are quite
soft, rub them through a hair sieve. Cut an old cock
in pieces and boil it for gravy, with one blade of
mace ; strain it, and pour it upon the pulp of the
onions, boil it gently with the crumb of an old
penny loaf, grated into half a pint of cream ; add
cayenne pepper and salt to your taste ; a few heads
of asparagus or stewed spinach both make it eat
well and look very pretty : grate a crust of brown
bread round the edge of the dish.

153. ONION SOUP (Kent, 1809)

Take half a pound of butter, put it in a stewpan
on the fire, let it all melt. Let it boil till it has done
making any noise, then have ready ten or twelve
middling-sized onions, peeled and cut small, throw
them into the butter, and let them fry a quarter of
an hour ; shake in a little flour and stir them round,
and let them cook a few minutes longer, then pour in
a quart or three pints of boiling water, and stir
well ; take a piece of upper crust of stale bread,
about as big as the top of a penny loaf, cut small, and
throw it in. Season it with salt to your taste, let it
boil ten minutes, stirring it often, then take it off
the fire, and have ready the yolks of two eggs beaten
very fine with half a tablespoonful of vinegar ; mix
some of your soup with them ; then stir the rest into
your soup, and mix it well and pour it into your tureen.

154. BROWN ONION SOUP (Eighteenth Century)

Skin and cut roundways in slices six large Spanish
onions, fry them in butter till they are a nice brown

and very tender, then take them out, and lay them
on a hair sieve to drain out the butter. When
drained, put them in a pot, with five quarts of
boiling water, boil them one hour and stir them
often ; then add pepper and salt to your taste. Rub
the crumbs of a penny loaf through a colander, put
it to the soup, stir it well to keep it from being in
lumps, and boil it two hours more. Ten minutes
before you send it up, beat the yolks of two eggs
with two dessertspoonfuls of vinegar and a little of
the soup, pour it in by degrees, and keep stirring it all
the time one way. Put in a few cloves if you choose.
N.B.—It is a fine soup, and will keep three or four
days.

155. WHITE ONION SOUP
(Eighteenth Century)

Take thirty large onions, boil them in five quarts
of water, with a knuckle of veal, a blade or two of
mace, and a little whole pepper. When your onions
are quite soft, take them up, and rub them through
a hair sieve and work half a pound of butter with a
little flour into them. When the meat is boiled so as
to leave the bone, strain the liquor over the onions,
boil them gently for half an hour, serve up with a
coffee-cup full of cream, and a little salt. Be sure
you stir the soup when you put in the flour and
butter, for fear of its burning.

156. OX-CHEEK SOUP (Ireland)

Put an ox-cheek into cold water in a tub to
soak for a couple of hours, then break the bones,
and wash it well in warm water ; put it into a soup-
pot, and cover it with cold water. When it boils,

skim it very clean, and put in herbs, a head of
celery, a turnip, carrots, two large onions, some
pepper, allspice, and lemon, thyme, marjoram, and
parsley. Cover the pot close, and let it boil slowly ;
skim well ; simmer about three hours ; take out
the head and let it boil slowly for about an hour.
If you wish to thicken it, put two ounces of butter
to melt in a pan, and then stir in as much flour as
will dry it up ; brown it when well mixed together,
and add it to the soup, stirring it well. Give it
half an hour longer to boil. Strain it, if you wish,
through a hair sieve.

157. OX-CHEEK SOUP (Eighteenth Century)

First break the bones of an ox-cheek, and wash it
in many waters; then lay it in warm water, and throw
in a little salt to fetch out the slime ; wash it out
very well. Then take a large stewpan, put two
ounces of butter at the bottom of the pan, and lay
the flesh side of the cheek down ; add to it half a
pound of shank of ham, cut in slices, and four heads
of celery ; pull off the leaves, wash the heads clean,
and cut them in with three large onions, two carrots,
and one parsnip sliced, a few beets cut small, and
three blades of mace ; set it over a moderate fire a
quarter of an hour ; this draws the virtue from the
roots, which gives a pleasant strength to the gravy.

I have made a good gravy by this method with
roots and butter only, adding a little browning to
give it a pretty colour. When the head has simmered
a quarter of an hour, put to it six quarts of water,
and let it stew till it is reduced to two quarts. If you
would have it like soup, strain and take out the
meat and other ingredients, and put in the white

part of a head of celery cut in small pieces, with a little browning to make it a fine colour; take two ounces of vermicelli, give it a scald in the soup, and put the top of a French roll in the middle of a tureen, and serve it up.

If you would have it like stew, take up the cheek as whole as possible, and have ready, cut in square pieces, a boiled turnip and carrot, a slice of bread toasted and cut in dice; put in a little cayenne pepper, and strain the soup through a hair sieve upon the meat, carrot, turnip, and bread.

158. PASSOVER BALLS FOR SOUP (Jewish)

Chop an onion and half a pound of suet very finely, stew them together until the suet is melted, then pour it hot upon eight spoonfuls of biscuit flour: mix it well together: add a little salt, a little grated nutmeg, lemon-peel, and ginger: add six beaten eggs: put the balls into the soup when it boils, and boil them for a quarter of an hour. The quantity of eggs and flour may appear disproportioned, but the flour employed is of a peculiar kind, used for the purpose in Jewish families. Nothing can exceed the excellence of the balls made after this recipe; they are applicable to any kind of soups.

159. PEA SOUP (Essex)

Four pints of water, one pint of dried peas, three onions, three carrots, two turnips, a bunch of herbs, sixpennyworth of beef bones (or stock from boiling salt beef). Soak the peas in two or three waters for twelve hours, wash the bones, put them in a clean saucepan with the water and peas, add

salt and pepper, skim well while boiling. Scrape
the carrots, peel the turnips, skin the onions, cut
them all in dice, add to the bones and peas, simmer
very gently for four hours. Remove the bones,
season with dried mint if liked, rub through a hair
sieve if a purée is required. The water in which a
joint of salt beef has been boiled, or one pint of
bone or vegetable stock can be used instead of the
bones.

160. COMMON PEAS SOUP (Eighteenth Century)

To one quart of split peas put four quarts of soft
water, a little lean bacon, or roast-beef bones, with
one head of celery; cut it and put it in with a
turnip, boil it till reduced to two quarts; then
work it through a colander with a wooden spoon;
mix a little flour and water, and boil it well in the
soup, and slice in another head of celery, with cayenne
pepper and salt to your taste. Cut a slice of bread
in small pieces, fry them a light brown, and put them
in your dish; then pour the soup upon it.

161. GREEN PEA SOUP (Essex)

Half a pint of shelled peas, one quart of the
green shells, one and a half pints of water, two
ounces of butter, one onion, two sprigs of mint, two
lumps of sugar, half a pint of milk, one teaspoonful of
cornflour. Shell the peas, rinse the empty shells,
and with a sharp knife remove the strings. Melt
the butter in a very clean saucepan, put in the peas,
the prepared shells, the onion sliced, and toss (to
absorb the flavour of the butter) over a slow fire
for a few minutes, *but do not brown*. Then add the
water, mint, sugar, and boil until tender. Rub all

through a hair sieve. Blend the cornflour smoothly
with the milk. Put the soup back into the saucepan, add the milk and cornflour, and stir until it
boils. Season and serve. Fried croûtons of bread
should be handed with this soup.

162. GREEN PEA SOUP (Hertfordshire)

Get some nice peas in their shells. Boil them
till they are quite tender, and pass through a fine
wire sieve ; then add a little strong white stock
and boil for an hour, colouring if required ; then
thicken and serve with some fried sippets.

163. GREEN PEAS SOUP (Eighteenth Century)

Shell a peck of peas and boil them in spring
water till they are soft, then work them through a
hair sieve ; take the water that your peas are boiled
in, and put in a knuckle of veal, three slices of ham,
and two carrots, a turnip, and a few beet leaves
shred small, and add a little more water to the meat ;
set it over the fire, and let it boil one hour and a
half ; then strain the gravy into a bowl, and mix
it with the pulp, and put in it a little juice of spinach,
which must be beaten and squeezed through a cloth ;
put in as much as will make it look a pretty colour,
then give it a gentle boil, which will take off the
taste of the spinach ; slice in the whitest part of a
head of celery, put in a lump of sugar the size of a
walnut. Take a slice of bread, and cut it in little
pieces, cut a little bacon the same way, fry them
a light brown in fresh butter ; cut a large cabbage-
lettuce in slices, fry it after the other, put it in the
tureen with the fried bread and bacon. Have ready

boiled, as for eating, a pint of young peas, and put
them in the soup, with a little chopped mint if you
like it, and pour it into your tureen.

164. GREEN PEAS SOUP WITHOUT MEAT
(Eighteenth Century)

In shelling your peas, separate the old ones from
the young, and boil the old ones soft enough to
strain through a colander ; then put the liquor and
what you strained through to the young peas, which
must be whole ; add some whole pepper, mint, a
large onion shred small, put them in a large saucepan, with near a pound of butter ; as they boil up,
shake in some flour, then put in a French roll, fried
in butter, to the soup. You must season it to your
taste with salt and herbs ; when you have done so,
add the young peas to it, which must be half boiled
first. You may leave out the flour if you do not
like it, and instead of it put in a little spinach and
cabbage-lettuce, cut small, which must be first
fried in butter and well mixed with the broth.

165. POTATO SOUP (Essex)

Two heads of celery, one carrot, one onion, one
parsley root, and some leeks. Boil together in some
stock with a little butter. Take some floury
potatoes, cook, and rub through a hair sieve. Boil
with the other ingredients.

166. POTATO SOUP (Ireland)

Two onions, three potatoes, two ounces of bacon,
all sliced thin, pepper, and salt. Two quarts of
water. Boil two hours.

167. RICE AND BONE SOUP (Sussex)

Well cover the bones with water. Take four carrots, two turnips, and two onions. Cut small. A small tablespoonful of salt and a teaspoonful of sugar. Boil the bones well and take off the fat. Then add the vegetables, and boil for another half hour. Then take away the bones and season the soup to taste.

168. SAGO SOUP (Hertfordshire)

Put two pints of good strong chicken broth in a pan, with a little parsley, onion, and celery ; bring to the boil and reduce it to one and a half pints ; strain and put back into the pan. Bring to the boil again. Then add four dessertspoonfuls of fine sago, simmer until the sago is quite cooked, season with salt and pepper, and just before serving put into the soup some chicken cut up in small dice, and half a teaspoonful of thick cream.

169. CREAM SAGO SOUP (Hertfordshire)

Take one quart of good veal stock nicely seasoned ; to it by degrees add two ounces of medium sago, first washed in boiling water. Simmer gently till the sago is quite dissolved and forms a sort of jelly ; add one gill of good cream, and just before serving, put in the yolks of two eggs well beaten. Care must be taken that the soup is not boiling when the eggs are added. Serve with fried sippets.

170. TASTY SOUP (Essex)

Take the liquor in which codfish has been boiled, and add to each quart half a teacupful of tapioca,

a carrot, half a head of celery, and a little parsley.
Cut the vegetables up very small and boil until
they are cooked. Then thicken with flour. Add
pepper and salt to taste, and serve with dry toast
cut into small fancy shapes. This is very tasty and
costs very little.

171. TOMATO SOUP (Hertfordshire)

Fry some onions and tomatoes till they are quite
tender, then pulp through a sieve and add some
strong stock ; when ready, thicken very slightly
and serve with some fried sippets.

172. TRANSPARENT SOUP (Eighteenth Century)

Take a leg of veal, and cut off all the meat as thin
as you can ; when you have cut off all the meat
clean from the bone, break the bone in small pieces,
put the meat in a large jar, and the bones at top,
with a bunch of sweet herbs, a quarter of an ounce of
mace, half a pound of Jordan almonds, blanched
and beaten fine; pour on it four quarts of boiling
water, let it stand all night by the fire, covered close.
The next day put it into a well-tinned saucepan,
and let it boil slowly till it is reduced to two quarts.
Be sure you take the scum and fat off as it rises all
the time it is boiling ; strain it into a bowl, let
it settle for two hours, pour it into a clean saucepan,
clear from the sediment, if any, at the bottom ;
have ready three ounces of rice boiled in water.
If you like vermicelli better, boil two ounces ; when
done enough, put it in and serve it up.

173. AN EXCELLENT WHITE SOUP
(Eighteenth Century)

To six quarts of water put in a knuckle of veal, a large old fowl, a pound of lean bacon, and half a pound of rice, a few pepper-corns, two or three onions, a bundle of sweet herbs, and three or four heads of celery in slices. Stew all together till your soup is as strong as you choose it, then strain it through a hair sieve into a clean earthen pot; let it stand all night, then take off the scum, and pour the soup clear off into a tossing-pan; put in half a pound of Jordan almonds beaten fine, boil it a little, and run it through a sieve, then put in a pint of cream and the yolk of an egg. Make it hot (but not boiling) and send it to table.

174. WHITE SOUP WITH POACHED EGGS
(Eighteenth Century)

Take veal stock or chicken broth: beat half a pound of almonds, and the breast of a fowl, very fine in a mortar: add these to the white stock, boil well, and strain off. Let it gently simmer on the stove, while you poach eight eggs: lay these in your soup, with a French roll in the middle, filled with minced chicken or veal. Serve very hot.

175. A GOOD VEGETABLE SOUP (Essex)

Boil bones for six or eight hours, then strain the liquor off. When cold, take all the fat completely off. Mince somewhat small a couple of turnips, a very little onion, a piece of shalot, and some outside pieces of celery. Let the stock boil for twenty minutes before it is required for dinner, then throw in the minced vegetables and a tiny bit of butter. Let the stock and vegetables boil rapidly for half an hour, and if the soup is not sufficiently thick with the vegetables, mix a teaspoonful of flour smoothly with cold water and strain it in, and let it simmer at once. Then strain it into the soup-tureen, in which you can put the toast that was left from breakfast, cut into tiny squares.

176. RICH VERMICELLI SOUP
(Eighteenth Century)

Into a large tossing-pan put four ounces of butter; cut a knuckle of veal and a scrag of mutton into small pieces, about the size of walnuts; slice in the meat of a shank of ham, with three or four blades of mace, two or three carrots, two parsnips, two large onions, with a clove stuck in at each end; cut in four or five heads of celery washed clean, and a bunch of sweet herbs, cover the pan close up, and set it over a slow fire, without any water, till the gravy is drawn out of the meat, then pour the gravy out into a pot or basin. Let the meat brown in the same pan, and take care it does not burn, then pour in four quarts of water; let it boil gently till it is wasted to three pints, then strain it, and put the other gravy to it, set it on the fire, add to it two ounces of vermicelli, the nicest part of a head of celery, cayenne pepper and salt to your taste, and let it boil for four minutes. If not a good colour, put in a little browning; lay a small French roll in the soup-dish, pour the soup upon it, and lay some of the vermicelli over it.

CHAPTER V

FISH RECIPES

NOTE.—Fish was very largely consumed in former days ; and it was, as a rule, so highly spiced and seasoned as almost (from our point of view) to swamp and destroy its flavour. Spices and condiments were indispensable to our forefathers ; and they would consider our modern treatment of fish insipid in the extreme. The days when herrings, dried or fresh, were the staple diet of the peasantry —when apprentices petitioned for special clauses in their indentures, that they should not be compelled to eat fresh salmon more than twice a week— are now so far beyond our ken as to be almost inconceivable. The following hints have been selected as those most feasible under present conditions, and largely deal with the utilisation of cold cooked fish—always a problem for the kitchen. Attention is especially directed to the easy and valuable recipe for preparing a " Finnan-Haddock," which, as usually cooked, is often a source of dyspepsia : to the excellent method for " Home-made Bloater Paste " ; and to " Sardine Sandwiches."

177. HOME MADE BLOATER PASTE (Yorkshire)

Put six large herrings into *boiling* water for ten minutes, then cut off their heads, skin them, and

draw out all the bones. Beat them in a mortar,
and add as follows : ten ounces of butter, three
dessert-spoonfuls of anchovy sauce, cayenne and
white pepper to taste.

178. TO BAKE COD (Middlesex)

The thickest part of the cod should be chosen for
this dish, which is to be filled with a stuffing of
grated bread crumbs, a bit of butter, the yolks of
three hard-boiled eggs, pepper, salt, grated lemon
peel and nutmeg, and an anchovy finely cut up,
binding the whole with the white of egg beaten up :
put the whole in a dish that will stand fire, with
bits of butter over the top of it, and bake it in the
oven for an hour. A Dutch oven is the best suited
for this dish, as it requires to be frequently basted
and turned : melted butter or oyster sauce may be
served with it.

179. TO DRESS A SALT COD
(Eighteenth Century)

Steep your salt fish in water all night, with a
glass of vinegar ; it will fetch out the salt and make
it eat like fresh fish. The next day boil it ; when it
is done enough, pull it in flakes into your dish, then
pour egg sauce over it, or parsnips boiled and beaten
fine with butter and cream. Send it to the table
on a hot-water plate, for it will soon grow cold.

180. TO DRESS CODS' SOUNDS
(Eighteenth Century)

Steep your sounds as you do the salt cod, and
boil them in a large quantity of milk and water ;
when they are very tender and white, take them

up and drain the water out, then pour the egg sauce boiling hot over them, and serve them up.

181. FISH CAKES (Middlesex)

Break up very fine any remains of cold fish, having carefully boned and skinned it. Pass through a sieve any cold potatoes, and mix an equal quantity of them with the fish. Moisten with any melted butter left over, or with a well-beaten egg, add a few bread crumbs to make the mixture firm. Season with pepper and salt. Make the mixture into balls or small round cakes. Roll in egg and bread crumbs, as for frying fish, and fry a light brown. Garnish with parsley and lemon.

182. TO CAVEACH FISH (Eighteenth Century)

Cut your fish into pieces the thickness of your hand, season it with pepper and salt, let it lie an hour, dry it well with a cloth, flour it, and then fry it a fine brown in oil. Boil a sufficient quantity of vinegar, with a little garlic, mace, and pepper, to cover the fish; add the same quantity of oil, and salt to your taste; mix well the oil and vinegar, and when the fish and liquor is quite cold, slice some onions to lay in the bottom of the pot, then a layer of fish, then onions, and so on till the whole fish is put up. The liquor must not be put in till it is quite cold.

183. FISH CUSTARD (Surrey)

Take any cold fish, remove all bones and skin, lay it in small pieces in the bottom of a pie-dish, with a little salt and pepper. Mix a dessertspoonful of flour smooth in a teacupful of milk, add one beaten egg, and a piece of butter about as big as a walnut, creamed but not oiled. Pour it over the fish, and bake half an hour or so in a moderate oven.

184.　FISH PIE (Cape Colony)

Remove all skin and bone from any kind of fish (cooked) ; break into small pieces, mixed with minced onion previously fried in butter ; add pepper, salt, and mustard, tomato sauce, half a well-beaten egg, and pack into a pie-dish. Cover with mashed potatoes, brush over with an egg. Bake for three-quarters of an hour.

185.　FISH PIE (Hertfordshire)

Put three-quarters of a pint of milk into a saucepan, with half a small onion, two cloves, a few thin strips of lemon peel, two or three pieces of parsley, and some salt and pepper, and let the milk simmer gently for twenty minutes. Make a paste in a saucepan with an ounce and a quarter of butter, and an ounce and a quarter of flour. Strain the milk and mix it gradually with the paste, thus making a thick sauce ; ascertain whether more pepper and salt is required, and add a teaspoonful of anchovy essence. Butter a pie dish, and place a layer of cooked fish which has been divided into flakes, in it, and cover it with some of the prepared sauce, a few shrimps, and a little chopped parsley ; then put more fish and the remainder of the sauce and some shrimps and parsley as before. Have in readiness some smoothly mashed potato, which has been well seasoned with salt, pepper, and nutmeg, and mix with some milk, butter, and the yolk of an egg ; then beat it until it is light and creamy. Cover the fish with this, mark the top with a fork, and after pouring a small quantity of warm butter over the surface of the potato, bake the pie in a quick oven until it is evenly browned.

186. FISH PIE (Ireland)

Line the bottom and sides of a deep fireproof china dish evenly with vermicelli, which has been previously boiled in salt and water, well drained, and then tossed in a little melted butter. Have ready some fillets of sole or whiting. Brush each fillet on both sides with melted butter, then dip them in fine bread crumbs, nicely seasoned with finely-chopped parsley, pepper, and salt. Fill up the dish with the fillets in layers, pour over them a gill of thick tomato sauce : spread vermicelli over the top, sprinkle with bread crumbs and chopped parsley, and put some small pieces of butter here and there. Bake in a steady oven half an hour, and serve in the dish in which it is cooked, garnished with parsley.

187. FISH PIE (Sussex)

Ingredients.—Fresh-water fish—either roach, jack, or eel ; one pound of onions, half a pound of rice, three eggs,. quarter of a pound of butter, puff paste. *Method.*—Boil rice. Lightly fry onions, cut into small pieces. Boil eggs hard, then slice them, and bone fish. Fill pie-dish, first with layers of rice, then onions, butter, fish, and eggs. So on. Cover in with puff paste, and bake. Very good, hot or cold.

6

188. FISH PUDDING (Surrey)

Take one pound and a half of cooked fish, half a teacupful of bread crumbs, two well-beaten eggs, half a teacupful of milk, one ounce melted butter, a little anchovy essence, a teaspoonful of chopped parsley, pepper, and salt. Break up the fish as finely as possible in a bowl, and add the rest—the eggs and milk last. When all is well mixed put it in a buttered mould, and let it steam for three-quarters of an hour. For a baked fish pudding, use an equal amount of well-mashed potatoes, and about twice as much milk and butter as is mentioned above.

189. FISH AND POTATO PUDDING (Kent, 1809)

Boil a quantity of potatoes, and bruise them like mashed potatoes. Mix with them a small portion of dried fish cut or grated very small, and a small quantity of dripping or butter. Put them into a tin dish, which may be put into a Dutch oven placed before the fire, until sufficiently browned, or in a common oven where a cottager's family bakes bread. If a few boiled eggs cut into small pieces be mixed with the mashed potatoes, the dish is much improved.

190. FISH SALAD (Devonshire)

One pound of cold, cooked fish, one potato (mashed), one lettuce, two tablespoonfuls olive oil, one tablespoonful vinegar, one hard-boiled egg, one teaspoonful made mustard, one tablespoonful milk, one piece cooked beetroot, two pickled gherkins, parsley, salt, pepper, castor sugar. Break up the fish

into small pieces, removing the skin and bones. Wash
the lettuce, or endive, tear into small pieces, dry in
a cloth. Mix the mashed potato with milk; stir
into it oil and vinegar; season with mustard, pepper,
salt, and sugar. Mix well to produce a smooth
dressing. Blend the salad with the fish, season with
the dressing. Pile up on a dish or salad bowl.
Garnish with slices of beetroot, and serve.

191. SCALLOPED FISH (Hampshire)

Take any cold fish remaining from the previous
day, carefully remove all skin and bones, and break
it as small as possible with two silver forks (steel
ones will injure the flavour). Mix into it any cold
melted butter left over, or use half a pint of milk
and two ounces of butter; add bread crumbs to
thicken it, and salt, pepper, and mace to taste.
When all is well mixed, take some scallop-shells,
or saucers, butter them well, and put in the mixture.
Scoop a little hollow in the centre at the top, and
put in a very small quantity of anchovy sauce
Dust over with very fine bread crumbs, and drop
some tiny bits of butter over. Bake in a moderate
oven, and serve very hot. These will be found most
savoury and appetising. A little chopped parsley
may be added at discretion, and grated cheese
may be dusted over along with the crumbs.

192. A GOOD WAY TO STEW FISH
(Eighteenth Century)

Mix half a tumbler of wine with as much water as
will cover the fish in the stewpan, and put in a little
pepper and salt, three or four onions, a crust of
bread toasted very brown, one anchovy, a good

lump of butter, and set them over a gentle fire ; shake the stewpan now and then, that it may not burn. Just before you serve it up, pour your gravy into a saucepan, and thicken it with a little butter rolled in flour, a little ketchup, and walnut pickle ; beat well together till smooth, then pour it on your fish, and set it over the fire to heat, and serve it up hot.

193. TO STEW FLOUNDERS, PLAICE, OR SOLES
(Eighteenth Century)

Half fry your fish a fine brown in three ounces of butter ; then take up your fish, and put to your butter a quart of water, and boil it slowly a quarter of an hour with two anchovies, and an onion sliced ; then put on your fish again, and stew them gently twenty minutes ; then take out your fish and thicken the sauce with butter and flour, and give it a boil ; then strain it through a hair sieve, over the fish, and send them up hot. *N.B.*—If you choose cockle or oyster liquor, put it in just before you thicken the sauce, or you may send oysters, cockles, or shrimps in a sauce-boat to table.

194. FLOUNDERS WITH SORREL
(Eighteenth Century)

Gut and cleanse the flounders well, then slash them crossways, three cuts only on one side, and lay them in your saucepan. Put in as much water as will just cover them, with a little vinegar, salt, and one onion. Let them boil quickly. Then boil four handfuls of sorrel, pick off the stalks, and chop it very small. Add to this about half a pound of melted butter, or more, according to the quantity of fish. Put it over your flounders, and serve away quick.

195. TO BAKE HADDOCKS (Middlesex)

Cut off the heads and fins of two or three haddocks, and put into a stewpan, with an onion, salt, pepper, and two anchovies cut up fine, a little flour, two tablespoonfuls of French white wine, and a little ketchup. Boil this all well up together, and when the fish has been skinned and cut into pieces, lay them in a deep pie-dish ; pour the above sauce over them, and bake in an oven. Strew the bottom of the dish with bread crumbs, and strew some more over the fish, having seasoned them well with pepper and salt and a little grated nutmeg.

196. FINNAN HADDOCKS STEAMED (Surrey)

Instead of boiling a finnan haddock the usual way, lay it in a deep basin or dish, and *pour boiling water upon it* to cover it completely. Cover it up close with a dish, lid, or thick cloth, and leave it for ten minutes. At the end of that time it will be better done, tenderer, and infinitely more digestible than if cooked the old way. Put on some butter, and a dash of pepper, and serve on a very hot dish.

197. BAKED HERRINGS (Eighteenth Century)

When you have cleaned your herrings, lay them on a board; take a little black pepper, a few cloves, and a good deal of salt; mix them together, then rub it all over the fish, lay them straight in a pot, cover them with alegar, tie a strong paper over the pot, and bake them in a moderate oven. If your alegar be good, they will keep two or three months. You may eat them either hot or cold.

198. TO BOIL HERRINGS (Eighteenth Century)

Scale, gut, and wash your herrings, dry them clean, and rub them over with a little vinegar and salt, skewer them with their tails in their mouths, lay them on your fish-plate. When your water boils put them in; they will take ten or twelve minutes boiling. When you take them up, drain them over the water, then turn the heads into the middle of your dish, lay round them scraped horse-radish. Parsley and butter for sauce.

199. FRIED HERRINGS (Eighteenth Century)

Scale, wash, and dry your herrings well; lay them separately on a board, and set them to the fire two or three minutes before you want them, it will keep the fish from sticking to the pan; dust them with flour. When your dripping or butter is boiling hot, put in your fish, a few at a time; fry them over a brisk fire; when you have fried them all, set the tails up one against another in the middle of the dish, then fry a large handful of parsley crisp, take it out before it loses its colour, lay it round them, and parsley sauce in a boat; or, if you like onions better, fry them, lay some round your dish, and make onion sauce for them : or you may cut off the heads after they are fried, chop them, and put them into a saucepan, with ale, pepper, salt, and an anchovy, thicken it with flour and butter, strain it, and put it in a sauce-boat.

200. TO MARINATE HERRINGS (Middlesex)

Clean the fish well without washing. Open them so as to remove the backbone, and season them well with salt, pepper, and onion chopped very fine. Roll them up tight, and place them in a jar, and pour over them some vinegar and water in equal quantities : tie over the jar with paper, and bake in a rather slow oven for an hour. When they are cold, pour over them a little cold vinegar. They may be pickled in the same way as mackerel. See Mackerel (No. 212).

201. HERRINGS AND POTATOES (Essex)

Wash, and boil some potatoes in their skins, carefully, so that they do not break or get too soft. Drain them, peel, and slice them rather thickly. Keep them hot. Fry lightly a chopped onion in one ounce of butter. Dust in some flour, and three tablespoonfuls of vinegar, salt and pepper, and a bay-leaf, and not quite a pint of water. Put the pan to simmer at the side of the stove. Take two red herrings, wash them well, cut them lengthways, and remove the bones. Cut up the flesh small, and let it simmer in the sauce for a few minutes. Put in the potatoes next, stirring carefully so as not to break them. Then add two ounces of butter and one gill of milk, and stir all well over the fire till it reaches boiling point.

202. POTTED HERRINGS (Lancashire)

Take six fresh herrings, wash, dry, and split them open, removing heads and backbones. Dust them with flour, pepper and salt, chopped parsley, or

powdered mace. Roll them up tightly with a small
piece of butter in the centre of each. Place them
in a pie dish, pour over them equal quantities of
vinegar and water, but not to cover them. Cover
the pie dish and bake in a slow oven, then remove cover and let them brown a little. Two bay
leaves may be put in the pie dish instead of mace.

203. KEDGEREE (Essex)

Boil two ounces of rice till tender and let it remain till cold. Mix with it a teaspoonful of curry
powder and some pepper and salt. Melt two
ounces of butter in an enamelled saucepan, break
two eggs into it and add the rice and stir until it is
stiff, which will be in a few minutes. Have a large
square of buttered toast ready on a hot dish, and
pile the kedgeree on it. Sprinkle chopped parsley
on the top, and serve very hot. The remains of a
cold finnan haddock, removed from the bones and
mixed with the kedgeree, makes a very palatable
supper-dish.

204. KEDGEREE (Kent)

Boil two tablespoonfuls of rice, add any fish previously cooked (salmon or turbot is best); it should
be well picked from the bone in shreds ; beat up
an egg and stir it in just before serving, but don't
let it boil after the egg is added. Serve with egg
sauce.

205. KEDGEREE (Sussex)

Take half a pound of cold fish, break it into
flakes, and remove all the bones. Then take three
ounces of cold boiled rice, and two hard-boiled eggs ;

cut the whites into dice and put them with the fish
and rice into a saucepan, with one and a half ounces
of butter, pepper, salt, and nutmeg. When well
heated, put the kedgeree into a dish, and squeeze the
yolks of eggs through a sieve over the top. Then
put it into the oven to brown.

206. BASHAWED LOBSTER (Cheshire)

Take any remains of lobster and cut them up.
Chop up a piece of onion about the size of a nut,
and a little parsley. Mix all together with a little
anchovy sauce and cayenne pepper. Cut up in
small pieces a bit of butter and mix, and then put
all into the shell of the lobster. Cover over the top
with fine breadcrumbs, and butter and shake a
few raspings on the top. Bake for about ten
minutes, or a little more, and serve hot.

207. LOBSTER FRITTERS (French)

Chop up the meat, with the red part and the
spawn, of two large lobsters, very fine, with finely
grated crumbs of bread, add a little butter, and
season with pepper and salt, and a very small quantity of chopped sweet herbs : make this into a kind
of paste with yolk of egg, and having formed it
into pieces about two inches in length and an inch
thick, dip them into a good thick batter, and fry.

208. SCALLOPED LOBSTER (Cheshire)

Line your dish well with lobster (tinned or
fresh) put some bread crumbs next, then lobster,
and so on, alternately with little bits of butter,
salt, and red pepper. Cover *well* with bread crumbs,

and then put little bits of butter all over, and pour
vinegar over all. Bake for about half an hour or
more, or brown nicely before the fire. You can
heat it up a second time, pouring in milk or gravy
or anything to moisten. One tin of lobster makes
two small dishes. Serve very hot. Excellent.

209. BOILED MACKEREL (Eighteenth Century)

Gut your mackerel and dry them carefully with
a clean cloth, then rub them slightly over with a
little vinegar, and lay them straight on your fish-
plate (for turning them round often breaks them)
into your fish-pan, and boil them gently fifteen
minutes. Put a little salt in the water when it boils,
then take them up and drain them well, and put the
water that runs from them into a saucepan, with
two teaspoonfuls of lemon pickle, one meatspoonful
of walnut ketchup, the same of browning, a blade
or two of mace, one anchovy, a slice of lemon ; boil
them all together a quarter of an hour, then strain
it through a hair sieve, and thicken it with flour
and butter; send it in a sauce-boat, and parsley
sauce in another. Dish up your fish with the tails in
the middle; garnish it with scraped horse-radish
and barberries.

210. MACKEREL FARCED (Eighteenth Century)

Take the roes out of four or six mackerel, fill
them with a farce of whiting, confine the farce in
them, and then marinate the fish in sweet oil, with
a sliced onion, parsley, sweet herbs, pepper, and
salt. Let them remain for two hours, then drain
and broil them carefully over a slow fire, that they

may be done carefully without scorching. Serve
with a rich sauce over them.

211. PICKLED MACKEREL (Essex)

Six smallish mackerel, four bay leaves, four
cloves, one level teaspoonful of peppercorns, one
pint vinegar, thyme, parsley, fennel (if possible),
salt, and pepper. Fillet the mackerel, wash and
dry them, strew over them the herbs finely minced,
and a little pepper and salt. Put in a dish with
a little butter, and bake till cooked. Try with a
skewer and see if they are done. Boil the vinegar,
bay leaves, cloves, and peppercorns together for ten
minutes. Stir in a teaspoonful of extract of meat,
and when cold, strain the liquor over the fish. Let
it stand for several hours before serving, then drain,
put on a clean dish, and garnish with parsley.

212. TO PICKLE MACKEREL (Middlesex)

Having cut and split the mackerel, cover them
with a little thyme, parsley, and shalots, chopped
fine : then fry the fish carefully : when done, pour
over them some vinegar boiled with black pepper,
a few cloves, and three or four bay leaves : this
liquor is not to be poured upon them until it is cold.

Another mode is to cut the fish into pieces, and to
cover them well with a mixture of black pepper
nutmeg, mace, and salt, reduced to a fine powder :
then fry them brown in oil, and when cold put them
into a jar, and fill it up with strong vinegar previously boiled. If it is intended to keep them for
some months before using, the top of the jar
should have a depth of at least an inch of good

sweet oil, and be carefully tied over with parchment.
This is a rich preparation. The quantities of spices
required for six common-sized mackerel are three
nutmegs, six blades of mace, and an ounce of black
pepper. A good handful of salt should be used.

213. RED MULLET (Eighteenth Century)

The red mullet is the only one worth using, the
grey mullet being somewhat poor and coarse.
Butter sheets of white paper, sprinkle them with a
little salt. Clean the mullet, wipe them dry, and
roll each in a separate paper. Broil (or bake)
them, and send them to table in the papers, and
serve with them a tureen of good melted butter
or Italian sauce.

214. FRIED PERCH OR TROUT (Eighteenth Century)

When you have scaled, gutted, and washed your
perch or trout, dry them well, then lay them separately on a board before the fire for two minutes
before you fry them. Dust them well with flour, and
fry them a fine brown in roast dripping or rendered
suet. Serve them up with melted butter and crisped
parsley.

215. PERCH IN WATER SOKEY (Eighteenth Century)

Scale, gut, and wash your perch, put salt in your
water : when it boils, put in the fish, with an onion
cut in slices, a handful of parsley picked and washed
clean and as much milk as will turn the water white ;
when your fish are done enough, put them in a soup
dish and pour a little of the water over them with
the parsley and the onions, then serve them up with

butter and parsley in a boat. Onions may be omitted
if you please. You may boil trout the same way.

216. SALMON IN BROTH (Seventeenth Century)

Boil it in wine, water, and vinegar till it be
tender, then put it into a piece of butter, which will
soak into the fish. Take it out and lay it on a
napkin, and eat it with vinegar : you may also
make an excellent sauce to it with butter and
anchovies.

217. SALMON CUTLETS (American)

Half a can of salmon mashed with a fork, one
cup of hot mashed potatoes with salt and pepper
to taste ; form into cutlets, dip in egg and bread
crumb, and fry in deep lard, or in cooking oil.

218. PICKLED SALMON (Essex)

Boil the salmon in salted water, with two lumps
of sugar and one gill of vinegar in it. Let it simmer
until done. Then take it out and put into vinegar
that has been well spiced with mixed pickling spice
and a small piece of ginger. The vinegar must
cover the fish. You can keep it thus until required.

219. ROLLED SALMON (Eighteenth Century)

Take a side of salmon ; when it is split, the bone
taken out, and scalded, strew over the inside some
pepper, salt, nutmeg, mace, a few chopped oysters,
minced parsley, and bread crumbs. Roll it up
tight, put it into a deep jar, and bake it in a quick
oven. Pour a good Italian sauce over it before
serving.

220. SALMON STEAK WITH CUCUMBER (Yorkshire)

Scale the fish and cut some slices about one and a half inches thick, and wipe them perfectly dry. Allow two ounces of good butter, the strained juice of a lemon, and a teaspoonful of white wine, to each pound of fish. Rub the bottom of a stewpan well with butter and lay in the fish, straining the lemon juice over it ; add a little salt. Lay over the fish a buttered paper, then put on the lid and allow twenty minutes for each pound of fish. When the fish is cooked, dish on a hot, dry dish. Garnish with little heaps of cucumber ; round it strain the gravy from the stewpan, through a tammy ; mix with it a tea-spoonful of finely chopped tarragon and chervil, and pour over fish.

221. SALMON TIMBALES (American)

Mash half a tin of salmon. Heat half a cup of cream, add three or four tablespoonfuls of butter. When the butter is melted, add salmon, salt, and pepper to taste. When taken from the fire add two eggs, then put it into buttered cups covered with buttered paper. Stand them in hot water in the oven for twenty minutes.

222. TO CAVEACH SOLES (Eighteenth Century)

Fry your soles either in oil or butter ; boil some vinegar with a little water, two or three blades of mace, a very few cloves, some black pepper, and a little salt ; let it stand till cold, and when cold beat up some oil with it ; lay your fish in a deep jar, and slice a good deal of shalots or onions between each fish ; throw your liquor over it, and pour some oil on the top. It will keep three or four months, thus made rich and fried in oil ; it must be stoppered well and kept in a dry place. Take out a little at a time when you use it.

223. SOLOMON GUNDY TO EAT IN LENT
(Yorkshire, 1769)

Take five or six white herrings, lay them in water all night, boil them as soft as you would do for eating, and shift them in the boiling to take out the saltness. When they are boiled, take the fish from the bone, leaving on the head and tail, and mind you don't break the bones in pieces. Take the white part of the herrings, a quarter of a pound of anchovies, a large apple, a little onion or shalot shred fine, and a little lemon-peel. Shred them all together, and mix them well, and lay them over the bones on both sides, in the shape of a herring. Then take off the peel of a lemon very thin, and cut in long bits, just so as it will reach over the herrings. You must lay this peel over every herring pretty thick. Garnish with a few pickled oysters, capers, and mushrooms, if you have any.

224. BAKED SPRATS (Eighteenth Century)

Rub your sprats with salt and pepper, and to every two pints of vinegar put one pint of red wine ; dissolve a pennyworth of cochineal, lay your sprats in a deep earthen dish, pour in as much red wine, vinegar, and cochineal as will cover them, tie a paper over them ; set them in an oven all night. They will eat well and keep for some time.

225. SARDINE SANDWICHES (Isle of Wight)

Take a dozen good-sized sardines, carefully remove the skin and backbone, and mash them up very fine with a fork. Add salt, pepper, and vinegar to taste, and mix it well in. Have thin white bread-and-butter cut, spread the mixture thinly over a slice, and cover it with another slice. When sufficient has been prepared, cut off the crust, cut the sandwiches diagonally into little three-cornered pieces not more than two and a half inches long by one and a half wide, and arrange them prettily upon a folded napkin with sprigs of parsley between. This is an enormous improvement upon the ordinary sardine sandwich, and excellent for afternoon tea, etc. Its only fault is that the sandwiches, which take a good while to prepare, are eaten up so rapidly !

226. CURRIED SARDINES (Kent)

One box of sardines ; strain off the oil into a small frying-pan ; add to this a dessertspoonful of curry powder previously mixed with cold water. Thicken the oil with a little arrowroot, previously mixed with water. As soon as the curry and oil are about as thick as good melted butter, the sauce is ready. Pour this over the sardines, and place them in the oven long enough to get heated through. When quite hot, serve with pieces of toast.

227. SARDINES ON TOAST (Cheshire)

Divide the sardines lengthwise ; remove the bones, tail, and skin ; put them in the oven between

two hot plates, with a little of the oil—let them be
quite hot. Cut some thin strips of bread the
length of the sardines, fry them in butter, and serve
with half a sardine on each. Add a little cayenne
and salt and a squeeze of lemon. Serve hot.

228. SARDINE TOAST (Essex)

Six sardines, two eggs, cayenne, buttered toast.
Scale and bone the sardines, boil the eggs hard
and chop them. Lay first the chopped egg on some
hot buttered toast, then the sardines seasoned with
cayenne, and put in the oven to get hot.

229. TWICE LAID (Kent)

Take remains of cold salt fish. Tear it into
flakes ; mix it with double its quantity of mashed
potatoes. Moisten with milk; season with pepper
and salt, roll into balls ; dip them in egg ; roll
them in bread crumbs, and fry them brown. Drain
and serve on a folded napkin.

CHAPTER VI

VEGETABLES AND VEGETARIAN DISHES

NOTE.—Our great-grandmothers had probably never heard of vegetarian diet : our grandmothers and mothers encountered it in a much less acute form than what prevails to-day. *Cooked* vegetables, up to about the end of the seventeenth century, were held in small esteem, although the peasantry employed them under the compulsion of Hobson's choice. Salad vegetables, uncooked, were largely used in preference. Both are now such staple articles of diet, that one can hardly conceive an adequate meal without them. Meanwhile, vegetarianism, whether as a matter of medical order, fad, or conviction, is continually on the increase.

The *strict* vegetarian of the twentieth century abstains, not only from fish, flesh, and fowl, and from all animal fats, however derived, but, I believe, in extreme cases, even from eggs and from milk. This renders his feeding very difficult to deal with, if he take his meals at home. For average vegetarianism, however, undertaken as a matter of expediency rather than conviction, there is a perfect wealth of choice. The main constituents of this *embarras de richesse* are vegetables and fruits (fresh, dried, or preserved), cereals and farinaceous foods of every kind, nut-foods, eggs, milk, butter, and cheese *ad lib.* The last article supplies that touch of tastiness (not to mention that amount of concentrated nutriment) in which so many vegetarian dishes are conspicuously lacking. Among those which follow, will be found many excellent *plats*, tried and tested, which will serve to vary the monotony of plainer dishes : for it should always be remembered that the vegetarian must make up in bulk for the absence of meat, and monotony ought above all things to be avoided. Nut-foods, which are quite modern, find practically no place here ; but the vegetarian cook is referred to the respective sections upon Egg-Dishes, Cheese Recipes, Salads, Savouries, Puddings, Sweet Dishes, Jams, Pickles, and Sauces, from which she may increase her repertory.

230. ARTICHOKES WITH CHEESE (Surrey)

Boil two pounds of Jerusalem artichokes, drain, and mash them up with one gill of milk. (Mashed cooked onions are an improvement : and yesterday's onion sauce is an admirable substitute for milk.) Turn the mixture into a well-buttered baking dish, dust the top well with grated cheese, and bake till the top becomes coloured.

231. BROAD WINDSOR BEANS PUDDING
(Middlesex)

Broad beans may be made into a pudding by pounding them in a mortar after boiling them and taking off the skins, then seasoning with salt and pepper, and a little butter, and tying them up in a cloth that has been floured and buttered. The pudding must be put into boiling water, and boiled for half an hour. When done, squeeze the water out by pressing the cloth, and take out the pudding, to which you can give any shape you please. Yolks of eggs beaten up, and the crumb of a roll soaked in cream, may be pounded with the beans to make a richer sort of pudding. This may be either boiled in a basin, or baked in an oven.

232. CABBILOW (Kent, 1809)

Mash boiled potatoes and boiled cabbages together, mixing with them slices of onions, and sprinkling the mess with pepper and salt, to which should be added a little butter or dripping. The dish is improved by being put into a Dutch oven to be browned, like mashed potatoes. (See the Irish dish, Kailcannon, No. 241.)

233. STUFFED CABBAGES (Middlesex)

Take two good-sized cabbages, soak them for twenty minutes in scalding water and salt, then dip them in cold water, take out a portion of the centre, fill it with chopped veal and fat bacon seasoned with salt, pepper, and other spices, and made into a stuffing with eight yolks of eggs : then tie up the cabbage to keep in the stuffing. Put at the bottom of a saucepan some slices of bacon, carrots, onions, and sweet herbs : over which place the cabbages, moistening them from time to time with good stock. Let the whole stew over a slow fire for at least an hour and a half, after which drain the cabbages, press them a little, and serve them up, without the herbs with which they have been cooked, with Espagnole, or any other such sauce. Remove the strings before serving.

234. CHESTNUTS AND BRUSSELS SPROUTS
(Devonshire)

Boil some chestnuts in water for two hours; remove the peel. Boil an equal amount of Brussels sprouts for half an hour, strain them well; be careful not to break them. Have ready a frying-pan with hot beef dripping or butter, put in both chestnuts and sprouts, and keep them moving until the fat is absorbed (do not brown them); then serve.

235. CHESTNUT TEA CAKES (Surrey)

Take some chestnuts, boil them till they burst, throw them into cold water and peel them. Pound them to a dry powder; add an equal quantity of self-raising flour, butter, eggs, and sugar according to taste and quantity; mix into a dough with milk, roll out and cut into small round cakes about half an inch thick, and bake in a brisk oven to a light golden-brown.

236. CUCUMBERS WITH EGGS
(Eighteenth Century)

Take five large young cucumbers, pare, quarter, and cut them into slices, about the size of dice; put them into boiling water, let them boil up; then take them out of the water, put them into a stew-pan, with an onion stuck with cloves, a good slice of ham, a quarter-pound of butter, and a little salt;

set this over a fire for a quarter of an hour, keep it close covered, skim it well, and shake it often, as it is apt to burn ; then dredge in a little flour, and put in as much gravy as will just cover the cucumbers ; stir it well together, and keep a gentle fire under it till no scum will rise ; then take out the ham and onion, put in the yolks of two eggs beaten with a teacupful of good cream ; stir it well for a minute, then take it off the fire, and just before you put it in the dish, squeeze in a little lemon juice. Have ready five or six poached eggs to lay on the top.

237. FRIED CUCUMBERS (Eighteenth Century)

You must brown some butter in a pan, and pare and slice (but not too thin) six middling cucumbers. Drain them from the water, then put them into the pan. When they are fried brown, put to them a little pepper and salt, a lump of butter, a spoonful of vinegar, a little shredded onion, and a little gravy (not to make it too thin), and shake them well together with a little flour. You may lay these round your mutton as a sauce, or they are proper for a side-dish.

238. DRIED HARICOT BEANS (Surrey)

Wash the beans (quantity according to requirements), and throw away all that *float* upon the water. Soak them for twelve hours at least (overnight for preference). Put them into cold water slightly salted, bring slowly to the boil, and let them simmer very gently until quite tender. To improve the flavour, for one pint of beans add twelve ounces of onions, and a muslin bag of dried herbs : allowing three pints of water to boil them in.

239. A HERB PIE FOR LENT (Eighteenth Century)

Take lettuce, leeks, spinach, beets, and parsley, of each a handful, give them a boil, then chop them small. Have ready boiled in a cloth one quart of groats, with two or three onions in them; put them in a frying-pan with the herbs and a good deal of salt, half a pound of butter, and a few apples cut thin; stew them a few minutes over the fire, fill your dish or raised crust with it ; one hour will bake it.

240. HOT POT (Vegetable) (Ireland)

One pound of potatoes, one pound of onions, half a pound of good cheese. Slice potatoes, ditto onions, ditto cheese, and fry them separately. Then line a dish with potato and fill in with onions mixed with cheese, pepper, salt, and sage. Cover with the potato to form crust. Bake. To be eaten very hot. If left, the cheese will get hard.

241. KAILCANNON (Ireland)

Take some well-boiled potatoes, mash them thoroughly, adding pepper, salt, and a small piece of butter. Then take a rather less quantity of boiled and chopped greens, or green cabbage, with a little fine chopped onion, mix well, and serve very hot. It can be served in a shape.

242. BOILED LETTUCES (Middlesex)

Wash and put them into boiling water, with a little salt, let them boil until tender ; strain them

in a colander, and chop them up; then put them
into a saucepan with some fresh butter, a spoonful
of flour, a little nutmeg, salt, and the juice of a
lemon; let the whole boil for a quarter of an hour.
This may be varied by omitting the lemon juice,
adding some good cream, and thickening with the
yolks of two eggs. (This is an excellent plan where
lettuces are " bolted " and unsuitable for serving
cold. Ed.)

243. STUFFED LETTUCES (Middlesex)

Choose some large cabbage lettuces, and having
boiled them a quarter of an hour, dip them into cold
water and let them drain; then open the leaves
without breaking them, and fill the centre part with
a good forcemeat, and tie them up; stew them for
a short time, then drain them on a cloth, dip them
in a batter, and fry to a good colour. When done,
cover them with bread crumbs, and serve with some
white sauce.

244. MACARONI RISSOLES (Kent)

Take one teacupful of butter beans, which have
been boiled till they are quite soft, half a teacupful
of boiled macaroni, half a teacupful of cold mashed
potatoes, the yolks of two eggs, pepper and salt,
half a teacupful of brown bread crumbs—that is to
say, the crumbs of bread which has been browned
and dried in the oven. Cut the macaroni up into
small pieces; mash the beans and potatoes; mix
all together with half the quantity of breadcrumbs,
bind them with the yolk of the egg, and shape them
into small balls. Roll the balls in bread crumbs,

fry them a deep golden brown, and serve very hot. They are very nice with bacon at breakfast, or they will take the place of a vegetable at lunch-time.

245. MACARONI WITH TOMATOES (Kent)

Boil a quarter of a pound of pipe macaroni in water till tender ; turn it out on to a dish, add pepper and salt, garnish with fresh tomatoes that have been baked in the oven with a little butter. Shake over the whole some grated Parmesan cheese, and serve very hot. It should have a light, cobwebby appearance, which is obtained by the cheese being dredged in while the macaroni is very hot, and therefore melting quickly.

246. MAIZE (American)

Strip the grain from the young cob, boil it like peas : drain it, toss in some melted butter, salt, and pepper, and serve very hot, sprinkled with chopped parsley. When green maize is not procurable (though it can easily be grown as a garden vegetable) the tinned preparations called *Succotash*, and *Wyndham Corn*, though not so cheap, make useful dishes, and supply a change from the more hackneyed vegetables.

247. BAKED MUSHROOMS (Surrey)

Carefully peel the mushrooms, and put them, hollow-side uppermost, on a buttered baking-sheet ; fill the cavities with butter, and set in a moderately hot oven. They should be ready in about twelve minutes. It will be seen that they must be fairly whole mushrooms, not stale or broken ones.

248. FRICASSEED MUSHROOMS (Eighteenth Century)

Peel and scrape the inside of the mushrooms, throw them into salt and water ; if buttons, rub them with flannel; take them and boil them with fresh salt and water. When they are tender, put in a little shredded parsley, and an onion stuck with cloves, and toss them up with a good lump of butter rolled in flour. You may put in three spoonfuls of thick cream, and a little nutmeg cut in pieces, but take care to take out the nutmeg and onion before you serve it at the table. You may leave out the parsley, and add a glass of wine if you like.

249. MUSHROOMS AU GRATIN (Ireland)

Take eight or ten large cup mushrooms. Cut off all the stalks and peel them, and also peel very carefully the cup-like part of the mushroom, so as not to hurt the rim. Next scoop out the inside of these cups, and chop it up with the stalk of the mushrooms. Take a piece of shalot about as big as a large nut, and a teaspoonful of chopped parsley, and a very little chopped thyme, with a little cayenne pepper. Add about three ounces of scraped bacon, fat and lean. Put all over the fire, and fry for a time. If the mass is too dry, it shows there is not enough bacon-fat ; if it be too moist, add bread-crumbs. Fill the cups of the mushrooms with this mixture, and shake over some fine bread-raspings. Place the cups so prepared in a covered stewpan, with some butter or oil, and let them cook very gently till the cup part of the mushroom is quite tender. Serve hot, with toast, either plain, or with some rich brown gravy poured round them.

250. SCALLOPED MUSHROOMS (Middlesex)

Put the mushrooms into a saucepan with fresh butter, chopped parsley, shalots, and a few mushrooms, also chopped up ; moisten them from time to time, with a little butter and water, mixed with flour, and stew them gently for about half an hour, then put them into scallop-shells or a dish, covered with crumbs of bread. Put them over a charcoal fire for a short time, and brown with a salamander.

251. MUSHROOM POWDER (Eighteenth Century)

Take about half a peck of large buttons or flaps, clean them (but you must not wash them), and set them one by one in an earthen dish or dripping pan. Let them stand in a slow oven to dry until they will beat to a powder, and when they are powdered, sift them through a sieve. Take half a quarter of an ounce of mace and a nutmeg, beat and grate them very fine, and mix them with your mushroom powder. Bottle it, and it will be fit for use.

252. BAKED ONIONS (Surrey)

Put four or five Spanish onions, with their skins on, in a saucepan of salted water ; let them boil quickly for one hour. Then take them out, dry them thoroughly, wrap each one separately in a piece of buttered paper (or a paper bag) and bake them in a moderate oven for two hours or longer. Remove the paper and serve the onions in their skins.

253. RISOTTO (Lancashire)

A quarter of a pound of rice, a small onion, some stock, salt, pepper, butter, grated Parmesan cheese. Chop up the onion and fry it in butter. Put the rice in a saucepan with the stock and fried onion, and boil gently until the rice is tender and has absorbed all the stock. Stir in the cheese, salt, and pepper, and serve very hot.

254. RISOTTO FOR TWO PERSONS (Hertfordshire)

One onion, two ounces of rice, boiled in stock, two tomatoes put through a sieve, one ounce of grated cheese. Cut the onion in rings and fry in butter, till pale yellow. Strain all, and add the cheese just before serving.

255. TO BOIL PARSNIPS (Eighteenth Century)

Wash your parsnips well, boil them till they are soft, then take off the skin, beat them in a bowl with a a little salt, put to them a little cream and a lump of butter; put them in a tossing-pan, and let them boil till they are like a custard pudding ; put them on a plate, and serve them up.

256. PARSNIPS FRIED TO LOOK LIKE TROUT
(Yorkshire, 1769)

Take a middling sort of parsnips, not over thick, and boil them as soft as you would do for eating ; peel, and cut them in two the long way. You must only fry the small ends, not the thick ones. Beat two or three eggs, put to them a tablespoonful of flour, dip in your parsnips, and fry them a light brown in butter. Have for your sauce a little vinegar and butter.

257. JUGGED PEAS (Surrey)

This is one of the best ways to cook peas, whether fresh, tinned, or bottled. Shell a pint of peas, put them into a clean two-pound pickle bottle or any jar with a closely-fitting top, adding a tablespoonful of butter, a teaspoonful of powdered sugar, a saltspoonful of salt, a dozen mint leaves, (and, at discretion, a very little black pepper). Cover the vessel tightly, and immerse it, to the extent of half its depth, in a pan of boiling water. Set the latter on the fire and boil briskly. Examine in half an hour : the peas, if very young, should be done by then ; if old, they will of course take longer.

258. PEAS PUDDING (Ireland)

Put a quart of dried peas rather loosely into a cloth, put them down in cold water slowly to boil till tender—good peas will take about two hours and a half. Rub through a sieve, adding an egg, an ounce of butter, some pepper and salt, and beat them well for about ten minutes. Flour the cloth, and tie the pudding tight as possible, and boil an hour longer. (Dried peas should always be soaked over-night for at least twelve hours.)

259. PEAS PUDDING HOT (Ireland)

This is an old recipe for peas pudding, to accompany cold pork. Put a breakfastcupful of split peas in a cloth : tie loosely to allow for swelling, and

boil *fast* for three hours in salted water. Turn out
and serve with melted butter.

260. STEWED PEAS (Eighteenth Century)

Take a quart of young peas, wash them, and put
them into a stewpan, with a quarter of a pound of
butter, three cabbage lettuces cut small, five or six
young onions, with a little thyme, parsley, pepper,
and salt, and let them stew all together for a quarter
of an hour; then put to them a pint of gravy, with
two or three slices of bacon or ham, and let them
stew all together till the peas are done enough; then
thicken them with a quarter of a pound of butter
rolled in flour.

261. BROWNED POTATOES WITH CHEESE
(Surrey)

Boil some potatoes in their " jackets," but do not
let them fall to pieces. Remove peel, and pare
them till all are the same size. Have a little butter
melted in a bowl, dip them in this, then roll them
in grated cheese, seasoned with pepper and salt.
Put them in a buttered tin in a good oven, and
when the cheese has coloured, serve " hot and hot."

262. CREAMED POTATOES (Kent)

Take six large potatoes, one ounce of butter,
a quarter of a pint of milk, the juice of half a lemon,
pepper, and salt. Peel the potatoes and boil them
for about five minutes, in order to make them a
little tender, but not at all breakable. Cut them
up into slices about a quarter of an inch thick.
Melt the butter in a small saucepan, throw in the

potatoes and stir them till they are well buttered, but not brown. Add the milk, pepper, and salt. Let the whole simmer till the slices of potato grow tender, and the sauce in which they are simmering is a little thickened. Then take the pan off the fire, add the lemon-juice, take out the slices of potato and range them on a dish. Boil up the sauce again with a pinch of flour to thicken it, pour it over the potato and serve at once.

263. CURRIED POTATOES (Hertfordshire)

Fry in dripping an onion, cut into thin slices. Cut up some boiled potatoes, and fry with the onion, dredge them with curry-powder, and add a little gravy, salt, and some lemon juice, if you have it. Allow this to stew for a quarter of an hour, and serve.

264. SEETHED POTATOES (Kent, 1809)

A number of small potatoes, or large potatoes cut in slices, are put into a cast-iron pot *without a lid*, with a sprinkling of salt, to which is sometimes added a small piece of butter. The pot without a lid is hung upon the crane which is found in the chimney of every cottage in Scotland, so as to be considerably above the fire, and to heat very slowly. No person who has not eaten potatoes prepared in this manner can conceive how delicious they are.

265. POTATO SANDERS (Surrey)

Mix with cold boiled potatoes, mashed up or passed through a sieve, enough flour to make a paste (*i.e.* nearly half their weight in flour). Dripping rubbed in,—about four ounces to the pound—will greatly improve the paste : but will be debarred from the strict vegetarian. Roll out the paste about half an inch thick, and cut it in small squares. Soak some bread crumbs in a very little water, just enough to moisten them well : mix in with them some minced parsley, herbs, a little minced onion, salt (see " Vegetable Goose," No. 273). Put a little of this mixture into each square of paste, roll up, and bake as a sausage roll.

266. STEWED POTATOES (Kent, 1809)

Take a pipkin, *having a lid made to fit close.* Lay in it one or two or more rows of potatoes, with the skins scraped off, and cut into slices. Sprinkle a little pepper and salt over them. Then lay a row of onions, then, if it can be afforded, a mutton chop. Then let there be layers of potatoes, onions, with pepper and salt and mutton, until the pipkin is filled. If mutton cannot be afforded, use a very small portion of dripping or mutton suet ; add a teacupful of water. Put the pipkin, *with the lid on,* covered with a piece of linen cloth, into a pan of water, *without a lid.* Let the water boil very slowly, or rather simmer, for five or six hours. Potatoes, when thus prepared, afford a most savoury and nourishing meal.

267. POTATOES WITH WHITE SAUCE (Middlesex)

Put into a saucepan a small slice of butter, with a little flour, diluted with a little stock : to which add some salt and pepper, and thicken it over the fire ; having boiled the potatoes, peeled them, and cut them into slices, pour this sauce over them, and serve hot. To vary the flavour, some minced capers or a little chopped parsley may be added to the sauce.

268. TO STEW SPINACH (Eighteenth Century)

Wash your spinach well in several waters, put it in a colander, have ready a large pan of boiling water, with a handful of salt, put it in, let it boil two minutes, it will take off the strong earthy taste ; then put it into a sieve, squeeze it well. Put a quarter of a pound of butter in a tossing-pan, put in your spinach, keep turning and chopping it with a knife until it is quite dry and green ; lay it upon a plate, press it with another, cut it in the shape of sippets or diamonds, pour round it very rich melted butter. It will eat exceedingly mild, and with quite a different taste from the common way.

269. SPINACH WITH POACHED EGGS
(Yorkshire, 1769)

Take two or three handfuls of young spinach, pick it from the stalks, wash and drain it very clean, put it into a pan with a lump of butter and a little salt, and keep stirring it all the time till it be done enough, then take it out and squeeze out the water. Chop it and add a little more butter, lay it in your dish in quarters, and botwixt every quarter (*sic*) a poached egg, and one in the middle. Fry some sippets of white bread and put them into your spinach, so serve it up.

8

270. SUCCOTASH (American)

Have green maize freshly cut, and take the cobs cleanly out of the outer leaves, etc. Add an equal quantity of soaked butter beans or haricot beans. Put them into a saucepan with only just enough water to cover them ; let them simmer till perfectly tender, then pour off the water and pour in the same amount of milk. Let the vegetables stew a little more, then add pepper and salt and a teaspoonful of cornflour mixed smooth in a little cold milk, and a lump of butter about as big as a large walnut. Mix well, let all boil up once, and serve very hot.

271. SCALLOPED TOMATOES (Sussex)

Put alternate layers of tomatoes and bread crumb in a pie-dish. Let the top layer be of tomato. Sprinkle bits of butter over. Season well and bake.

272. VEGETABLE CURRY (Kent)

Cut onions into thin slices, and fry a good brown in butter ; add a breakfast cup of milk in which a teaspoonful of curry has been mixed. Let all boil together for twenty minutes, stirring the whole time. Then add the vegetables,—previously par-boiled—and let all simmer for an hour. Potatoes, peas, beans, carrots, and turnips may be used. Broad beans alone make a delicious curry.

273. VEGETABLE GOOSE (Surrey)

Soak half a pound of bread crumbs in cold water, squeeze them nearly dry and mash them. Mix in one onion chopped small, one teaspoonful chopped parsley and herbs, one ounce of butter, pepper and salt to taste. Put in a buttered dish and bake in good oven for about one hour.

274. VEGETABLE HOT POT (Kent)

Take two large potatoes, one stick of celery, one large carrot, one large onion, butter, pepper, and salt. Slice the vegetables, put them in layers in a pie-dish, with a layer of potatoes at the top. Pour in sufficient boiling water to cover them. Set the dish in a cool oven and let it simmer for one and a half hours. Lay little pieces of butter on the top, and serve very hot. This method of cooking the vegetables preserves the flavour far better than boiling would do.

275. VEGETABLE PIE (Surrey

Required, one onion, one carrot, one turnip, one stick of celery, one handful of green peas (if in season), half an ounce of sago, one ounce of butter, pepper and salt, pie-crust. Cut all the vegetables small, and stew them with the sago and butter in a *very little* water until nearly cooked. Then put them in a pie-dish, cover with crust, and bake about half an hour. Any other vegetables may be used at pleasure. Mushrooms are always an improvement.

276. VEGETABLE-MARROW AU GRATIN (Sussex)

Take some very small marrows, slice them in rounds about half an inch thick, and lay them in a pie-dish. Pour tomato sauce over till they are hidden, then cover with bread crumbs and grated cheese, and sprinkle little bits of butter over. Bake in a good oven until you find the marrow tender on trying it with a fork.

CHAPTER VII

SALADS

NOTE.—Although our ancestors were exceedingly fond of salads, and included much more under this head than we ever dream of using—they rarely troubled to write down any formal recipe. Their gardens were full of " salletings,"—not only lettuce, cucumber, radish, mustard, cress, water-cress, beet, celery, onions, and " love-apples " (tomatoes)—but a great many salad-plants of which we in England now hardly know the names. A sorrel-bed was a common thing—for sorrel, as Evelyn observed, " imparts so grateful a quickness to the salad that it should never be left out." Chervil, purslane, burnet, lambs' lettuce, " small-mustard," tarragon, dandelion, and various other plants, were welcome ingredients in the salad-bowl. And I conjecture that these wise folk also included cold cooked potatoes, old or new, cold cooked onions, and any such left-over vegetable odds and ends. Their salad dressings would seem to have been quite simple—oil, pepper, and vinegar, salt and mustard, plus an occasional hard-boiled yolk and a spoonful of cream. For the most part, I imagine, they did not bother about dressings at all. They preferred uncooked to cooked vegetables, as has already been said, and the mere plain green foodstuffs sufficed them. The Mayonnaise Sauce recipe given on page 120 will be found particularly good.

277. APPLE SALAD (Sussex)

Two cupfuls of sour apple, half a cupful of celery, half a cupful of English walnuts, two tablespoonfuls of salad dressing, one cupful of whipped cream, one teaspoonful of sugar. Salt and pepper.

278. CHEESE SALAD (Sussex)

Rub the yolk of a hard-boiled egg with a dessert-spoonful of butter, add salt, sugar, pepper, mustard, about half a pound of grated cheese, and a dessert-spoonful of vinegar.

279. ENDIVE SALAD (Middlesex)

Take some fine white endives, carefully wash and drain them, and lay them in a salad-bowl. Chop some shalots, wash them in several waters, and squeeze out the water in a cloth. Add them to the endive, together with some chopped tarragon, chervil, and burnet. Season with thin mayonnaise sauce, and add two finely chopped Chili capsicums.

280. GERMAN SALAD (Hertfordshire)

One tablespoonful of salad oil, one and a half tablespoonfuls light claret, one ounce chopped onion, one teaspoonful French mustard, one table-spoonful of white wine, the yolk of one boiled egg, passed through sieve. Take boiled potatoes, sliced beetroot in dice, sliced cucumber ; mix all together.

281. HARICOT SALAD (Kent)

One pint of white haricots, well boiled. Sprinkle over them one teaspoonful of salt, and half a teaspoonful of pepper ; add a very finely-chopped onion, or a few drops of shalot vinegar, one tablespoonful of vinegar, two of oil, and sprinkling of very finely chopped parsley.

282. WINTER SALAD (Surrey)

Take some white haricot beans, French beans, potatoes, beetroot, and onions. Blanch all the vegetables separately, cool, and drain them. Chop the onions, and put them in the corner of a cloth ; dip this in cold water, and press the water out of the onion. Do this two or three times, which will render the onion more digestible. Cut the potatoes and beetroots in half-inch discs. Put all into a salad-bowl, adding some chopped chervil ; season with salt, pepper, oil, and vinegar, and mix the whole well.

283. WINTER SALAD (Middlesex)

Cut up small some endive and celery, add two tablespoonfuls of russet apples cut into dice. Stir well and cover these with half a pound of grated nuts, and mix mayonnaise sauce with the whole.

284. SALAD DRESSING (Kent)

Take the yolks of two hard-boiled eggs ; bruise them very carefully until they are in a fine powder, entirely free from lumps. Then add gradually a tablespoonful (or a little more, according to taste) of the best salad oil, and stir it well until it is the

consistence of a smooth paste ; then add a tablespoonful of freshly mixed mustard. After this is
well mixed, stir in very gradually two tablespoonfuls
of white vinegar and a teaspoonful of Chili vinegar ;
then add a little salt, a few grains of cayenne pepper
and a few drops of anchovy sauce. When these
are all well mixed, stir in gradually a large teacupful or more of good sweet cream. Add a small
lump of sugar. This mixture will keep a week if
well corked. It is thicker and better if used the
day after it is made.

285. CHEAP SALAD DRESSING (Ireland)

Take one hard-boiled egg, one tablespoonful of
flour, the same of vinegar (or more *ad lib*), one
breakfastcupful of milk, one dessertspoonful of
butter, one teaspoonful of mustard, a pinch of salt,
a little sugar. Blend the flour and milk. Blend
to a paste, in separate bowl, a *hot* yolk of egg,
with butter, mustard, and salt. Then add blended
milk and flour. Boil the mixture, keeping it stirred
until it thickens. When cold, add vinegar to it :
and if still too thick, put a little cold milk. The
white of an egg can be chopped up and added, or
used for decoration.

286. MAYONNAISE SAUCE (Isle of Wight)

Whisk the yolks of six eggs, add to them one
dessertspoonful of made mustard, one saltspoonful
of salt, and a pinch of cayenne, stirring all the time.
Put them into an enamelled saucepan, then add a
quarter of a pint of salad oil, whisking all the time ;
next, a quarter of a pint of milk or cream, one table-

spoonful of vinegar, and the same of Worcester sauce. Last, add a quarter of a pint of vinegar. Continue to stir gently all the time you are mixing, or the sauce will curdle. Now put the saucepan over a slow fire and whisk until it becomes thick. It must not boil. Take it off the fire, continue stirring gently till it cools. Then put it into wide-mouthed bottles, cork closely, and it will keep two or three months. (This is a yacht steward's recipe, and most excellent.)

CHAPTER VIII

CHEESE DISHES

NOTE.—The vast majority of cheese-made dishes are quite modern. Either cheese, in former days, was eaten to the very rind, careless of its hardness, staleness, or "blue-vinny" appearance: or it was little esteemed as a combined flavouring and nutriment when used in small quantities along with vegetables, eggs, etc. Nowadays it is not only, in grated form, a chief ingredient of many vegetarian dishes, but a most valuable adjunct to all sorts of home-made savouries. And as these recipes afford the means of utilising odd bits of hard, dry cheese, the careful cook will gladly avail herself of them. I have included one form of serving cheese, which will be found exceedingly palatable, simple, and digestible: the "Creamed Cheese," No. 288. No one who has ever tried this is likely to revert to the toasted cheeses and "Welsh Rabbits" which he (or she) has so frequently relished—and regretted.

287. CHEESE BISCUITS (Sussex)

Take nine ounces of flour, six ounces of grated cheese, three ounces of butter, one or two tablespoonfuls of milk, two eggs, pepper, and salt. Roll out very thin and bake fifteen or twenty minutes.

288. CREAMED CHEESE (Cheshire)

This is the simplest, easiest, most digestible, and economical, way of serving "Welsh Rabbit," and one very little known at all. Scrape or thinly flake some cheese into a breakfast-cup or small bowl, until it is three-parts full. Fill it up with *boiling* water, cover it with a saucer, stand it on a hob, or stove, or in the fender before an open fire, for about ten minutes. At the end of that time, pour off the water (with which will go all the oily matter of the cheese) and you will find the cheese like a thick cream at the bottom. Pour this upon a piece of *hot* toast upon a *hot* plate, pepper and salt it to taste, and serve. The above quantity is enough for one person. Canadian Cheddar will serve, though English Cheddar is better. As a lunch or supper dish it is most excellent.

289. COTTAGE CREAM CHEESE (Rutlandshire)

Take some milk which has gone sour suddenly, and reduce it to curds and whey by boiling. Place the curd on a cloth to drain thoroughly, and when it is dry as you can get it, press it down tightly in a wooden box, with clean fresh hazel leaves laid here and there in layers. Keep a good weight upon the top of the curd, and turn it when thoroughly dry. It will be fit to eat in a couple of days.

290. CHEESE FRITTERS (Sussex)

Take two tablespoonfuls of flour, a little made mustard, cayenne pepper, salt, one egg, and one ounce of Parmesan cheese. Add as much milk as will make it into a stiff batter. Heat some lard

very hot, and drop the batter into it a spoonful
at a time. The fritters should be a golden brown
when done.

291. MACARONI CHEESE (Boiled) (Isle of Wight)

Half a pound of tomatoes, one tablespoonful curry
powder, a quarter of a pound of macaroni, two ounces
butter, salt and pepper, two ounces grated cheese.
Put the macaroni into salted boiling water, boil it
thirty minutes, and drain it. Scald the tomatoes,
peel and slice them. Put the butter in a saucepan
to melt, add sliced tomatoes, and macaroni, stir
well together, add pinch of salt and curry powder.
Lastly, with two forks, stir in the grated cheese for
five minutes, then serve.

292. MACARONI CHEESE AND TOMATOES (Devonshire)

Half a pound of macaroni, one pound of tomatoes,
two ounces cheese (Parmesan), two ounces Gruyère,
half an ounce of butter, one shalot, pepper, salt,
browned bread crumbs. Wash the macaroni, cut it
up into small pieces and boil it in salted water till
tender. Scald the tomatoes, and then they will
easily peel ; slice them, chop the shalot finely,
place the various ingredients respectively in layers
in a greased pie-dish. The last layer must be the
macaroni. Then on the top put a little grated
cheese, the brown bread crumbs, and the butter.
Bake half an hour in a brisk oven.

293. CHEESE PUDDING (Isle of Wight)

Two ounces of grated cheese, two ounces of breadcrumbs, one ounce of butter, one teaspoonful made

mustard, half a gill of milk, one egg, cayenne pepper, salt. Put butter and milk into saucepan, make quite hot, pour over crumbs and cheese, then add yolk of egg and mustard mixed. Whip white of egg and add lastly, or it may be piled on the top (when pudding is cooked) with a little grated cheese, and just set. Bake pudding twenty minutes.

294. CHEESE PUDDING (Kent)

Two eggs, half a teacupful of cream or good milk, and a little salt and pepper. Two large tablespoonfuls of grated cheese. Mix all together, and bake for twenty minutes in quick oven.

295. CHEESE PUDDINGS (Surrey)

(1) Grate three ounces of cheese, mix with two ounces of bread crumbs, two well-beaten eggs, one and a half pints of milk, pepper and salt to taste, and a squeeze of lemon juice. Bake in a well-buttered dish from a half to three-quarters of an hour.

(2) Three ounces of grated cheese, three ounces of bread crumbs, a little made mustard, salt to taste. Pour over as much boiling milk as it will absorb, and two well-beaten eggs. Bake in a buttered pie-dish about twenty minutes, and serve immediately and very hot.

(3) One teacupful of milk, one teaspoonful of flour, one well-beaten egg, one ounce creamed butter, four ounces of grated cheese. Mix well, and bake ten to fifteen minutes. To be served and eaten at once.

296. GLOUCESTER RABBIT

Make some buttered toast, cut it into rounds or squares, put it to keep hot in the oven. Put half an ounce of butter in a small saucepan to melt, stir in two tablespoonfuls of grated cheese, half a small teacupful of milk and two tablespoonfuls of fresh bread crumbs—enough to make it as thick as cream. Add salt and pepper, pour the mixture on to the toast, and serve it immediately.

297. RAMAKINS (Surrey)

Beat up two eggs thoroughly, add in two ounces of grated cheese, two tablespoonfuls of cream or milk, one teaspoonful of flour (mixed smooth first in a drop of milk). Pepper and salt to taste. While you are doing this, cream two ounces of butter in a cup, on the stove or in the oven, and add that last : mix all well together, pour into buttered patty-pans, and bake a quarter of an hour or twenty minutes in a good hot oven. The ramakins should be a golden brown. These never fail to please.

298. CHEESE STRAWS (Essex)

Rub one and a half ounces of butter into three ounces of flour, with the finger-tips. Add one and a half ounces of American Cheddar, grated, quarter of a teaspoonful of baking powder, a little cayenne, a small pinch of salt, and a little water, enough to mix it into a very dry dough. Roll it out an eighth of an inch thick, and cut it into sticks two and a half inches long. Bake it like pastry, but don't let it colour.

299. CHEESE STRAWS (Isle of Wight)

Two ounces of butter, two ounces of flour, one
yolk of egg, three ounces of cheese (two ounces of
Parmesan and one ounce of Cheddar), one tablespoonful of cold water, cayenne pepper, salt. Rub
the butter into the flour, add the grated cheese,
pepper, and salt, mix to the consistency of pastry
with the yolk and water ; roll out, and cut into rings
and straws, allowing six straws to one ring. When
served, the straws are placed through the rings.
Bake a short while in a quick oven.

300. CHEESE STRAWS (Kent)

Two ounces of butter, two ounces of flour, two
ounces of breadcrumbs, two ounces of grated cheese,
half small saltspoonful of mixed salt and cayenne ;
mix all to a paste, roll it out quarter of an inch in
thickness ; cut it into narrow strips, lay them on
a sheet of paper, and bake for a few minutes. Arrange the straws on a napkin and serve hot.

301. CHEESE STRAWS (Staffordshire)

Half pound of dried flour, quarter pound of butter,
quarter pound of grated cheese, teaspoonful mustard, cayenne, saltspoonful of salt. Rub butter
into the flour, and then mix the whole well together. Beat the whites of two eggs with half a pint
of cold water, and stir in enough to form a firm paste.
Knead it well. Roll it out the eighth of an inch
thick, and cut it into straw-like strips, about five
inches long. Bake in a quick oven a pale brown

colour—about five minutes. Pile them on a dish prettily, and serve hot or cold. Must be kept in a dry place.

302. CHEESE STRAWS (Surrey)

Three ounces of flour, two ounces of butter, the yolk of one egg, three ounces of grated cheese, cayenne, and salt. Rub the butter into the flour, add the cheese and seasoning. Mix into a stiff paste with the yolk of egg. Roll out and cut into narrow strips about two inches long. Bake a pale fawn colour on a greased tin or baking sheet. To be served hot.

303. CHEESE STRAWS (Yorkshire)

Grate two ounces of Parmesan cheese into a bowl. Mix with it a pinch of salt, a little cayenne, and two ounces of flour, and rub in two ounces of butter. Make the ingredients into a stiff paste with the yolk of one egg, cut them about five inches long, and bake them. When they are a pale brown colour they are done. They will take about ten minutes.

304. CROUSTADES (Yorkshire)

Make a good paste, roll it out very thin, line small patty pans or moulds with it. Grate two ounces Parmesan cheese into a basin, and mix with it one ounce warmed (but not oiled) butter, the yolks of two eggs and white of one, a saltspoonful of salt, and a pinch of cayenne. If the eggs are small, three yolks will be required instead of two. Put a small spoonful of the mixture into the pans, and bake in a moderate oven. When they are set and the pastry is lightly coloured, they are done enough.

305. STEWED CHEESE (Surrey)

Take four ounces of grated cheese, two ounces of butter, one tablespoonful of cream ; stir them together in a saucepan until nearly boiling. Add the beaten-up yolk of an egg, stir well, and pour the mixture upon a very hot dish. Serve with dry hot toast.

CHAPTER IX

EGG DISHES

NOTE.—Countless as are the various methods of serving eggs, there yet seems room for more. As is pointed out in the Cakes section, our grandmothers used eggs with what we should consider reckless extravagance, merely as ingredients in made dishes. They do not appear to have considered eggs seriously as articles of food. However, a few interesting egg-dishes are here set forth, which will help towards the (always too monotonous) breakfast and luncheon table, or towards the enlargement of the vegetarian menu.

Eggs have been divided by a humorist into seven classes : viz.

New-laid Eggs.
Breakfast Eggs.
Fresh Eggs.
Cooking Eggs.
Shop Eggs.
Election Eggs.
Eggs.

And nowadays, when the origin of those harmless necessary edibles is so frequently " wrop in mystery," it behoves one to be exceedingly careful. You should break all eggs, of whose antecedents you

are not absolutely certain, one by one into separate
cups, lest a single tainted specimen should ruin all.
And it is usually cheaper, in the long run, to procure
the best eggs only ; for those coming under the
category of cooking eggs are hardly ever to be
depended on. We are not of the same mind as
those Tartar tribes who bury their eggs in the earth
till they shall be " high " enough to suit the tribal
tastes ; and even the notorious " curate's egg,"
which was " good in parts," displeases our fastidious
fancy. It is therefore advisable to lay in a stock
of eggs when they are cheap and plentiful, and to
preserve them against the dear days, first testing
each by any of the different recognized methods.

306. BAKED EGGS (Kent)

Beat up four eggs well. To each egg allow two
tablespoonfuls of new milk and half a teaspoonful
of fine-chopped parsley ; season with pepper and
salt to taste. Melt some butter (or dripping) in an
enamelled pie-dish ; pour in mixture, and bake
quickly in a quick oven.

307. BIRDS' NESTS (Essex)

Boil four eggs eleven minutes, let them get quite
cold, then shell the eggs and coat them over with
egg, and roll in sausage meat. Drop them in a pan
with plenty of lard, and brown them well. Lift
them up and drain them, cut them in halves, and
serve on buttered toast. These are very nice eaten
cold, served up on a dish with watercress.

308.　CHEESED EGGS (Surrey)

Boil six eggs hard, and when they are cold, remove
the shells. Cut them in slices, arrange these in
layers in a well-buttered baking-dish, with pepper
and salt. Dust grated cheese over each layer, and
moisten with white sauce. On the top, put a layer
of cheese, and over that a little (melted) butter.
(Sliced tomatoes may at pleasure be included in this
dish.) Bake until lightly coloured.

309.　CURRIED EGGS (Essex)

Four hard-boiled eggs, one sour apple, one large
onion, one ounce of butter, one ounce of flour, one
dessertspoonful of curry powder, one tablespoonful
of cream, one small teaspoonful of salt, half a pint
of milk, or milk and water, quarter of a pound of
Patna rice. Boil the eggs for ten minutes, shell
and lay them in cold water, to keep white. Peel
and chop finely the apple and onion, fry them in the
butter for five minutes, using a saucepan ; stir in
curry powder, then the flour and salt ; lastly, the
milk, and simmer gently for a quarter of an hour.
Add the cream and the eggs, which should be cut
in quarters. When quite hot, serve in a border of
boiled rice.

310.　CURRIED EGGS (Yorkshire)

Slice finely a couple of onions, and fry them a
delicate brown in two ounces of butter ; rub together till smooth, two ounces of curry powder,
two spoonfuls of good vinegar, and a teaspoonful
of castor sugar. Stir into it, over the fire, about

a breakfastcupful of good stock, and bring it to the
boil. When nicely blended, break into it five
or six eggs, and let them cook gently in this about
one or two minutes. Serve at once, with curried
rice.

311. EGGS À LA DUCHESSE (Kent)

Boil several new-laid eggs for ten minutes ; take
off the shells, and cut them in half (long-ways) ;
take out the yolks ; have ready some bread crumbs
soaked in milk, and mix (together with the yolks)
a little pepper, salt, and a little lemon peel and
parsley chopped fine. Put a layer of this mixture
at the bottom of a pie-dish ; then fill the whites
with the force-meat, and build them up in a pyramid
with some pieces of butter put on them and a few
bread crumbs, and then let them be in the oven to
get brown—not long enough for the white of egg
to get hard.

312. A PRETTY DISH OF EGGS (Yorkshire)

Break some eggs into a small pie-dish without
injuring the yolks, drop lightly some warm butter
on them, and strew bread crumbs lightly over them ;
put into the oven till the whites of the eggs are set,
and serve with a wreath of parsley. Of course, you
can put any quantity of eggs, but I should say about
one ounce of bread crumbs to four eggs.

313. BROWN FRICASSEE OF EGGS (Yorkshire, 1769)

Take eight or ten eggs, according to the bigness
you design your dish : boil them hard. Put them
in a stewpan of cold water, take off the shell ; then

fry them in butter till they be of a deep brown.
Have a little brown gravy and a lump of butter,
thicken it up with flour. Lay two or three eggs in
the middle of the dish, then cut the others in two,
and set them with the small ends upward round the
dish. Fry some sippets and lay round them.
Garnish with crisp parsley.

314. WHITE FRICASSEE OF EGGS (Yorkshire, 1769)

Take ten or twelve eggs, boil them hard and peel
them, put them in a stewpan with a little white
gravy. Take the yolks of two or three eggs, beat
them very well, and put to them two or three tablespoonfuls of cream, a tablespoonful of white wine,
a little lemon juice, shred parsley, and salt to taste.
Shake all together over the stove till it be as thick
as cream, but don't let it boil. Lay some of the
eggs whole in the dish, lay the rest round, cut in
halves and quarters; but you must not cut them
till you lay them in the dish. Garnish with sippets.

315. OMELETTE (Kent)

The yolks and whites of six eggs (these will
suffice for three or four persons), well beaten for
at least three minutes with three tablespoonfuls
of milk, some chopped parsley and onion, half a
teaspoonful of salt, a little pepper. When this is
ready, put a piece of butter as large as a walnut
into the frying-pan over a brisk fire, and when the
butter is hot, throw in the mixture of eggs, stirring
it, or rather, putting it together with a spoon or
ladle, to give it the shape, which can be finished
doing when it is thrown off the frying-pan on the

dish, for it must not be kept more than two minutes on the fire.

316. OMELETTES (Surrey)

To prepare a plain omelette, see that the frying-pan is thoroughly clean. Place in it about one ounce of butter. Break three eggs separately to see that they are fresh, beat them up with a little chopped parsley, and a pinch of pepper and salt. The eggs should not be beaten too much, or the white of them separates, and you produce a watery mixture which destroys the flavour and appearance of the omelette. When the butter is melted, pour the mixture into the frying-pan, and stir it till it begins to set or thicken. Shake the pan occasionally, and fold over the omelette neatly in an oval shape. When it is of a golden colour, turn it quickly into a hot dish. To be able to prepare a plain omelette is to be able to prepare any kind. If you require a cheese omelette, introduce into the mixture about a dessertspoonful of grated cheese, with a little pepper and salt, and sometimes a few grains of cayenne. In a sweet omelette, no pepper and salt, but a little grated sugar, and just before the omelette is folded in the pan, distribute evenly over it a little jam. If a bacon omelette, a few pieces of previously cooked bacon cut into small dice, and so on. In preparing an omelette, remember five things : a clean pan; mixture not to be too much beaten; omelette must not be too large (three eggs are better than six); it should not be too much cooked; it must be eaten immediately, or it becomes tough and flabby.

317. PALESTINE EGGS (Surrey)

Trim and boil twelve good-sized Jerusalem artichokes, and set them to cool. Boil six eggs hard and
let them get cold (they can be plunged into a bowl
of cold water), then cut them up. Slice the artichokes, lay them in a buttered baking-dish ; strew
the chopped eggs over them ; next, put a layer of
sliced tomatoes ; last, a layer of grated cheese.
Bake until lightly coloured, and serve very hot.

318. SCALLOPED EGGS (Devonshire)

Four new-laid eggs, half a teaspoonful made
mustard, four tablespoonfuls white crumbs, half an
ounce of butter, four tablespoonfuls chopped
cooked ham, bacon, game, or chicken, two tablespoonfuls hot milk or stock ; salt and pepper. Mix
crumbs, ham, and seasoning ; put half aside. Mix
the other half with mustard, a little oiled butter,
and enough milk to form a stiff paste. Butter
four saucers or scallop-shells, spread them thickly
with the above paste, leaving a hollow for the raw
egg. Shake over each egg some of the dry mixture
laid aside. Put a few pieces of butter here and
there. Bake until set ; about ten minutes.

319. SCOTCH EGGS (Middlesex)

Boil them hard, and when the shell has been removed, cover them thickly with a forcemeat made
as follows :—Take some veal or calves' kidney, with
a slice of ham, a bit of butter, shalot, cayenne, and
a green onion, all finely minced together, and mixed
to a proper consistency with the yolks of eggs ;

dredge them with flour, and fry in boiling lard, or
beef dripping : serve up with a rich gravy.

320. SCOTCH EGGS (Scotland)

Take as many eggs as required, allowing a half
egg for each person and boil until hard. Then put
into cold water and take off the shells when quite
cold. Cover each egg with sausage meat, or well-
seasoned rissole mixture, being careful to cover
the egg completely, keeping them an oval shape.
Flatten them at both ends, dip each into beaten
egg, then into bread crumbs. Do this twice, so as
to have a firm cover. Fry in boiling fat until brown.
Cut them open with a sharp knife, and serve on a
dish with good thick gravy.

321. SCRAMBLED EGGS (Cheshire)

Beat up four eggs, add salt and pepper, put them
into a stewpan with two ounces of butter, keep
stirring constantly with a wooden spoon till the eggs
are nearly set ; then (1) serve as they are on a very
hot dish, or (2) add two tablespoonfuls of tomato
sauce, and stir for two minutes *off* the fire.

322. EGGS STEWED IN GRAVY (Yorkshire, 1769)

Pour a little gravy into a little pewter (or earthenware) dish, and set it on a stove. When it is hot,
break in as many eggs as will cover the dish bottom,
keep pouring the gravy over them with a spoon till
they are white at the top. When they are set
enough, strew over them a little salt : fry some
square sippets of bread in butter, arrange the eggs
on them, and serve up.

323. EGG AND TOMATO MOULD (Yorkshire)

One pound of tomatoes, four eggs, half a tea-cupful thin cream or milk, one clove garlic or onion. Scald and peel the tomatoes, cut into small pieces, simmer with the butter and seasoning. Remove the garlic as soon as it has flavoured the tomato. Mash the tomato as it cooks, with a wooden spoon. Let it boil ten minutes, then add the cream or milk, and four hard-boiled eggs (chopped), thicken the whole with a cornflour liaison. Pour into a wetted mould to stiffen. When cold, turn out and garnish with parsley and rubbed egg yolk.

324. EGGS AND TOMATO SAUCE (Yorkshire)

Place one pound of stewed and pulped tomatoes and a slice of onion into a stewpan, with two ounces of butter rubbed into one teaspoonful of flour; add pepper and salt, and a little water if necessary. Stir well. Poach as many eggs as are required, and lay them on hot buttered toast. Pour the tomato sauce round, and scatter chopped parsley over the eggs to serve.

325. EGGS IN THE TURKISH WAY (Surrey)

Put an onion cut into slices, with some fine herbs and butter, into a saucepan, adding a little flour, salt, and pepper: when these have been on the fire a few minutes, add a glass of white French wine and the whites of a dozen hard-boiled eggs cut into slices: when these ingredients are well united, add the yolks, which had been previously set aside, and serve up very hot.

CHAPTER X

SAVOURIES

NOTE.—Under this heading I include several pleasing little recipes which were received too late for insertion under other groupings : they are genuine country concoctions, and will be found to afford a light variety to the usual staple articles of diet. Although they have about them a somewhat more modern feeling than the majority of recipes in this book, I have the donors' words for it that these savouries have long been used with much success. In any case, they carry their own commendation to the " knowledgeable " cook.

326. ANCHOVY CREAMS (Hertfordshire)

Take a quarter of a pint of cream ; put into it a little anchovy sauce, enough to give it a delicate pink colour and flavour ; whip stiffly, and place on croûtes of fried bread.

327. ANCHOVY FILLETS AND GREEN BUTTER
(Hertfordshire)

Green butter is made thus : Take some good fresh watercress and pick all the leaves off the stalks, chop them finely, then dry in a cloth, and add them to some fresh butter till it becomes a bright green colour. Season with cayenne pepper and salt, and mould it with an ordinary butter spoon. Dish these in a pile, and on each lay two small anchovy fillets crossways.

328. BREAD AND CHEESE CUSTARD (Kent)

Take half a pound of grated Cheddar cheese, half a pound of bread crumbs, one pint of milk, one egg, pepper, and salt. Mix the cheese, crumbs, pepper, and salt together. Boil the milk and pour it over them. Leave the mixture to grow cold, and then beat the egg and stir it in. Put all in a deep dish, and bake to a good brown in a hot oven. Lay little pieces of butter on the top, and serve hot.

329. BOUCHES À L'INDIEN (Hertfordshire)

Pieces of puff paste filled with any sort of minced white savoury meat and moistened with curry sauce—whether made as tartlets, turnovers, sausage-rolls, or fried rolls—are excellent.

330. BEEF AND HAM ROLL (Hertfordshire)

One pound of beef steak or veal, one pound raw ham, five ounces of white crumbs, one egg, mace, pepper, salt, and cayenne to taste, one ounce parsley scalded and chopped. Mince the raw meat, including fat, but not gristle ; add the other ingredients, and beaten egg, and mix well. Form firmly into the shape of a pillow, wrap in a greased paper, tie lightly in a cloth, and boil for two hours. Always serve it cold ; but sprinkle, whilst hot, browned bread crumbs on the top.

331. FRICATELLES (Hertfordshire)

Take any remains of the cold meat from a veal pie, season it highly, chop it, and mix with a raw egg. Lay the mixture on a square slice of bread, and fry in a little butter, or clarified fat. Garnish with parsley.

332. JAMAICA FRITTERS (Devonshire)

A small slice of cold meat (about one ounce), one egg, half a slice of bread. Mince the meat finely, pour boiling water on the bread; when soaked, pour off superfluous water. Beat the egg, add to the bread parsley or any other flavouring. Have ready boiling fat in frying pan. Drop the mixture in by tablespoonfuls, turn when sufficiently set, so as to brown both sides—or it may be made in one large fritter, filling the bottom of the pan. Any sort of meat or fish may be used. The above is enough for two persons.

333. HADDOCK SOUFFLÉ (Hertfordshire)

Boil a dried haddock, remove all skin and bones, pound it with a lump of butter, and a dash of cayenne pepper; pass it through a sieve, mix it with three yolks of eggs, then add their whites whisked to a very stiff froth; half fill some little cases with the mixture, and bake at once. (Filleted dried haddock may be treated as above.)

334. KEBOBS (Hertfordshire)

Cut a few pieces the size of an egg from a leg or loin of mutton; chop a small onion, with seasoning to

taste, and lay this on the meat before rolling it up ;
leave it covered for an hour, and then thread the
pieces on a skewer, leaving a little space between ;
grill or broil slowly, turning often, and as soon as it
begins to brown, baste it with a little tomato juice
diluted with mutton stock.

335. ONION AND KIDNEY SAVOURY (Isle of Wight)

Take a Spanish onion, cut out the centre, and
insert a kidney which has been carefully washed
and skinned. Bake in rather a hot oven, basting
freqüently with cooking butter ; serve with thick
brown gravy.

336. POTTED LIVER (Hampshire)

Cook the liver, and mince it with a good-sized
piece of fat bacon. Mix with it salt, cayenne pepper,
nutmeg, and a little clove. Pound in a mortar, put
into pots, and cover with melted butter.

337. LIVER AND POTATO TURNOVERS
(Hertfordshire)

Boil some potatoes dry and floury ; mash them
smoothly, make into a paste with an egg, adding a
little salt and pepper. Roll out, and cut into
rounds about five inches across, prepare a stuffing
thus. Carefully chop or mince some boiled liver,
add a few breadcrumbs, season with a little chopped
onion and powdered sage, lay a little mixture on
each round, fold over and wet the edges of one half
to make it adhere to the other ; brush over with
milk and bake in a quick oven.

338. DRESSED OYSTERS (Kent)

Mix in a sherry glass one eggspoonful of tomato ketchup and an equal amount of lemon juice. Add one teaspoonful of French vinegar, a little pepper and salt, and a suggestion of cayenne. For each glass take four oysters—beard them carefully—and previous to placing them in the glass put in the juice from their shells. Serve at once in sherry glasses.

339. FINE PATTIES (Eighteenth Century)

Slice either cold turkey, lamb, or chicken, with an equal quantity of the fat of lamb, or of loin of veal, or the inside fat of a sirloin of beef; add a little parsley, thyme, and shredded lemon peel, put it all in a marble mortar, and pound it very fine, season it with white pepper and salt; then make a fine puff paste, roll it out in thin square sheets, put the forcemeat in the middle, cover it over, and close it evenly all round. Just before the patties go into the oven, wash them over with the yolk of an egg. Bake them twenty minutes in a quick oven ; have ready a little white gravy, seasoned with pepper, salt, and a little shalot, thickened with a little cream and butter ; as soon as the patties come out of the oven, make a hole in the top, and pour in some gravy ; you must take care not to put too much gravy in for fear of its running out at the sides, and spoiling the patties.

340. SAVOURY PATTIES (Yorkshire, 1769)

Take the kidney of a loin of veal before it is roasted, cut it in thin slices, season it with mace, pepper, and salt, and make your patties with good shell (puff) paste. Lay a slice in every patty, and either bake or fry them.

341. SAVOURY MUTTON ROLLS (Hertfordshire)

Cut some mutton into slices, trim off all fat and season nicely; chop some capers with a little lemon peel and lay them on the mutton; roll up and put on a skewer. Place it in the oven with just enough gravy to cover, and bake for about a quarter of an hour; slip the rolls off the skewer, and serve with thick gravy.

342. BAKED PIG'S FRY (Hertfordshire)

Cut up a pound of pig's fry, lay it in a pie-dish; chop finely two onions and a few sage leaves, season to taste; mix these ingredients and sprinkle over the meat. Cut up a pound and a half of part boiled potatoes, and cover over the meat with them; fill the dish with water or stock, bake for two hours and a half in moderate oven.

343. SAVOURY PUDDING (Sussex)

Half a pound of stale bread, three eggs, three ounces of flour, three ounces of suet, one ounce of fine oatmeal, one pint of milk, a small shalot chopped very fine, a little salt, a pinch of sweet marjoram, and enough lemon to give a flavour. Mix all thoroughly well together, not too moist: turn into a basin or (better) a floured cloth, and boil or steam for three hours.

344. ITALIAN RICE (Middlesex)

Melt one ounce of butter in a stewpan, take one onion about the size of a golf ball, mince it very finely, and fry it in the butter. When it is a golden yellow, stir in four ounces of hot, well-boiled rice. Work it well with a fork, at the same time shaking in two heaped tablespoonfuls of grated cheese. Serve it piled on a flat dish, garnished with sliced hard-boiled eggs.

345. SAVOURY RICE (Isle of Wight)

Wash three ounces of rice, and boil it in milk until tender, adding pepper and salt. Butter a pie-dish, spread half the rice on it, sprinkle an ounce of grated cheese on it, add the rest of the rice and another ounce of cheese, put little pieces of butter on the top, and brown in the oven.

346. SAVOURY RICE MOULD (Hampshire)

This is a very tempting and nutritious dish. To half a teacupful of rice boiled in milk, add two ounces of minced cold mutton, one ounce of ham, one hard-boiled egg minced, one tablespoonful of chopped parsley, one raw egg, pepper and salt to taste. If not moist enough, add a little milk. This may be baked in a pie-dish or steamed in a mould.

347. FRIED SANDWICH (Hertfordshire)

Well season a slice of cold meat or ham, spread a layer of mashed potato over each side, trimming it neatly into shape, spread with beaten raw egg, and cover with crumbs ; make the fat very hot before frying the sandwich.

10

348. SARDINE PUFFS HOT (Hertfordshire)

Take some pastry (the remains of any puff paste
will do) or a nice short crust, have a tin of sardines
which have been skinned and freed from bone,
mash up on a plate with a little pepper and salt,
and when well mashed put about a dessertspoonful
of the mixture into the paste, which has been cut
with a round cutter, and form into a puff. Egg and
breadcrumb the puffs, fry a delicate hue in some
clean lard, and serve up on a dish paper. Garnish
with fried parsley.

349. SAVOURY TOAST (Hertfordshire)

One ounce of butter, three hard-boiled eggs put
through a sieve (or chopped very fine), one teaspoonful of anchovy sauce, one teaspoonful of chopped
capers, a little pepper and salt (and cayenne pepper
if liked) ; mix well together, make very hot, and
serve on squares of hot buttered toast.

350. MOCK CRAB TOAST (Derbyshire)

Pound two ounces of cheese with a dessertspoonful of anchovy sauce, the same of made mustard,
the same of vinegar, a pinch of Nepaul pepper, and
a little salt, the yolk of an egg, and a tablespoonful
of butter. Mix thoroughly in a basin and then
spread on buttered toast ; put it in the oven and
bake for about ten minutes. Serve piping hot.

351. FRENCH TOAST (Lancashire)

One pound of beef, half a pint white bread-crumbs,
half a pound of tomatoes. Mince the beef, mix
with the bread crumbs and tomatoes chopped up

(previously scalded to remove skins); bind with one beaten egg. Press into pillow form, place in a baking tin, cover, and bake one hour. Remove cover, put a little butter on the top, and let it bake until brown. Make a nice gravy.

352. EXCELLENT HAM TOAST (Hertfordshire)

Take a quarter of a pound of lean ham, mince it very finely or pass through a mincing machine. Put this in a shallow saucepan, with the beaten yolks of two eggs, half an ounce of butter, two table-spoonfuls of cream, and a *soupçon* of cayenne to taste. Stir over the fire till it thickens. Have ready some nicely trimmed pieces of toast, spread the mixture on this and serve hot. Set all on a nice d'oyley, and garnish with sprigs of parsley.

353. TOMATO AND MUSHROOM SAVOURY (Isle of Wight)

Cut as many rounds of bread as you require, butter them, and place a mushroom upon each. On the mushroom place a tomato which has been peeled, season with pepper and salt, and bake.

354. SAVOURY TOMATOES (Hertfordshire)

For each small tomato allow a slice of bacon, or ham ; take out the pulp of the tomatoes, mix it with a few white bread crumbs, a little grated cheese, cayenne, salt, and sugar ; a little cream or part of an egg may also be used if convenient, but it is not necessary ; refill the tomatoes, fold the bacon round, and fry ; or, if frying is not liked, put a little fat or butter in a saucepan with the balls. Cover the

pan closely, and let it cook gently for twenty
minutes to half an hour, shaking the pan to prevent
burning. Serve each ball on toast or bread.

355. SAVOURY TONGUE (Hertfordshire)

Take some cold cooked tongue, and cut it into
dice, and for every half-teacupful allow a teacupful
of good stock. Chop a little onion finely and put it in
with the stock ; add pepper and salt to taste. Make
it thoroughly hot, mix the meat with the well-beaten
eggs, in the proportion of one egg to each cupful of
tongue, and add to the stock. Stir well, and then
put into small patty pans, sprinkle thickly with
breadcrumbs, and scatter small bits of butter over
the top. Bake for a quarter of an hour in a quick
oven.

356. A NICE WHET BEFORE DINNER
(Eighteenth Century)

Cut some slices of bread half an inch thick, fry
them in butter, but not too hard ; then split some
anchovies, take out the bones, lay half an anchovy
on each piece of bread ; have ready some Cheshire
cheese grated and some chopped parsley mixed
together, lay it pretty thickly over the bread and
anchovy, baste it with butter, and brown it with a
salamander ; it must be done on the dish on which
you send it to the table.

357. SCOTCH WOODCOCK (Hertfordshire)

Take two slices of toasted bread, rather thick,
butter them on both sides, spread them with anchovy
paste and place one piece on top of the other, and

cut them into fingers or squares. Take the yolks
of two eggs well beaten, and a quarter of a pint of
cream ; or if cream is not at hand, the yolks of
three eggs, and a little milk will do ; set over the
fire to thicken (but do not let it boil, else it will
curdle); it should be a nice thick custard. Pour
this over the toast, and send to table as hot as
possible.

CHAPTER XI

SAUCES

NOTE.—Voltaire's celebrated sneer about the "fifty religions and only one sauce" (*i.e.* melted butter) of the English, was in reality undeserved. Our forefathers were particularly keen on sauces : and some of these sauces were frequently so elaborate, so expensive, and so tedious in preparing, that I have refrained from setting them down. Life went more leisurely in those days, and the twentieth-century housewife finds it easier to purchase a bottle of some well-known condiment, such as Worcester or Wiltshire sauce, to expenditure of much time and trouble in the concoction of appetising relishes. After all, "hunger," as the proverb says, "is the best sauce." Amongst those here contained, however, will be found some very meritorious recipes, calculated to mitigate the monotony of cold mutton, or to add a pleasing asperity to unexhilarating fish. I have included two or three ketchups and bottling sauces. An excellent Mayonnaise Sauce will be found in the salad section of this book.

SAUCES FOR MEAT

358. SAUCE FOR ANY KIND OF COLD MEAT
(Kent)

Mix in a basin one tablespoonful of grated horse-radish, the same amount of red-currant jelly, the

grated rind of one orange (or lemon) and its juice,
and a little raw mustard.

359. SIMPLE SAUCE FOR COLD MEAT (Kent)

Three teaspoonfuls of pale brown sugar, one teaspoonful of made mustard, four dessertspoonfuls
of vinegar. Mix thoroughly.

360. SHARP SAUCE FOR COLD MEATS
(Middlesex)

Into a quart of white wine vinegar, put eight
cloves of garlic, twelve shalots, a small clove of
ginger, a little salt, and the peel of a lemon: boil
them together for a short time ; then strain and
bottle for use.

361. SAUCE FOR ROAST MEAT IN GENERAL
(Eighteenth Century)

Wash an anchovy clean, put to it a glass of red
wine, a shalot cut small, a little lemon-juice, and
some gravy. Stew them together, strain off, and
mix into the sauce the gravy that runs from the
meat.

362. CUMBERLAND SAUCE (Hertfordshire)

Half a pound of red currant jelly, half a pint of
Madeira, juice of a lemon; mix together with the juice
of four to six oranges, one dessertspoonful of French
mustard, the rind of one orange cut in Julienne
shreds. Mix well, and stir all together in a lined
pan over the fire till hot, but not boiling.

363. DEVIL SAUCE (Ireland)

Cut up some young onions very fine, and moisten them with a little French vinegar, and boil for five or six minutes. Add some cayenne pepper, good strong gravy, wine, and anchovy butter, which last consists of filleted anchovies pounded very well in a mortar with butter and cayenne.

364. GHERKIN SAUCE (Hertfordshire)

Half an ounce of butter, half an ounce of flour, one dessertspoonful of gherkin, three-quarters of a pint of water, pepper and salt, the yolk of one egg, one dessertspoonful of lemon juice. Mix well in a lined pan and stir till it is hot, but not boiling.

365. GOOSEBERRY SAUCE (Eighteenth Century)

Put some scalded gooseberries (passed through a sieve), a little juice of sorrel, and a little ginger, into some melted butter.

366. " GUBBINS " SAUCE (Middlesex)

Fill a basin with boiling water and put a soup-plate on the top. When the plate is quite hot, melt in it a piece of good butter, the size of a walnut. When the butter is melted, stir in two teaspoonfuls of made mustard, one dessertspoonful of good wine vinegar, one teaspoonful of good Devonshire cream. Add salt and black pepper. This is the best possible sauce for grilled meat or " devilled " bones.

367. HORSERADISH SAUCE (Middlesex)

One teaspoonful of mustard, one tablespoonful of vinegar, three ditto of cream, one teaspoonful of salt, one saltspoonful of pepper. Add grated horseradish, stirring it in very smoothly till the whole be of the consistency of thick clotted cream.

368. INDIA SAUCE (Kent, 1809)

To a pint of the best vinegar, slice in two heads of garlic, three tablespoonfuls of soy, five of walnut pickle, and an ounce of cayenne pepper. Put it into a bottle and shake it well.

369. ITALIAN SAUCE (Essex)

Put into a stewpan over a slow fire one tablespoonful of salad oil, and a handful of finely chopped onions. Add half a teacupful of broth and eight tablespoonfuls of glaze. If too thick when it has done boiling, add a very little water; but it is better fairly thick. Seasoning: chopped parsley, cayenne, and one teaspoonful of lemon juice.

370. PIQUANT SAUCE (Hertfordshire)

Half a pint of brown gravy, one teaspoonful of tarragon vinegar, one tablespoonful malt vinegar, pepper and salt, half an ounce of butter, one teaspoonful of chopped onion, one teaspoonful of French mustard. Mix well and stir till hot (but not boiling) in a lined pan.

371. SAVOURY SAUCE (Hertfordshire)

Half an ounce of butter, half an ounce of bacon, one carrot, one onion, one turnip, one sprig of parsley, one of thyme, pepper and salt, half a pint of stock, six pepper-corns, three-quarters of an ounce of flour. The flour to be mixed smooth with a little stock, and added last of all, when the other ingredients have been boiled and strained off.

372. TOMATO SAUCE (Sussex)
(To eat with Mutton)

Pare half a dozen ripe tomatoes ; put them into a saucepan with a little piece of butter, two chillies, and salt. Shake some flour in, add half a teacupful of gravy. Boil all together ten minutes, keeping it stirred, and send to table hot.

373. WHITE SAUCE (Kent, 1809)

To a pint of cream put a tablespoonful of anchovy juice, a tablespoonful of ketchup, a tablespoonful of soy, and a little flour and butter as for melted butter.

374. WHITE SAUCE FOR FOWLS (Eighteenth Century)

Take a scrag of veal, the neck of a fowl, or any bits of mutton or veal you have ; put them in a saucepan, with a blade or two of mace, a few black pepper-corns, a head of celery, a bunch of sweet herbs, a slice of the end of a lemon ; put in a quart of water, cover it close, let it boil till it is reduced to half a pint ; strain it, and thicken it with a quarter of a pound of butter, mixed with flour ; boil it five or six minutes, put in two spoonfuls of pickled mushrooms ; mix the yolks of two eggs with a teacupful of good cream and a little nutmeg, and put this in your sauce ; keep shaking it over the fire, but do not let it boil.

375. SAUCE FOR WILD FOWL (Eighteenth Century)

Take a proper quantity of veal gravy, add some pepper and salt, squeeze in the juice of two Seville oranges, and a little red wine, and let it all boil some time together. This is a good sauce for wild duck, teal, etc.

376. GRAVY WITHOUT MEAT (Kent, 1809)

Four large onions sliced into two quarts of water, a bundle of sweet herbs, a burnt crust of bread, two ounces of butter, some pepper and salt. When boiling, strain it, and add to it a tablespoonful of ketchup.

377. SAUCE FOR A GOOSE (Yorkshire, 1769)

Take the juice of sorrel, a little butter, and a few scalded gooseberries. Mix all together, and sweeten to your taste. You must not let it boil after you put in the sorrel, if you do it will take off the green. This is to be served separately.

SAUCES FOR FISH

378. DUTCH SAUCE (Middlesex)

Mix well together half a pound of butter, two tablespoonfuls of flour, and the yolks of five or six eggs ; then put this paste into a saucepan with some salt, whole pepper, the juice of three lemons, and half a tumbler of water ; put it on a red fire, and keep stirring until it has become sufficiently thick to lay on the vegetables or fish, over which you may throw it.

379. CUCUMBER GARNISH FOR FISH (Devonshire)

Peel and cut a cucumber into one and a half inch
lengths. Quarter these and remove the seeds, cut
the pieces into fancy olive shapes. Lay them in cold
water with a pinch of salt, and bring it to the boil ;
skim, and let the cucumber cook until tender, then
serve round the salmon.

380. GENEVA SAUCE FOR FISH

Take a few mushrooms, onions, carrots sliced,
parsley, a sprig of thyme, a bay-leaf, two ounces of
ham, two cloves, a blade of mace, and some pepper-
corns ; set the whole over the fire with a little butter.
When it becomes clear, add a tablespoonful of flour,
stir it well over the fire a few moments, and add
enough good *consommé* to bring it to the consistency
of cream. With this put half a bottle of sherry or
Madeira. Let the whole simmer until the roots are
done, then skim it well and strain it over whatever
fish you have occasion to dress. When the fish is
done, take it up carefully with a slice, drain it
and put the sauce into a stewpan. Boil it and
skim off the fat. The moisture from the fish will
thin your sauce, therefore reduce it by boiling.
Add a little flour and butter kneaded together;
finish with a little anchovy, butter, lemon juice,
and cayenne, and mask the fish with it.

381. SAUCE FOR FISH (Scotch)

Brown four ounces of butter slightly, add to it an
English pint of water, a little flour and pepper,
three tablespoonfuls of ketchup. The fish must be
well drained from the cold water before they are put

into the sauce. After they have boiled a few minutes, put in three or four pickled walnuts cut in small pieces. This sauce will be sufficient for four good haddocks, and may do to serve cod's head in.

382. A VERY NICE SAUCE FOR MOST SORTS OF FISH (Eighteenth Century)

Take a little gravy made of either veal or mutton, put to it a little of the water that drains from your fish ; when it is boiled enough, put it in a saucepan, and put in a whole onion, one anchovy, a spoonful of ketchup, and a glass of white wine ; thicken it with a good lump of butter rolled in flour and a spoonful of cream ; if you have oysters, cockles, or shrimps, put them in after you take it off the fire, (but it is very good without). You may use red wine instead of white, by leaving out the cream.

383. WHITE FISH SAUCE (Eighteenth Century)

Wash two anchovies, put them into a saucepan with one glass of white wine and two of water, half a nutmeg grated, and a little lemon peel ; when it has boiled five or six minutes strain it through a sieve, add to it a spoonful of white wine vinegar, thicken it a little, then add a quarter of a pound of butter rolled in flour ; boil it well, and pour it hot upon your dish.

384. OYSTER SAUÇE (Ireland)

Strain the liquor from the oysters, and wash them in cold water. Simmer the liquor with a little mace and lemon-peel ; add a little flour, and some butter rubbed in flour ; when this is boiled, put in the oysters and give one boil more.

385. EGG-SAUCE FOR A SALT COD
(Eighteenth Century)

Boil your eggs hard, first half chop the whites, then put in the yolks, and chop them both together, but not very small; put them into half a pound of good creamed butter, and let it boil up; then put it on the fish.

386. LOBSTER SAUCE (Eighteenth Century)

Boil half a pint of water with a little mace and whole pepper, long enough to take out the strong taste of the spice; then strain it off, melt three quarters of a pound of butter smooth in the water, cut your lobster in very small pieces, stew it all together tenderly, with an anchovy, and send it up hot. (The butter in above two recipes can be reduced *ad lib.*)

387. LOBSTER SAUCE—ANOTHER WAY
(Eighteenth Century)

Bruise the body of a lobster into thick melted butter, and cut the flesh into it in small pieces, stew all together and give it a boil ; season with a little pepper, salt, and a very small quantity of mace.

388. SAUCE FOR SALMON (Eighteenth Century)

Boil a bunch of fennel and parsley, chop them small, and put them into some good melted butter, send it to the table in a sauce-boat ; have another with gravy sauce. To make the gravy sauce, put a little brown gravy into a saucepan, with one anchovy, a teaspoonful of lemon pickle, a tablespoonful of liquor from walnut pickle, one or two tablespoonfuls of the water that the fish was boiled in (it gives a pleasant flavour), a stick of horseradish, a little browning and salt ; boil this three or four minutes, thicken it with flour and a good lump of butter, and strain it through a hair sieve. *N.B.*—This is a good sauce for most kinds of boiled fish.

BOTTLING SAUCES

389. BLACK BUTTER (Middlesex)

Put any quantity of butter required into a saucepan, and heat it over the fire until the colour has turned ; just before it is taken off, add a little vinegar, salt, and pepper. This is the common mode of making black butter. But where a fine flavour is required, a tablespoonful or more of the vinegar must be used, according to the quantity of butter. Take a pint of white wine vinegar, put into it a small quantity of the usual sweet herbs, a few cloves, salt, pepper, and a sliced shalot. Let these stand in the sun for a fortnight, or infuse near the fire. Then strain clear off, and put into another bottle. This vinegar may be used with a variety of sauces.

390. BROWNING FOR MADE DISHES
(Eighteenth Century)

Beat small four ounces of fine lump sugar, put it in a clear iron frying-pan, with one ounce of butter, set it over a clear fire, mix it very well together all the time ; when it begins to be frothy, the sugar is dissolving, hold it higher over the fire, have ready a pint of red wine ; when the sugar and butter are of a deep brown, pour in a little of the wine, and keep stirring it all the time ; put in half an ounce of

Jamaica pepper, six cloves, four shalots peeled,
two or three blades of mace, three spoonfuls of
mushroom ketchup, a little salt, the rind of one
lemon ; boil it slowly for ten minutes, pour it into a
basin ; when cold, take off the scum very clean, and
bottle the sauce for use.

391. EXCELLENT BOTTLING SAUCE (Kent, 1809)

One quart bottle of porter or ale, two pounds of
anchovies, one bottle of port wine, one quart of
vinegar, a quarter of an ounce of mace, half an ounce
of allspice, two or three Jamaica peppers, the rind
of five or six lemons pared thin ; all put together and
boiled down to half, strained through a cloth bag,
boiled again with white pepper. Bottle it when
cold. It will keep very long.

392. BOTTLED FISH SAUCE (Kent)

Half a pint of walnut pickle, six anchovies pounded,
three cloves of garlic pounded, three *not* pounded,
one spoonful of cayenne pepper, all mixed well,
and bottled for use. A tablespoonful in a boat of
melted butter is sufficient.

393. FISH SAUCE FOR BOTTLING (Kent, 1809)

Take walnuts fit for pickling, beat them well in
a mortar till they are pulped, squeeze the juice from
them and let it stand a day. Pour it off clear, and
to every pint of liquor put one pound of anchovies
with an ounce of shalots ; set it on the fire till the
anchovies are quite dissolved, strain it clear, and to
every quart put a quarter of an ounce of cloves, mace

and allspice, and half a pint of white wine vinegar.
Let them boil all together for a quarter of an hour,
then put in glass bottles for use.

394. KING'S OWN SAUCE (Hampshire)

Fill a quart bottle with nasturtium flowers, and
half an ounce of shalots ; cover them with vinegar and
let it stand two months.   Then strain, and add to the
liquor one ounce of salt, one teaspoonful of cayenne
pepper, and four ounces of soy.   To be eaten with
either hot or cold meat.

395. LIVER KETCHUP (Lancashire)

Take a bullock's liver, wash it extremely well,
then put it with some salt in four quarts of water.
Let it simmer away one-half, carefully skimming it
all the time.   Strain it through a hair-sieve, and
let it stand till next day, then pour it gently into a
saucepan with spice, a clove of garlic, a few bay
leaves, and a bit of horseradish.   When boiled
enough to season it, let it stand till cold and bottle
it for use.

396. MUSHROOM KETCHUP (Surrey)

Having skinned and peeled some large field mushrooms, crush them into a pulp, adding a tablespoonful of salt to every quart of pulp : let them
stand for a day and a night, then pour off the clear
liquor, and add to every quart about twenty cloves,
thirty peppercorns, and the same quantity of allspice : boil very gently for about half an hour,
then put into bottles with the spices.   Some persons
add port wine, but this rather injures than improves

11

the flavour, and is objectionable for many sauces.
A little mace may be added, but it is not essential.

397. TOMATO SAUCE FOR BOTTLING (Essex)

Take ten pounds of ripe tomatoes, and to this
quantity allow one pint of best brown vinegar, half
a pound of white sugar, two ounces of salt, one
ounce of garlic, one ounce of allspice, half an ounce
of black pepper, half an ounce of cloves, and a
quarter of an ounce of cayenne pepper. Wipe the
tomatoes clean, and bake them in an oven till they
are soft enough to be rubbed through a fine sieve
which will retain the seeds and skins. Boil the juice
for one hour, then add the other ingredients. All
the spices must be ground, and the garlic peeled
and pounded to a pulp.

Now boil the whole mixture together, stirring
constantly to prevent burning, and continue the
boiling till you get a thick smooth mass free from
watery particles ; it will take about five hours
boiling. If you desire a bright colour, add a little
prepared cochineal. This is one of the very best
keeping tomato sauces you can make.

It is to be bottled without further straining.
The bottles must be absolutely dry inside before
you put the sauce in them. When cold, cork
securely and seal or resin over the corks.

SWEET SAUCES

398. BRANDY SAUCE (Hertfordshire)

Take a quarter of a pound of fresh butter, beat
it to a cream, add two and a half ounces of crushed
loaf sugar, and a glassful of brandy, mix all well

together. The spirits must be added but a little at a time.

399. CARAMEL SAUCE (Hertfordshire)

Make a caramel with twelve lumps of sugar, a tablespoonful of water, and a little lemon juice ; boil until it gets a nice brown, then add a quarter of a pint of milk, add this to two yolks of eggs beaten well. Strain through muslin. This makes a nice sauce to any plain pudding.

400. GINGER SAUCE (Hertfordshire)

Two ounces crystallised ginger, two ounces loaf sugar, half a pint of water, a few drops of caramel. Boil, stirring constantly, in lined pan.

401. ORANGE SAUCE (Sussex)

The unexpected virtues of orange sauce were first appreciated by a Patagonian explorer, who, left stranded with his only remaining stores, a Westphalian ham and a few oranges, concocted a sauce with the fruit which proved a most ideal accompaniment to the ham. It improves the flavour of wild duck, of goose, turkey, and saddle of mutton ; and is a first-rate sauce with plum-pudding, while in America they use it as a wholesome adjunct to stewed raisins, prunes, and stewed grapes, both as a breakfast and a luncheon dish.

To make orange sauce, mix one level tablespoonful of flour with half a cupful of sugar. Add at once half a pint of quite boiling water, and the grated rind of half an orange. Stir and boil four minutes, and add the juice of an orange, and a large dessertspoonful of butter, and pour while hot over a well-beaten egg. This will be only sufficient for four persons. The sauce, poured over apple pudding, apple pie, or stewed apples, gives a pineapple flavour to the whole.

402. RASPBERRY SAUCE (Hertfordshire)

Two tablespoonfuls of raspberry jam, one ounce of loaf sugar, gill of water, one tablespoonful of lemon juice. Boil quickly in lined pan.

403. SARACEN SAUCE (Fourteenth century, modernised)

Take rose-hips, and clean them (by pulping through a sieve). Take the same amount of blanched almonds, fry them in oil, and bray them with the hips in a mortar. Boil them up with red wine, and put in sufficient sugar, and powdered hot spices (such as ginger, pepper, etc.). Mix all stiff with rice-flour, colour with alkanet or cochineal, and serve.

404. SAUCE FOR HOT PUDDING (Hertfordshire)

Glass of wine, two yolks of eggs, lemon juice, a little sugar ; whisk till thick.

CHAPTER XII
PICKLES

NOTE.—The love of pickles is sometimes considered the sign of a depraved taste : certainly it is a very widespread depravity. The desire for something at once hot, sour, salt, and pungent, would seem to be an inherent principle of human nature. We do not go to such lengths as the Germans in their affection for vinegary compounds : but (among our working classes in particular) we undoubtedly give way to an omnivorous appetite for pickles.

That the home-made pickle is superior from every possible point of view to the " boughten " one, as they say in the West Country, is a foregone conclusion. Although all pickly concoctions tend towards obscure dyspeptic ailments, yet the home-made article, partaken of in moderation, is at least not actively deleterious : containing no artificial colourings, no illicitly procured greens of vivid hue, no doubtful ingredients of any sort : just good plain vegetables in a good clean pickling mixture. Any reader who makes proof of the praiseworthy pickle prescriptions herewith, will unquestionably reap the reward of her labours.

405. PICKLED BEET ROOT (Middlesex)

Boil the root until the skin can be removed easily : having removed the skin, cut the root into slices, and put them into salt and water for twelve hours, drain them, put them into a jar, and pour over them (cold) white wine vinegar, previously boiled with whole pepper and ginger. For a quart of vinegar, use half an ounce of pepper, and a good-sized piece of white ginger : if the beet root be red, use black pepper : but if white, the contrary. Any other root, such as carrot, parsnip, turnip, etc., may be pickled in the same manner.

406. PICKLED CABBAGES (Middlesex)

Shred the inner leaves of good firm red cabbage, sprinkle them plentifully with salt, and let them lie on a sieve for a day : put them into the jar, and cover with vinegar which has been boiled with whole black pepper, ginger, and cloves. The proportions are half an ounce of pepper, a drachm of ginger, and a drachm of cloves, to a quart of vinegar. The quantity of cloves may be increased for those who like the flavour. The vinegar should be poured over cold. Do not, either in this or in any other recipe for pickling, strain off the spices : they are to be put into the jar with the vinegar.

407. PICKLED RED CABBAGE (Essex)

The ingredients are red cabbages, salt, water, and vinegar. To each quart of vinegar, half an ounce of ginger well bruised, one ounce of whole black pepper, and, when liked, a little cayenne. Take off the outside decayed leaves of a nice red cabbage, cut it into quarters, remove its stalks, and cut it across in very thin slices. Lay these on a dish and strew them plentifully with salt, covering them with another dish.

Let them remain for twenty-four hours, turn into a colander to drain, and if necessary wipe them lightly with a clean soft cloth; put them in a jar. Boil up the vinegar with spices in the above proportions, and when cold pour it over the cabbage. It will be fit for use in a week or two. If kept for a very long time, the cabbage is liable to get soft and to discolour. To be really nice and crisp and of a good red colour, it should be eaten almost immediately after it is made. A little bruised cochineal boiled with the vinegar adds much to its appearance. Tie down with bladder and keep in a dry place.

408. PICKLED CAULIFLOWER (Middlesex)

Having trimmed the cauliflower, put it into salt and water for twelve hours : then put it either whole, or in detached parts, according to the size, into a jar, and pour over (cold) white wine vinegar, previously boiled with whole white pepper. In this, as in all other cases, tie over with wet bladder and leather : and whenever the bladder is removed to take out any of the pickle, wet the bladder again so that it may adhere firmly. The cauliflower is sometimes about half boiled in strong salt and water, before the vinegar is put upon it.

409. CHUTNEY (Kent)

Five pounds of apples (green), five pounds of tomatoes, two and a half pounds of sugar, two and a half pounds of sultanas, four ounces of garlic, or ten ounces of onions, ten ounces of salt, two ounces of cayenne, two ounces of ginger, three pints of vinegar.

410. BENGAL CHUTNEY (Surrey)

One pound of brown sugar, half a pound of salt, half a pound of mustard-seed, washed and pounded : half a garlic, or quarter of a pound of onions chopped finely, quarter of a pound of powdered ginger, half a pound of raisins, stoned and chopped, one ounce of cayenne pepper, three pints of vinegar ; thirteen large sour apples, peeled, cored, and cut up, then boiled till tender in the vinegar, and, when tender, bruised with a spoon to a smooth pulp. When cold, mix all the ingredients together, and cover them lightly for a day or two. Then put into jars and cover down tightly. It is best to make half this quantity at a time. Mustard flour may be used instead of mustard seed, and onions instead of garlic.

411. BENGAL CHUTNEY (Devonshire)

Three quarters of a pound of Demerara sugar, six ounces of mustard seed, two ounces of dried chillies, four ounces of onions, six ounces of stoned raisins, fifteen large unripe sour apples, six ounces of ground ginger, one bottle best vinegar. The sugar must be made into syrup ; the onion and ginger must be finely pounded in a mortar ; the mustard-seed must be washed in cold vinegar and dried in the sun ; the apples to be peeled, cored, and sliced, and boiled in half a bottle of vinegar. When the apples are cold, put them into a large pan and gradually mix in all the ingredients, including the half bottle of vinegar. It must be well stirred until all is thoroughly blended. Then bottle for use. One pound of tomatoes added to the apples and raisins (after they are cooked), put through a sieve, then gradually mixed all together, is a great improvement.

412. TOMATO CHUTNEY (Sussex)

Ingredients.—Three and a half pounds of green tomatoes, one teaspoonful of mustard-seed, one teaspoonful of ground ginger, one teaspoonful of allspice, one onion, one quart of vinegar, ten cloves, and a pound of brown sugar.

Method.—Peel and cut the tomatoes, put into the preserving pan with vinegar and spices. When nearly boiling, add sugar, and the onion whole. Boil gently for about two hours. Remove the onion before it breaks. Put into small pots and tie down. If ripe tomatoes are used, less vinegar is required.

413. TO PICKLE GHERKINS (Surrey)

Put a quantity of spring water into a large earthen pan. To every gallon put two pounds of salt: mix them well together, and throw in five hundred gherkins. When they have lain two hours in the salt and water, put them to drain. When they are quite dry, put them into a jar. Take one gallon of white wine vinegar, put it into a saucepan with half an ounce of cloves, half an ounce of mace, one ounce of allspice, one ounce of mustard-seed, one stick of horseradish cut in slices, two or three races of ginger, six bay leaves, one nutmeg cut in pieces, and a handful of salt. Boil up all together, and pour it over the gherkins. Cover them close down and let them stand twenty-four hours. Then put them in your saucepan, and do not let them boil (for that

would spoil them), but simmer till they are of a fine
green. Put them hot in the jars, over which put
plates. When cold, cover them with bladder.

414. INDIAN PICKLE (Middlesex)

Boil in salt and water, for a quarter of an hour,
a cauliflower, two summer cabbages, six heads of
celery, a quart of French beans, and two sticks of
sliced horseradish ; drain and dry in the sun, or by
the fire, until very crisp, having first divided the
vegetables into small neat pieces : half a pound of
garlic is to be put into salt for three days, and dried
in the same way : have ready in a jar half a pound
of bruised and washed whole ginger, two ounces of
bruised mustard-seed, two ounces of turmeric, two
ounces of black pepper, a quarter of an ounce of
cayenne pepper, and an ounce of allspice : sprinkle
these with salt, and let them stand for a day before
the vegetables are added : then put in the vegetables,
and pour over them, boiling hot, two quarts of the
strongest white wine vinegar.

415. LEMON PICKLE (Eighteenth Century)

Take two dozen lemons, grate off the outer rind
very thin, cut them in four quarters, and leave
the bottoms whole ; rub on them equally half a pound
of bay salt, and spread them on a large dish. Put
them in a cool oven, or let them dry gradually by the
fire till all the juice is dried into the peels ; then put
them into a well-glazed pitcher (or jar), with one ounce
of mace, half an ounce of cloves beat fine, one ounce
of nutmeg cut in thin slices, four ounces of garlic
peeled, half a pint of mustard-seed, bruised a little

and tied in a muslin bag ; pour four quarts of boiling
white wine vinegar upon them, close the pitcher
well up, and let it stand five or six days by the fire ;
shake it well up every day ; then tie it up, and let
it stand for three months to take off the bitter taste.
When you bottle it, put the pickle and lemon in a
hair sieve, press them well, to take out the liquor,
and let it stand till another day, then pour off the
clear part, and bottle it ; let the rest stand three or
four days and it will refine itself, then pour it off and
bottle it ; let it stand again, and bottle it, till the
whole is refined : it may be put in any white sauce,
and will not hurt the colour. It is very good for
fish sauce and made dishes ; a teaspoonful is enough
for white, and two for brown sauce for fowl. It is a
most useful pickle, and gives a pleasant flavour ;
be sure you put it in before you thicken the sauce, or
put any cream in, lest the sharpness make it curdle.

416. LYONS PICKLE (French)
(Generally called Yellow Pickle)

Take a large cauliflower, two heads of cabbages,
and five or six carrots cut into neat pieces, a quart
of French beans sliced, a pint of green peas (if in
season) and three or four ounces of garlic : cover
a sieve with a layer of salt, and put them upon it ;
then sprinkle them with salt plentifully. After they
have lain in this way for two days, divide them into
two or three sieves, and place them in the sun to dry
for ten or twelve days : put them into a jar with a
quarter of a pound of white mustard-seed or three
ounces of the seed, and one of ginger, two ounces of
turmeric, and two teaspoonfuls of cayenne pepper ;

a quart of young onions prepared as for pickling may
be added. Pour over sufficient boiling vinegar to
cover them completely, and leave about an inch or
two of liquid above the vegetables.

417. TO PICKLE MUSHROOMS (Sussex)

Put the smallest you can get into a pan of spring
water, and rub them with a piece of flannel dipped
in salt, and when well washed, set them on the fire
in a pan of boiling water, with a little salt in it.
When they have boiled five or six minutes, lay them
on a colander to drain. Then lay them between
two cloths till they are cold. Put them in wide-
mouthed bottles with a few blades of mace and some
sliced nutmeg; fill the bottles with vinegar, and cork
them down.

418. TO PICKLE MUSHROOMS BROWN (Surrey)

Shake a little salt over, and leave them till next
day; then stick an onion full of cloves, which put
with them into a skillet, and let them stew very
well; then add some vinegar, and let that also stew
for some time.

419. NASTURTIUM BUDS (SEEDS) PICKLED
(Yorkshire, 1769)

Gather your little knobs quickly after the blossoms
are off, put them in cold water and salt for three days,
shifting them once a day. Then make a pickle for
them (but don't boil them at all), of some white
wine and some white wine vinegar, shalot, horseradish, whole pepper, salt, and a blade or two of
mace. Then put in your seeds, and stopper them
close up. They are to be eaten as capers.

420. PICKLED YOUNG ONIONS (Middlesex)

Peel them, and steep them in strong salt and
water for four days, changing the water two or three
times ; wipe them perfectly dry and put them into
milk which is scalding hot, until the milk becomes
cold : now drain them, and dry each separately in
a cloth ; after which put them into jars, pour as
much white wine vinegar (which has been boiled with
white pepper), as will cover them completely ; tie
over first with wet bladder, and then with leather,
and keep the jars in a dry place for use : a little
ginger may be added. Some persons put the onions,
without peeling, into cold water, and keep them on
the fire till the water boils : then they take off the
outer skins, and steep them in salt and water
before adding the vinegar.

421. PICKLED PRUNES (Ireland)

One pound of prunes, half a pound of sugar, a
little cinnamon, a few cloves. Wash the prunes,
prick them with a needle. One pint of vinegar to
four pounds of prunes. Boil all together without
the prunes ; throw it boiling over them. Let it
stand a night, then boil all together very slowly
till the skin is a little broken. When done, cover
it well.

422. TO PICKLE SAMPHIRE (Eighteenth Century)

Wash your samphire well in sour small beer,
then put it into a large preserving pan, dissolve a
little bay salt and twice the quantity of common

salt in sour beer, then fill up your pan with it, cover
it close, and set it over a slow fire till it is of a fine
green. Drain it through a sieve, and put it into
jars. Boil as much white wine vinegar as will be
sufficient to cover it, with a race or two of ginger,
and a few peppercorns. Pour this hot upon your
samphires in the jars, and tie them down.

423. PICKLED GREEN WALNUTS (Surrey)

Gather green walnuts before the inner shell is
formed, which may be known by pricking them with
a pin ; if it goes through easily, they are young
enough to pickle. Prick them in several places
with a needle or pin, to allow them to imbibe the
salt, and put them in strong brine for a fortnight,
making fresh salt and water every three days :
drain them, and put them in a jar, sprinkle them
with salt, and pour over (hot) vinegar boiled as for
cabbage ; some shalots, garlic, or onion may be
boiled in the vinegar, if the flavour is not disliked.
Some persons dry the walnuts in the sun for three
or four days, after having left the brine, and before
the vinegar is added.

424. RIPE WALNUT PICKLE (Middlesex)

Pound the rinds of ripe walnuts in a mortar with a
little salt ; then add water by degrees, and continue
to pound the whole together ; pass the whole through
a sieve, so as to get out a strong liquor ; boil this
with ginger, horseradish and sweet herbs, white
pepper, a few cloves, and salt, for half an hour very
slowly ; strain and put it into bottle, adding tho

spice ; the trouble of pounding may be avoided by putting the rinds bruised into a tub with a little salt, and sufficient water to cover them, and straining off the liquor at the end of a few days. (This is so far as the recipe goes : but I presume the kernels are separately pickled as above (see " Green Walnuts "), and this liquor is subsequently added. Ed.)

425. VEGETABLE MARROW PICKLE (Sussex)

Take a good-sized marrow and cut it up into small cubes, none more than two and a half inches long. Put it into a preserving pan, with a layer of Demerara sugar upon each layer of marrow, and enough vinegar to cover it. Let it cook thus until completely tender ; then add some stoned raisins, mixed spices, ginger, salt, and pepper, and let it go on boiling until it is quite thick and stiff. Take it off and let it cool down a little before bottling.

426. PICKLING MIXTURES (Surrey)

I

Twenty quarts of spring water, three pounds of coarse brown sugar, quarter of a pound of saltpetre, two pounds of bay salt.

II

One stone of common salt, quarter of a stone of bay salt, four ounces of saltpetre, half a pound of brown sugar, to four gallons of water.

III

Half a pound of salt, two ounces of ginger, two ounces of shalots, two ounces of mustard-seed, one ounce of white pepper, one tablespoonful of cayenne pepper, boiled together in two quarts of vinegar. All the vegetables except onions may be put in it, merely first wiping them dry. Put the pickle before the fire for nine days to give it a good colour. It will keep for years.

CHAPTER XIII

PUDDINGS

NOTE.—The pudding, from time immemorial, has been an English dish *par excellence*; and our forefathers simply ran riot in puddings. I have declined the insertion of puddings which would make the boldest stand aghast, from their daring novelty in the way of ill-matched ingredients, or their excursion far afield into realms of indefensible costliness. The vast number of recipes which are offered to the reader, represent a wide and comprehensive range, the Poles of the pudding world; it will be seen how many counties have contributed their quota to this remarkably extensive list. I should like to underline the respective merits of very many: but here, as in all else, "the proof of the pudding is in the eating." As sheer curiosities, I have included two rice puddings—one boiled, one baked, dating from about the year 1820, in Dublin. These are, I fancy, quite unparalleled, and I am loth that the recipes should be lost.

427. ALBERT PUDDING (Yorkshire)

Take six eggs, six apples, six ounces of bread finely grated, six ounces stoned currants (raisins ?), four ounces of sugar, a little salt and nutmeg.

To be boiled slowly for three hours. Eaten with
melted butter.

428. APPLE AMBER (Hertfordshire)

Strip of rough puff pastry, one pound of apples,
two ounces of butter, two ounces of sugar, two eggs,
two ounces of bread crumbs, a little grated lemon
rind. Line the sides of a pie-dish with the strip of
pastry, decorating the edge. Peel, core, and cut
up the apples. Stew these until quite tender, add
the sugar, butter, bread crumbs, and yolks of eggs.
Place this mixture in the pie-dish and bake for half
an hour. Beat up the whites stiffly, and two
tablespoonfuls of sugar. Pile this meringue on top
of the apple mixture, and set slowly in a cool oven.
Decorate with cherries, and angelica. *N.B.*—This
pudding is excellent hot or cold.

429. BUTTERED APPLES (French)

Take some middle-sized apples, peel and core
them, and put them on little round slices of bread
which have had all the crust taken off. Put in each
apple as much butter and sugar as it will hold.
Cook them in a good oven on a buttered tin, and
before serving put a teaspoonful of red currant
jelly in each apple.

430. APPLE DOWDY (Essex)

Take about one and a half pounds of apples,
slices of stale bread and butter, a little nutmeg,
one gill of water, one gill of golden syrup, two ounces
of Demerara sugar. Well butter a deep baking

tin or pie-dish. Line the bottom with the thin slices of bread and butter. Peel, core, and slice the apples, and nearly fill the dish with them. Grate over a little nutmeg. Now mix the syrup and water, pour it in over the apples. Put the sugar in a layer on the top, and cover all with more bread and butter. Cover the top over with a tin plate or lid, and bake in a moderate oven about two hours. Then loosen the edges with a knife, put on a hot dish, and serve with sugar and cream ; or it can be served in the dish it is cooked in.

431. EGG AND APPLE PUDDING (Yorkshire)

Beat an egg well, add one gill of milk or water, seven tablespoonfuls of flour, one saltspoonful of salt, mix well together. Pare and cut into pieces three middle-sized apples, stir them into the batter. Boil in a cloth for one and a quarter hours ; if in a basin, ten minutes longer. Eat with melted butter flavoured with lemon. (Sugar seems to have been omitted. Ed.)

432. GRANDMOTHER'S APPLE PUDDING
(Somerset)

Take half a pound of plain flour, three ounces of minced suet, three ounces of cold boiled potato, a little salt ; apples. Peel, core, and cut up the apples, rub the potato in the flour (as you would butter), add the chopped suet and salt. Wet with a little water, roll out on to a floured board. Grease a pudding basin, line it with the crust, put the apples in with a little sugar, wet the edges and put

on the top crust. Flour a thick pudding-cloth, tie
down, put into boiling water and boil for three
hours. This can be made the day before it is
wanted, and not boiled till the next day, when it
will turn out a nice biscuit colour. Can be made
two days before boiling, but not longer, as the
potato turns sour. Same crust can be used for all
boiled suet-puddings.

433. ROYAL APPLE PUDDING (American)

Line a pie-dish with a good paste and bake it a
golden brown. Make a good custard with three yolks
of eggs and half a pint of milk, with sugar to taste.
Have ready half a pound of good thick apple sauce.
When the paste is baked, put a layer of apple sauce,
then a layer of red currant jelly, and over this pour
the custard. Have ready baked straws of pastry cut
the length and width of the tart. Put them lattice-
fashion over the custard, then set in oven for five
minutes.

434. AUNTIE'S PUDDING (Hertfordshire)

Well butter a plain mould, stick alternate rows
of split raisins and sliced candied peel round it.
Pour a breakfastcupful of fresh milk, which has been
warmed and mixed with a piece of butter the size of
a walnut, over a teacupful of white breadcrumbs, let
it soak for a time, then add two beaten eggs, any
flavouring that is liked—crushed ratafia biscuits are
very nice—beat all well together, pour it into a
mould, cover it closely and allow it to steam for
two hours. Serve orange sauce round.

435. AUSTRALIAN PUDDING (Essex)

Line a pudding basin with good suet paste, then set a lemon, end up, in the bottom, with a little peel cut off to flatten it, so that it will keep steady. Put a deep layer of well-picked sultanas around it, up to about the top of the lemon: then a layer of paste, then a thinner layer of sultanas, and so on till the basin be full (it should not be too large a basin). Cover with paste, like any other boiled pudding, and steam or boil for two and a half to three hours. When cooked, turn it out upon a hot dish, and let it be cut at table with a very sharp knife, so that a little slice of the lemon goes with each helping. This is particularly good.

436. AUSTRIAN PUDDING (Hertfordshire)

Mix together one pound of dried and sifted flour, two teaspoonfuls of baking powder, six ounces of suet, two teaspoonfuls of chopped candied peel (lemon) and a tablespoonful of moist sugar. Mix a teacupful of treacle with a breakfastcupful of warm milk, stir it smoothly into the other ingredients, pour into a well-greased mould, cover with a cloth, and boil for three hours.

437. BAKEWELL PUDDING (Derbyshire)

A quarter of a pound of flour, two ounces of butter, a pinch of salt, a little water. Rub the butter into the flour, add the water and mix from the centre. Do not make it too moist. Flour a board, and work the paste till quite smooth. Roll it out, and line the edge of a pie-dish with a broad band of paste. Cut the remainder into rounds with a cutter, and

put them overlapping one another all round edge
of pie-dish, lifting the first so that the edge is complete. Mark each round of paste with top of paste-
brush handle, and make a line with a skewer as
ornamentation.

Put about two tablespoonfuls of jam into bottom of
pie-dish. For filling mixture, take two ounces of
butter, two ounces of castor sugar, two ounces of
flour, one egg, one teaspoonful baking powder,
eight drops essence of lemon. Cream the butter and
sugar together. Add the egg *whole* and beat well.
Mix the flour, baking powder, and essence of lemon
together, and add to the above and mix well. Put
this mixture on the top of the jam in the pie-dish,
and spread it with a knife, evenly covering all the
jam. Bake in a good oven for half an hour. This is a
a very old recipe.

438. BETSY SOUFFLÉ (Hertfordshire)

Take three ounces of sponge-cake crumbs, and
on them pour one pint of hot milk ; cover and set to
cool. Beat up two eggs, leaving out the white of
one, with one teaspoonful of brandy, and add to
the cake and milk. Line the bottom of a pie-dish
with apricot jam, and pour the above mixture on
the top. Bake in a steady oven for half an hour.
Beat up the second white of egg to a stiff froth, pile
it on pudding, and just brown in oven. Serve hot
or cold.

439. CREAM BLANC MANGE (Somerset)

To one ounce of Nelson's gelatine add half a pint
of new milk. Let it soak for thirty minutes. Boil

two or three laurel leaves in a pint of cream and half a pint of milk. When boiling pour over the soaked gelatine. Stir it till it dissolves ; add four ounces of lump sugar and a tablespoonful of brandy. Strain it through muslin. Stir occasionally until it thickens, then pour into wet moulds.

440. BOLTON PUDDING (Isle of Wight)

Three ounces of flour, one ounce of butter, one and a half ounces of sugar, one egg, one small teaspoonful of baking powder, three tablespoonfuls of milk, a little jam. Butter a basin and place the jam at the bottom. Rub the butter in the flour, add the sugar and baking powder, mix up with the beaten egg and milk, pour into the buttered basin. Steam for one and a half hours ; serve with sweet sauce.

441. BONITA PUDDING (Ireland)

Take two eggs, juice of two lemons, rind of one, half a pound of castor sugar, quarter of an ounce of gelatine, melted in less than half a tumbler of water (small teacupful). Cream the yolks and sugar, add lemon juice, rind, and gelatine. Mix well, leave till beginning to thicken, then stir in whites beaten stiff. Pour into glass dish, and leave to set. Serve with whipped cream when cold. This is very good ; but be careful that the whites are not added till the mixture is getting thick, or it will set in two layers, instead of being of one consistency throughout.

442. BRADFORD PUDDING (Hertfordshire)

Take three eggs and their weight in butter, sugar,
and flour ; cream the butter and sugar well together,
add the grated rind of a lemon, a good tablespoonful
of cream, and one of brandy ; sprinkle in the flour,
fill some small buttered moulds with the mixture,
stand them on sand on a baking tin to prevent
the puddings getting too brown, and bake about
fifteen minutes. Pour some sherry over them, or
some wine sauce round them.

443. BREAD-PUDDINGS (SMALL) (Cheshire)

I

Pour one pint of boiling water over half a pint of
fine bread crumbs ; add three eggs well-beaten, the
rind of half a lemon, and sugar to taste. Butter
some small moulds, or " castle-pudding " tins, fill
them with the mixture, and bake it a light brown.
Turn the puddings out on a hot dish, and sprinkle
sifted sugar over, or put a little warmed jam on
the tops.

II

Butter well some small plain moulds, and put in
each a layer of fine bread crumbs half an inch thick ;
then a layer of jam ; and so on till the moulds are
nearly full. Beat up an egg, and add to it half a
pint of milk, with sugar and flavouring to taste.
Pour this very slowly into the moulds, and bake about
twenty minutes. Turn out the puddings and serve
with sweet sauce.

444. BROWN BETTY (Yorkshire)

Take two dozen fine large apples, and cut them into thin slices, pare them if preferred ; crumb up a loaf of stale bread. Take a deep pudding-dish, put in a layer of bread crumbs, then one of apples, sprinkle over them some brown sugar, put in a piece of butter and any spice that may be preferred, then sprinkle in a very little cold water. Put in another layer of crumbs, apples, sugar, butter, spice, and water again ; go on until the dish is full, making the top layer of apples. Bake in a quick oven. Eat hot with sugar and wine sauce.

445. CABINET PUDDING (Kent, 1809)

Line a mould with stoned raisins, first buttering the mould well; then put thin slices of bread, some chopped lemon peel, and pour in a glass of brandy. Beat six eggs, yolks and whites, and milk enough to fill the mould ; sweeten it to taste, set it in a basin half filled with boiling water, put it in the oven to bake.

446. CANTERBURY PUDDING (Kent)

Take half a pound of suet, chopped fine, half a pound of grated bread, half a pound of sugar, the juice and rind of one lemon grated fine, three eggs, and a large wineglassful of brandy ; to be boiled an hour and three-quarters, and served with sweet sauce.

447. CARROT PUDDING (Yorkshire, 1769)

Take three or four clean red carrots, boil and peel them. Take the red part of the carrots, beat

it very fine, put it to the crumb of a penny loaf,
six eggs, half a pound of clarified butter, two or
three tablespoonfuls of rosewater, a little shredded
lemon-peel, a little grated nutmeg. Mix all well together, bake the pudding with a puff-paste round
your dish, and have a little white wine, butter,
and sugar for the sauce.

448. CARROT PUDDING (1815)

Wash and scrape your carrots, and boil them till
quite soft, in a good quantity of water ; take off
the outsides, and grate a quarter of a pound of the
middle part of the carrots ; add to it a quarter of
a pound of clarified butter, four eggs well beaten,
and candied orange and lemon peel finely cut ; sugar
and brandy to your taste ; bake it in a dish with
a puff paste at the bottom.

449. CASTLE PUDDING (Lancashire)

One and a half ounces of flour, one and a half
ounces of castor sugar, one ounce of butter, one teaspoonful of baking powder, one egg, a little milk,
flavouring. Cream the butter and sugar, add the
egg and part of flour, then the rest of the flour and
baking powder. Pour into cup-shaped tins. Bake
for about twelve or fifteen minutes. Serve with
clear arrowroot sauce or jam sauce.

450. CAROLINA SNOWBALLS (American)

Boil some rice in milk until quite soft ; prepare
some large apples as for apple dumplings, and
having placed as much of the rice on a small cloth

as will entirely cover the apple like a crust, tie each
up closely, and boil for two hours ; serve with
melted butter and sugar, or with wine sauce.

451. CAULIFLOWER PUDDING (Seventeenth Century)

Boil the cauliflowers in milk, then lay them
(without leaves or stalks) in a pie dish. Take
three gills of cream, the yolks of eight eggs, and the
whites of two. Season with nutmeg, sugar, mace,
cinnamon, sack (sherry), or orange-flower water.
Put it in the oven, bake it as you would do a custard,
and grate sugar over it when it comes out of the
oven. Serve with a sweet rich wine sauce.

452. CITRON PUDDINGS (Kent, 1809)

The yolks of three eggs, beat in half a pint of
cream, one spoonful of flour, two ounces of citron,
cut thin, sugar to the taste ; put them into large
cups, buttered ; bake them in a pretty quick oven,
turn them out and grate some sugar over them.
For sauce, melted butter, wine, and sugar.

453. CHOCOLATE MOULD (Devonshire)

One pint of milk, two tablespoonfuls of cocoa,
two tablespoonfuls of cornflour, two tablespoonfuls
of sugar. Mix the cocoa and cornflour to a smooth
paste with a little cold milk, bring the remainder
to boiling point, and add the sugar, then pour
slowly on the paste, stirring all the time ; return to
the saucepan and cook very slowly ; stir all the
time, as it easily sticks. Pour into a wet mould.

454. CHOCOLATE PUDDING (Hertfordshire)

Take about half a pound of stale bread, and break
it into small pieces. Pour over it a pint of boiling
milk, and let it stand to cool. Then beat with a
fork. Add two ounces of sugar, an ounce of oiled
butter, and a dessertspoonful of cocoa. Stir it all
together over the fire, until the cocoa tastes cooked.
Remove it from the fire, and when thoroughly cooled
add two well-beaten eggs. Pour the mixture in a
buttered pie-dish, and bake in a moderate oven for
half or three-quarters of an hour. Serve hot.

455. CORNISH PUDDING (Cornwall)

Work four ounces of dripping or lard with one
pound of pastry flour, then add one pinch of salt,
two ounces of sugar, and a teaspoonful of baking-
powder. Beat up one egg with a little milk; grease
a pudding basin and put an inch layer of preserve
or marmalade at the bottom. Flavour the pudding
mixture with lemon, and arrange on the jam so as to
half fill the mould. Cover with a cloth, dipped into
boiling water and floured, and steam for three hours.
The pudding will quite fill the basin when cooked,
and should turn out well with jam on the top.
Serve with any sweet sauce.

456. COLCHESTER PUDDING (Essex)

Take one pint of milk, two ounces of tapioca, the
rind of one lemon, vanilla, two tablespoonfuls of
castor sugar, stewed fruit, custard, whites of two
eggs. Put a layer of any stewed fruit in a glass dish.
Put the milk in a clean pan on the fire, pare the

lemon rind very thinly and put it in. Bring the milk
slowly to the boil, strain out the rind, and sprinkle
in the tapioca. Simmer this very slowly in the milk
till it is soft and creamy. Keep the lid on, but stir
it frequently. Then add sugar and vanilla to taste.
Pour it on to the fruit; it should be just thick enough
to flow over it nicely. If too thick, add a little more
milk. Let this get cold, then pour over a good
boiled custard. Lastly, beat up the whites of the
eggs to a very stiff froth; sweeten with the castor
sugar, and add a few drops of vanilla. Colour the
froth a pale pink with a few drops of cochineal.
Heap it over the top of the custard.

457. CUMBERLAND PUDDING (Hertfordshire)

Mix together in a basin six ounces of bread
crumbs, four ounces of beef suet, four ounces of
sugar, six ounces of sour apple, chopped, a tablespoonful of treacle, the grated rind of a lemon, a
little mixed spice, and a teaspoonful of baking
powder. Bind together with two eggs beaten up
with half a teacupful of milk. Turn into a greased
mould, cover with a greased paper, and steam in a
saucepan, for not less than two hours. Serve with
some liquefied apple jelly as sauce.

458. DAME BLANC PUDDING (Hertfordshire)

Boil a pint of milk, having put into it three ounces
of sweet almonds, one ounce of bitter almonds;
then pour the milk on to three yolks of eggs, add
some gelatine, let cool, then add three whites
whipped stiff, and a little cream. When the mould is
turned out, cover with red currant jelly and sherry.

459. AN EXCELLENT DATE PUDDING (Hertfordshire)

Procure one pound of dates at about 2*d.* per pound, scald them in boiling water for a moment, and set near the fire to dry; remove the stones, and chop the fruit small. Put six ounces of flour in a basin, add a pinch of salt to it, and a little baking powder, mix in four ounces of finely chopped suet, add the chopped dates, about a quarter of a grated nutmeg, and two ounces of brown sugar. Moisten the pudding with as little water as possible or, better still, one egg, and boil the whole in a buttered basin for four hours. Serve with a little scalded cream, or a nicely flavoured cornflour sauce.

460. DEVIL'S FOOD (American)

Take a cupful of brown sugar, three eggs, one cupful of butter, two cupfuls of flour, two teaspoonfuls of baking powder, half a cupful of milk. Stir this into a batter, and let it cool. Next take a quarter of a cake of chocolate, half a cup of milk, one cupful of brown sugar. Melt this, but do not let it boil; then mix all together and bake. (Breakfastcups are probably meant. Ed.)

461. DEVON " STIR-UP " PUDDING (Devonshire)

One breakfastcupful of flour, one apple cut up, one tablespoonful of currants, one tablespoonful of suet chopped, half a teaspoonful of baking powder, and a pinch of salt. Mix all together to a stiff paste with a little water, and steam in a basin for one and a half hours. Serve with a sauce of treacle and milk in equal parts—heated, but not boiled. This pudding is also excellent when made with rhubarb, gooseberries, or any sort of fruit. The above quantities make a small pudding sufficient for two or three persons.

462. DEVONSHIRE WHITE-POT
(Eighteenth Century)

Take a penny white loaf sliced very thin ; make two quarts of new milk scalding hot, then put it to the bread, and break it up and put it through a colander. Then put in four eggs, a little spice, sugar, raisins and currants, and a little salt, and bake it, but not too long, or it will whey (*i.e.*, curdle).

463. ELIZABETH'S PUDDING (Hertfordshire)

One pound of stale bread, one pound of stewed rhubarb, two ounces of sugar, two ounces of suet, one egg. Soak the bread in just enough milk to cover. When quite soft, squeeze dry and break up with a fork ; add the chopped suet, sugar, and beaten egg. Line a greased pie-dish with the mixture. Pour in the stewed rhubarb, or any other stewed fruit sweetened. Cover with another layer of bread. Bake in a moderately hot oven for one hour and a half. Serve hot.

464. EXETER PUDDING (Hertfordshire)

Take three tablespoonfuls of white bread crumbs, three of sago, three of finely minced suet, and four of white sugar. Mix these ingredients with two well-beaten eggs, a cupful of milk, adding a few drops of almond essence, and a pinch of salt. Butter a mould, put in a layer of sponge rusks and ratafias, spread a layer of raspberry jam over, then a layer of the above mixture at the top. Cover with a buttered paper, let it stand a few hours, or over night, then bake in a moderate oven for forty minutes. For a sauce, boil a pound of red currants and raspberry jam with an equal quantity of water and some lumps of sugar; strain and pour round the pudding.

465. FAVOURITE PUDDING (Hertfordshire)

The necessary ingredients are one egg, one third of a pint of milk, a quarter of an ounce of gelatine, and one ounce of castor sugar. Soak the gelatine in a small quantity of the milk, beat the yolk of an egg, and add it to the milk with the ounce of sugar. Bring the rest of the milk to the boil, and pour it over the gelatine, etc.; stir well and let the mixture boil again. Directly it reaches boiling point, pour it over the well-beaten white of egg, mix the whole thoroughly, and pour into a mould. The pudding must not be stirred or shaken till cold, when it should be turned out, and it will look like a thick cream, surmounted by a clear jelly.

466. FIG PUDDING (Ireland)

Take a quarter of a pound of bread crumbs, a quarter of a pound of figs, three ounces of suet, three ounces of brown sugar, salt, two eggs, juice of one lemon, peel of half a lemon. Mince suet and figs. Pass all the dry ingredients through mincer, mix well, add eggs well beaten. Beat all well. Steam in buttered mould three or four hours.

467. FRIAR'S OMELETTE (Essex)

Make six moderate-sized apples into sauce, sweeten with powdered loaf sugar, stir in two ounces of butter, and, when cold, mix with two well-beaten eggs. Butter a tart-dish, and strew the bottom and sides thickly with bread crumbs to the depth of a quarter of an inch; put a little dissolved butter on the top, and bake for an hour in a good oven. When done, turn out and sift sugar over it.

468. FRUIT PUDDING (Hertfordshire)

Dip a pudding basin or plain mould into cold water. Line it with slices of bread, fill half full of hot, stewed fruit, add a thin layer of thin bread, then more stewed fruit nearly to fill the basin. Cover with slices of bread and press it down with a plate and weight. Turn out next day, and serve with a custard or whipped cream round it.

469. GERMAN PUFFS (Hertfordshire)

Cream two ounces of butter, adding three table-spoonfuls of sugar, and the yolks of three eggs ; then, by degrees, add three teacupfuls of milk, the same of flour, a saltspoonful of salt, and when they are all well beaten together, the stiffly-beaten whites of three eggs, flavoured with vanilla. Half fill some well-greased teacups, and bake for about twenty minutes. Serve immediately with sweet sauce.

470. GERMAN TREACLE PUFFS (Hertfordshire)

Half a pound of flour, half a pound of treacle, a quarter of a pound of suet, a quarter of a pound of peel, one teaspoonful baking powder ; steam three hours ; lemon sauce.

13

471. GERMAN PUDDING (Hertfordshire)

Cook four ounces of rice in one and a half pints
of milk, until the milk is all absorbed. Let it cool
a little, turn into a basin and add a quarter of a
pound of beef suet, finely chopped, six ounces of
sultanas, one ounce of finely chopped candied peel,
half an ounce of ground sweet almonds, three ounces
of castor sugar, and the well-beaten yolks and whites
of four fresh eggs. Pour into a well-buttered mould,
being careful not to fill within half an inch of the
top ; cover with a buttered paper and steam for three
hours.

472. PRESERVED GINGER PUDDING (Essex)

Take two eggs and their weight in butter, sugar,
and flour, one teaspoonful of baking powder, and
three ounces of preserved ginger. Beat the butter
to a cream, add the sugar and flour, with which the
baking-powder should be mixed, then the preserved
ginger cut into small dice. Beat the eggs, yolks and
whites separately, and add the yolks first to the
pudding, then the whites. Pour into a buttered
mould and steam for one and a half hours. Turn it
out to serve, and pour round a nice cream sauce.

473. A GOOD PUDDING (Devonshire)

Two ounces of butter, four ounces of flour, three
ounces of castor sugar, two eggs, one tablespoonful
of raspberry jam. Cream the butter and sugar,
and let it stand for fifteen minutes, then add the
flour and eggs alternately, and lastly mix in the
jam. Steam for two hours.

474. HELSTON PUDDING (Yorkshire)

Two tablespoonfuls each of flour, sugar, bread crumbs, ground rice, currants, and sultanas, three tablespoonfuls of chopped suet, one tablespoonful cut candied peel, pinch of salt. Mix up with milk in which one teaspoonful of carbonate of soda has been dissolved. Boil or steam in a greased basin for two or three hours.

475. HOMINY SNOWBALLS (Sussex)

Take one pint of milk, two tablespoonfuls of hominy, and sweeten with white sugar. Put it into a jug, or jar, which must stand in a saucepan of boiling water. Let it simmer for two and a half hours, then turn it out into teacups. These are subsequently turned out, when the hominy is set, and a little jam should be put on the top of each "snowball."

476. KENTISH PUDDING-PIES

Thinly pare half a lemon, boil the rind in a pint of milk, and strain it out. Add to the milk three ounces of ground rice and a pinch of salt, and boil it for a quarter of an hour, stirring continually. Then add (with care not to curdle the eggs) one ounce of butter, two ounces of sugar, two well-beaten eggs. When the mixture is cold, line some patty-pans with good paste, fill them with the mixture, and bake in a moderate oven for about twenty minutes.

477. LEMON PUDDING (1815)

Put half a pound of fresh butter and half a pound of lump sugar into a saucepan, and keep it stirred

over the fire till it boils ; put it into an earthen jar,
and grate the rind of a large lemon into it, and let
it stand till it is cold ; beat eight eggs and squeeze
the juice of a lemon on them, mix the sugar and
butter with them, put them in a dish with a good
puff paste at the bottom, put bits of candied lemon
peel in the dish upon the paste. To be baked in
the usual manner.

478. BAKED LEMON PUDDING (Hampshire)

One pint of milk, two eggs, one lemon, bread,
sugar to taste. Boil the milk and put into it about
two ounces of bread cut in dice, and the grated rind
of one lemon. Add the beaten yolks of the eggs,
pour the mixture into a buttered pie-dish, and bake
gently in a slow oven until set. Now whip the white
of the eggs, with the lemon juice, till stiff ; replace
in the oven till lightly browned, and serve either
hot or cold. This is equally good made with orange
instead of lemon.

479. COLD LEMON PUDDING (Hertfordshire)

Put the rind of three lemons in a pint of milk,
and strain it on the yolks of six eggs, well beaten ;
sweeten to taste. Dissolve an ounce of gelatine
in a little milk, and add it to the custard. Beat
the six whites and mix all together in a basin.
Stir it frequently till nearly cold, when put it in a
mould till wanted.

480. LIGHT PUDDING (Kent)

Break into a basin the yolks of two eggs, one
spoonful of flour, the same of sifted sugar. Mix the

whole ; beat the whites to a firm froth, add them to
the other, put some jam in a pie-dish, put the
mixture on it, and bake for ten minutes.

481. LIGHT PUDDING (Sussex)

Take four ounces of grated apples, two ounces of
bread, four ounces of sugar. Beat together and add
two eggs. Bake in a buttered dish.

482. LISTER PUDDING (Westmorland)

A quarter of a pound of flour, two ounces of castor
sugar, two ounces of butter, one teaspoonful of
baking powder, one egg, three tablespoonfuls of
milk, a little jam. Rub the butter into the flour,
add the rest of the ingredients. Take a buttered
basin and line with jam or split raisins. Put in
the mixture and steam one and a quarter hours.
Serve with white sweet sauce or jam sauce.

483. MARGUERITE PUDDING (Surrey)

Take a quarter of a pound of flour, rub in two
ounces of butter ; add two ounces of castor sugar,
and one small teaspoonful of baking powder ; lastly
add a well-beaten-up egg, with enough milk to
moisten the whole. Pour into a buttered mould,
half-filling it only, as the pudding will rise : steam
for one hour ; warm about a small teacupful of jam
or marmalade in the oven, turn out the pudding on
a hot dish, and pour the jam over it. This is very
light and good.

484. MARMALADE PUDDING (Devonshire)

Eight ounces flour, four ounces of bread crumbs, four ounces of suet, two large tablespoonfuls of marmalade, two tablespoonfuls of Demerara sugar, one egg, a teacupful of milk, one teaspoonful of carbonate of soda. Mix flour, bread crumbs, suet, and sugar together. Beat the egg, add the marmalade, stir well and mix in. Then warm the milk, put in the soda, stir into the mixture to a soft dough, place in a greased basin (not quite to fill it), cover with greased paper, and steam two and a half hours.

485. MARMALADE PUDDING (Isle of Wight)

Three tablespoonfuls of marmalade, two ounces of moist sugar, one ounce of candied peel, three ounces of bread crumbs, three ounces of flour, a quarter of a pound of suet, one lemon, pinch of salt, and one egg. Time to boil or steam, three and a half hours. Chop the suet finely, rub the bread crumbs through a sieve, put the flour, salt, and suet into a basin and rub together with the fingers. Add the bread crumbs, moist sugar, candied peel, and marmalade, and cut the lemons in halves and squeeze the juice also into the basin ; add the egg, and mix all well together. Butter a pint basin and turn the mixture into it. The basin must be quite full for boiling, but need not be full for steaming. When done, turn out carefully on to a hot dish, and serve with sweet sauce or marmalade sauce.

486. MATTRESS (Durham)

Two teacupfuls flour, two ounces dripping or butter, one teacupful castor sugar, one teaspoonful of baking-powder, one egg, and enough milk with egg to fill a teacup. Rub the dripping into the flour, add the baking powder and sugar, and mix. Beat the egg, add the milk, and mix together. Bake on a shallow tin from twenty to thirty minutes : spread thickly with jam. If served hot, warm the jam before spreading.

487. MOUNTAIN PUDDING (Isle of Wight)

Butter a pie-dish and line it with ratafias ; grate the rind of a lemon over them. Mix two ounces of flour with a little cold milk to a smooth paste, and add cold milk gradually to make a pint; boil this for ten minutes, stirring all the time. Pour the mixture gently over the ratafias and leave them to soak for ten minutes. Beat the whites of two eggs (the yolks are added to the flour mixture after it is cooked) to a stiff froth, stir two ounces of castor sugar to this, and add a little cornflour or arrowroot to make the icing stiff. Arrange it on the pudding in four or five little moulds, and put the pudding in the oven till these are slightly browned. Serve cold. This icing will take no harm if made two or three hours before it is wanted.

488. MUFFIN PUDDING (Kent, 1809)

Spread some butter entirely over a basin, and cover it with raisins stoned, then fill the basin with thin slices of bread. Pour over it a pint of milk, with four well-beaten eggs, nutmeg, and sugar. Cover with a cloth and boil.

489. MYSTERIOUS PUDDING (Surrey)

Two eggs, their weight in flour, butter, and castor sugar ; a tablespoonful of marmalade and a teaspoonful of baking powder. Beat the butter and sugar to a cream, add the flour (in which has been mixed the baking powder) and the marmalade. Beat the eggs well, yolks and whites separately, adding whites lastly when the pudding is well mixed. Pour into a buttered basin, and steam for one and a half hours. Turn out, spread a little marmalade over the top, and pour sweet sauce round (this sauce is not essential).

490. NEWARK PUDDING (Hertfordshire)

One cupful of fine bread crumbs soaked in a pint of milk, two well-whisked eggs, a tablespoonful of rice flour, a quarter of a pound of raisins, stoned and cut in pieces, a few drops of vanilla or almond essence, and a pinch of carbonate of soda. Mix all to a smooth batter, pour into a buttered pie-dish, and bake gently for upwards of an hour.

491. NORFOLK DUMPLINGS

Take baker's dough and form dumplings the size of a large egg. Then put plenty of sugar, butter, and spices into a pan of hot milk, baste the dumplings well with the milk, and bake a golden brown. The dumplings, when cooked, should be double the size they were when put into the oven.

492. NOTTINGHAM PUDDING

Peel six good apples, take out the cores and leave the apples whole; fill up with sugar where the core was taken out; place them in a pie-dish, and pour over them a light batter, prepared as for a batter pudding, and bake an hour in a moderate oven.

493. OXFORDSHIRE PUDDING

Wash some rice well in several waters, and tie it up, but not too tightly, in a pudding cloth : put it on in cold water, and let it boil for two hours ; mix some well-washed currants with the rice, and eat with sweet sauce, or cold butter and sugar.

494. PATRIOTIC PUDDING (Yorkshire)

Two ounces of flour, two ounces of butter, one and a half ounces of castor sugar, one egg, half a teaspoonful baking powder, half a teaspoonful of lemon juice, salt, a little milk. Cream the butter and sugar, add the beaten egg and milk alternately with the flour, lastly add the baking powder. Put some jam into the bottom of a greased basin. Pour the mixture in and steam for one hour.

495. PINEAPPLE PUDDING (Hertfordshire)

Take two ounces of butter, the same of flour, half a pint of milk, and four ounces of pineapple cut up into dice. Take slices of pineapple, the yolks and whites of three eggs, and a tablespoonful of castor sugar. Take flour and butter together in a stewpan and mix well, and let it boil. Stir it well and add the eggs one by one, and beat them well in ; then stir well in the juice of pineapples and sugar. Put the mixture into a mould and put paper on top, and steam it for three-quarters of an hour. Serve sauce with it, composed of half a pint of liquor of the pineapple, two ounces of sugar, and some lemon juice, all boiled together till clear. A ginger pudding, with preserved ginger, can be made the same way.

496. CHRISTMAS PLUM PUDDINGS (Hertfordshire)

Five pounds of suet, three pounds of bread crumbs, one and a half pounds of cornflour, one and a half pounds of flour, three pounds of raisins, three pounds of sultanas, three pounds of currants, two pounds of candied peel, four pounds of Demerara sugar, one pound of sweet almonds, two pounds of apples, eight lemons, two nutmegs, one pint of milk, twenty-four eggs, half a pound of baking powder, one pint of brandy. This makes eight good-sized puddings.

497. CHRISTMAS PLUM PUDDING (Ireland)

Crumb of three household loaves, three pounds of sultanas, two pounds of Valentia raisins, one pound Demerara sugar, one and a half pounds of butter, twelve eggs, half a pound of mixed candied peel, allspice to taste. Mix all dry ingredients first, melt butter and mix in, then add the eggs, and flavour with whisky or sherry. (It will be seen that the above contains no flour or suet, and is therefore exceptionally light.)

498. VEGETABLE PLUM PUDDING (Kent)

One pound of mashed potatoes, half a pound of mashed carrots, half a pound of flour, half a pound of bread crumbs, half a pound of suet, one pound of sugar, one pound of currants, one pound of raisins, half a pound of mixed peel, one nutmeg (grated), a quarter of a pound of almonds (grated), three eggs. Boil in basins ten hours.

499. POLKA PUDDING (Kent)

Put a tablespoonful of arrowroot into a pint of cold milk. Beat six eggs well ; add to them three ounces of fresh butter cut into small bits, a dessert-spoonful of rosewater, a few drops of lemon or ratafia, a teacupful of sugar. Boil two pints of milk, when boiling stir in the other ingredients without taking it from the fire, boil till thick, then put it in a mould. Freeze it, if you have ice.

500. POMMES AU RIZ (Hertfordshire)

Take three tablespoonfuls of ground rice, a pint and half of milk, a dozen fair-sized apples, and yolks of three eggs. Cook the rice in the milk. Peel eight of the apples and cook them in a little water and sugar to taste, and, as these will be too juicy, crush and add the other four apples, having previously peeled and cored them. Mix the rice and the apples, and the yolks of the eggs, and cook for five minutes, stirring all the time, then place in a pie-dish, and brown in the oven. Just before serving spread some jam over the top.

501. POUDING À LA MONSIEUR PLARCH
(Hertfordshire)

Two ounces of chopped apples, two ounces of sugar, four ounces of breadcrumbs, tablespoonful of marmalade, two eggs, a little baking powder. Steam.

502. POTATO PUDDING (Ireland)

A pound of potatoes boiled and beaten fine, six ounces of butter melted in one pint of milk, twelve

eggs, half the whites, the peel of three lemons, and
the juice of one.   Sugar to taste.   Boil or steam.

503. BOILED PUDDING TO BE EATEN COLD (Kent)

Four eggs, one pint of milk, one ounce of sugar, a
little grated lemon peel, two ounces of raisins, four
large spoonfuls of marmalade, six ladies' fingers
(Savoy sponge cakes).   Sweeten the milk with sugar,
add the lemon peel, stir in the eggs, having well
beaten them ; line a buttered mould with the raisins
stoned and cut in half ; spread the slices of sponge
biscuits with the marmalade, and place in the mould;
pour in the custard ; tie the pudding down with
paper and a cloth, and boil gently for one hour.
When cold, turn out carefully.

504. PUDDING TO BE EATEN COLD (Shropshire)

Rice and milk boiled together with a laurel leaf,
pretty stiff.   Add a good bit of butter, white sugar
powdered, six yolks and three whites of eggs.   Put
all in a flat dish alternately with jam.   Put it for
a few minutes before the fire to dry the top ; beat
up the remaining three whites, pour them over
and bake.   To be eaten cold.

505. QUAKING PUDDING (Eighteenth Century)

Boil one quart of cream, and let it stand till
almost cold.   Beat four eggs for half an hour, with
one and a half teaspoonfuls of flour, and then mix
them up with your cream.   Add sugar and nutmeg
to taste : tie the pudding close up in a well-buttered
cloth, let it boil one hour and then turn it out
carefully.

506. QUEEN OF PUDDINGS (Surrey)

One pint of bread crumbs, one quart of milk, one
teacupful of white sugar, yolks of four eggs, grated
rind of one lemon. Beat the yolks, sugar, and lemon
together, and stir in the crumbs. Bake to a light
brown colour. Then beat the whites of the four
eggs to a stiff froth, with four tablespoonfuls of sugar.
Spread currant jelly over the top of the pudding;
spread over this the beaten whites, and set it back
in the oven long enough to brown slightly. Serve
cold. A little vanilla may be used in place of
lemon.

507. QUEEN'S PUDDING (Kent)

Half a pint of cream, one pint of milk, sugar, to
boil together for a quarter of an hour. Add the
yolks of three eggs well beaten, then place in a
shape, covered with a piece of thin paper. Boil for
one hour, serve it with sauce made of red currant
jelly and sherry.

508. RASPBERRY PUDDING (Hampshire)

Two eggs, their weight in butter and castor sugar,
the weight of three eggs in flour, two tablespoonfuls raspberry jam, half a teaspoonful carbonate
of soda. Put the soda in the flour dry, rub in the
butter, add the sugar, jam, and eggs. Mix, put in
buttered basin, steam or boil for two hours.

509. RASPBERRY PUDDING (Hertfordshire)

Half a pound of bread crumbs, a quarter of a
pound of butter (creamed), a quarter of a pound of
sugar, one tablespoonful flour, four tablespoon-

fuls raspberry jam, half a teaspoonful baking powder, two eggs. Mix all thoroughly and put into a mould, and steam for two hours.

510. RAILWAY PUDDING (Ireland)

Required, two ounces of butter beaten with a teacupful of flour ; add a teacupful of castor sugar, a small tablespoonful of baking powder, half a teacupful of milk, and one egg. Bake fifteen to twenty minutes on two flat tins. Spread with jam and fold over.

511. REFORM PUDDINGS (Yorkshire)

The weight of two eggs in ground rice, the same in sugar, the same in butter. First work the butter to a cream, then put in the sugar and ground rice, and lastly the two eggs well beaten. Put in buttered cups and bake twenty minutes.

512. REGENCY PUDDING (Kent, 1809)

A quarter of a pound of flour, a quarter of a pound of suet, a quarter of a pound of currants, a quarter of a pound of apples chopped fine, a little sugar, two eggs. Boil it two hours.

513. RICE CAKE MOULD (Hertfordshire)

I

Stew enough rice in milk to fill a quart mould. When middling stiff and cool, add six yolks and four whites whipped stiff. Flavour with essence of lemon. Butter the mould well, strew it with breadcrumbs, turn the rice into it. Bake about three-quarters of an hour. Serve with hot apricot sauce.

II

Three eggs and their weight of ground rice, also the same weight of sugar ; beat all well together and bake in a mould.

514. RICE CHEESE PUDDING (1815)

Steep a quarter of a pound of ground rice in milk over the fire till it is quite soft ; put it into an earthen pot, and add a quarter of a pound of butter, keep stirring it till the butter is melted, cover it close and let it stand till the next day ; then add a quarter of a pound of currants, washed and dried thoroughly, three eggs well beaten, two tablespoonfuls of ratafia or brandy, and sugar and nutmeg to your taste ; bake it in patty pans with puff paste at the bottom. *N.B.*—Be careful not to have more milk than the rice requires ; if it is too thin, the currants will sink to the bottom.

515. BAKED RICE PUDDING (Ireland)

Wash a quarter of a pound of rice ; put it on the fire in a quart of water ; when hot, pour the water off. Add two quarts of milk, some laurel leaf or bitter almonds, some lemon peel, and cinnamon. Let it boil till the rice is quite soft. While hot, put in a quarter of a pound of butter, sweeten it, and when cold add the beaten yolks of twelve eggs and half the whites, a glass of whisky or brandy and some saffron. Butter the dish and put paste round the edge. To take an hour and a half to bake. (*See note at head of this chapter.*)

516. BOILED RICE PUDDING (Ireland)

One pound of rice steeped a few hours in soft water ; then carefully strain off the water ; and take three pints of good milk, a stick of cinnamon, some laurel leaves, and boil well. Have ready beaten up ten or twelve eggs ; add currants, raisins, sugar, nutmeg. Have ready your pudding cloth dipped in boiling water, well squeezed, and then flour it and pour in your pudding. An hour's constant boiling will be sufficient. Tie your cloth well.

Sauce.—Whisky, sugar, and melted butter. To make this pudding dark as rich plum pudding, take a little dark sugar, put it in a saucepan to burn on the fire ; add a glass of whisky ; keep stirring till very brown. Throw it into your pudding while boiling hot. (*See note as above.*)

517. SMALL RICE PUDDINGS (Kent, 1809)

A quarter of a pound of butter, the yolks of four or five eggs, one pint of milk and a little cream, one ounce of almonds, pounded or chopped fine, a quarter of a pound of rice boiled up with a laurel leaf. Bake them in small tins.

518. PUDDING À LA ROYALE (Hertfordshire)

Make some custard, add a little gelatine and whipped cream, and some fine brown breadcrumbs. Set in a mould and serve with some sauce round.

519. SANDOWN PUDDING (Isle of Wight)

Butter a cake-tin and line it with sponge fingers or boudoir biscuits, put in two ounces of glacé cherries and two ounces of ratafias. Make a pint of custard and add to it three ounces of gelatine ; pour into the mould or tin, leave it to cool, and serve as a cold pudding with whipped cream.

520. SNOWBALLS (Surrey)

Take a pint of milk, boil it and sweeten to taste. Mix three tablespoonfuls of ground rice with a little cold milk. Pound a dozen and a half sweet, and half a dozen bitter, almonds in a mortar, add these to the rice, together with a dessertspoonful of orange-flower water, then pour the boiling milk over the rice, stir and return all to the saucepan ; keep stirring until it thickens. Allow it to boil for two or three seconds. Fill wet teacups with the mixture, and when quite cold turn out the snowballs and ornament the top of each with almonds, garnish them with strawberry jam, and pour cream round them.

521. SNOWDON PUDDING (Devonshire)

A quarter of a pound of raisins, half a pound of sugar, half a pound of suet chopped finely, half a pound of bread crumbs, the rind and juice of a lemon, half a wine-glass of brandy (this is not essential). Mix with two eggs well beaten, pour into a buttered basin lined with the raisins (split), boil two hours, and serve with lemon sauce.

522. SPONGE PUDDING (Devonshire)

Half a pound of flour, three ounces of sugar, three ounces of butter, one teaspoonful of ground ginger, one teaspoonful of bicarbonate of soda, one teacup-

14

ful of milk. Mix dry ingredients together, then rub
in the butter, and add the soda (ready dissolved in
warm milk). Beat it to a soft batter, steam it in a
buttered basin for two or three hours. Serve with
sweet sauce.

523. SPOONFUL PUDDING (Seventeenth Century)

To one spoonful of flour and one spoonful of
cream or milk, add an egg, a little nutmeg, ginger,
and salt. Mix all together, with a few currants if
you choose, and boil it in a basin half an hour.
(A tablespoon is presumably indicated. Ed.)

524. SUFFOLK DUMPLINGS

Take one pound of dough, divide it into six equal
parts, mould these into dumplings and drop them
into fast-boiling water. Boil quickly for ten to
fifteen minutes, and serve them the instant they are
dished. They should each be slightly torn apart
with two forks, to let the steam out, directly they
are taken out of the saucepan, or they will be sad
(heavy) in the middle.

525. SUNDAY PUDDING OR FRITTERS
(Isle of Wight)

A quarter of a pound of flour, a quarter of a pound
of sugar, two ounces of butter, four eggs, one pint of
milk. Beat the butter and sugar to a cream, add
the flour and eggs singly. Bake in saucer tins,
half full, for fifteen minutes. Eat them with jam
or cream.

526. SWEETMEAT PUDDING (Hertfordshire)

Melt half a pound of butter in a jam-pot in a pan
of hot water, add a quarter of a pound of sugar,
beat well the yolks of eight eggs without the whites,
add to the butter and sugar a quarter of a pound of
candied lemon-peel, a quarter of a pound of candied
orange peel, and a quarter of a pound of candied citron
very finely chopped or shredded. Bake one and a
half hours.

527. TAPIOCA SOUFFLÉ (Hertfordshire)

Soak a tablespoonful of tapioca in cold water;
when soft set it to boil, and when of the consistency
of porridge, sweeten to taste. Flavour with vanilla
or lemon peel. When it is cold, whisk four eggs,
whites and yolks separately, beat up the eggs,
adding the whites last. Bake in a soufflé mould
for twenty minutes. Serve at once.

528. TREACLE PUDDING (Lancashire)

Two tablespoonfuls of golden syrup or treacle,
two tablespoonfuls of chopped suet, six tablespoonfuls of flour, one and a half teaspoonfuls of baking
powder, one egg. Mix flour, suet, and baking-
powder, and a pinch of salt. Stir in treacle, beaten
egg, and a little milk. Place in a greased basin,
cover with paper, and steam about two hours.

529. TOWN PUDDING (Kent)

Six ounces of suet, half a pound of grated bread
crumbs, six ounces of moist sugar, half a pound of
apples after being pared and cored; one teaspoonful

finely cut lemon rind ; small pinch of salt. Mix ingredients thoroughly, and press them tightly into a mould (well buttered), tie floured cloth over, and boil for four hours. Turn out carefully. No other moisture required.

530. WELSH PUDDING (Shropshire)

Half a pound of chopped suet, three quarters of a pound of bread crumbs, half a pot of orange marmalade, a *little* moist sugar, three eggs. Beat well together and boil three hours in a mould.

531. WHITE POT (Yorkshire, 1769)

A layer of white bread cut thin at the bottom of the dish, a layer of apples cut thin, a layer of suet, currants, raisins, sugar, and nutmeg ; then the bread, and so on, as above, till the dish is filled up. Beat four eggs, and mix them with a pint of good milk, a little sugar and nutmeg, and pour it over the top. This should be made three or four hours before it is baked.

532. DR. WILSON'S PUDDING (Hertfordshire)

Make hot fruit juice, cut rounds of bread the size of the mould, soak them in juice, fill the mould, put a weight on the top ; then put it on the ice or in a very cold place, turn out, serve with whipped cream or custard over it.

533. YEAST PUDDING (Ireland)

Mix dough as for rolls, or procure some from the baker ; make it up into dumplings, and boil for about twenty minutes.

CHAPTER XIV

PASTRY AND SWEET DISHES

UNDER this heading are a few recipes which do not fall exactly under the head of puddings ; some of these will be found a most welcome change from the ordinary round of things, especially the fruit dishes and the "Treacle-George," which is immensely popular in those families favoured by its acquaintance.

For making short crust, good beef-dripping is much superior to lard or butter ; a mixture of beef and mutton dripping, *plus* bacon-fat or lard, run down and clarified, is the best thing possible for meat-pies. For puff pastry the best lard or butter only should be used : it is cheapest in the end. Flour should be slightly warmed before using, as directed for cakes. But the baking is quite as important as the making : and if an oven door be left ajar, or open too long, or if articles are taken out of the oven, and carelessly set in a draughty place, the best batch of pastry may be ruined.

PASTRY

534. OBSERVATIONS ON PIES (Eighteenth Century)

Raised pies should have a quick oven, kept well closed up, or your pie will fall in at the sides ; it

should have no water put in till the minute it goes
to the oven, or else it makes the crust sad, and it is
a great hazard of the pie running. Light paste
requires a moderate oven ; but not too slow, or it
will make it sad, and a quick oven will catch and
burn it, and not give it time to rise. Tarts that
are iced, require a slow oven, or the icing will
brown, and the paste not be nearly baked. This
sort of tarts ought to be made of sugar paste,
rolled very thin.

535. APPLE TART (French Method)

Scald eight or ten large apples, and when cold
mash them with a spoon : then add to them the
yolks of four and the whites of two eggs, and mix
the whole well together, adding grated nutmeg and
sugar to taste : cover the inside and edges of a
tart-dish with puff-paste, filling the dish with the
mixture ; bake for an hour, and before serving
cover with powdered sugar.

536. ALMOND CHEESECAKES (Yorkshire)

Four ounces of almonds blanched and beaten in a
mortar along with four ounces of sugar ; add four
ounces of butter, the grated rind of a lemon, and
three eggs, all beaten well together in a mortar.
Put a thin puff paste at the bottom of tins, and
insert the mixture.

537. APPLE CHEESECAKE MIXTURE
(Gloucestershire)

Four ounces of apple pulp, two ounces of castor
sugar, two eggs, two ounces of butter. The grated

rind and juice of a lemon. Pare, core, and slice half
a pound of apples and stew with little water till
soft. Weigh four ounces, put back the apples in
pan—add sugar and butter and stir (one way only)
till butter is melted. Put mixture in basin, add
grated rind and juice of lemon and beaten eggs.
Stir with a wooden spoon till well mixed. Line
tart tins with short pastry, place a little mixture
in each, and bake in quick oven.

538. LEMON CHEESECAKES (Hertfordshire)

Half a pound of sugar, two ounces of butter, rind
of two lemons, half a dozen grated almonds, juice
of three lemons, three eggs, one cracker biscuit.
Grate lemons, almonds, and biscuits, then mix
together and stir over the fire until it thickens.

539. LEMON CHEESE (Isle of Wight)

Put into a saucepan half a pound of castor sugar,
two beaten eggs, three ounces of butter, and the
juice and rind (grated) of a lemon. Bring it to the
boil slowly, until it looks thick (like honey). Then
put into jars, and cover down. This is used for
filling open tarts and cheese cakes.

540. LEMON CURD (Essex)

Take two ounces of fresh butter, three beaten
yolks of eggs, the juice and grated rind of two lemons,
half a pound of castor sugar. Mix well, and put
the mixture into a jar, and stand it in a saucepan
of boiling water over a slow fire, till the mixture
is like a thick cream. Put it into pots and cover
closely.

541. POTATO CHEESECAKES (Hertfordshire)

Boil a quarter of a pound of mealy potatoes, mash
them well, then add to them two tablespoonfuls of
brandy, a quarter of a pound of sugar, a quarter of
a pound of butter, four eggs and the rind of half an
orange. Mix these ingredients well together, and
bake in hollow patty pans with puff paste.

542. GROUND RICE CHEESECAKE MIXTURE
(Gloucestershire)

Four ounces of ground rice, four ounces of butter,
two eggs, four ounces of sugar (castor), small
teaspoonful of baking powder. Mix well together
and use as above.

543. CODLING PIE (Eighteenth Century)

Gather small codlings, put them in a small preserving pan with cold water, lay vine leaves on them,
and cover them with a cloth wrapped round the cover
of the pan to keep in the steam ; when they grow
softish, peel off the skin, and put them in the same
water as the vine leaves, hang them up a great
height over the fire to green. When you see them a
fine green, take them out of the water, and put them
in a deep dish, with as much powder or loaf sugar, as
will sweeten them. Make the lid of rich puff paste,
and bake it ; when it comes from the oven, take off
the lid, and cut it in pieces like sippets, and stick
them round the inside of the pie, with the points
upward. Pour over your codlings, a good custard
made thus : Boil a pint of cream, with a stick of
cinnamon, and sugar enough to make it a little
sweet ; let it stand till cold, then put in the yolks

of four eggs well beaten, set it on the fire, and keep stirring it till it grows thick, but do not let it boil, lest it curdle ; then pour it into your pie. Pare a little lemon-peel thin, cut the peel like straws, and lay it over the top of your codlings.

544. EGG PIES (Yorkshire, 1769)

Boil half a dozen eggs, half a dozen apples, one and a half pounds of beef-suet, a pound of currants, and shred (finely mince) them. Season with mace, nutmeg, and sugar to your taste, a tablespoonful or two of brandy, and sweetmeats, if you please. Make into pies (like mince-pies).

545. LEMON PIE (Surrey)

Take two lemons, grate off the outer peel, chop the rest very fine. Put two tablespoonfuls of corn-starch to a teacupful of hot water, and boil ; when cool, add two teacupfuls of white sugar, and the beaten yolks of four eggs. Then add the chopped peel and the juice. Stir well together, bake till the crust is done. Beat the whites of eggs to a stiff froth ; stir well in five tablespoonfuls of sugar ; pour this over the pie while hot, and set it back in the oven to brown.

546. LEMON TARTLETS (Lancashire)

Take the juice and grated rinds of two lemons. Clean the grater with bread, only using sufficient crumbs to take off all the lemon peel. Beat all together with two eggs, half a pound of loaf sugar, and quarter of a pound of butter. This is sufficient to make twelve tarts.

547. MINCEMEAT PIE WITHOUT MEAT
(Eighteenth Century)

Chop fine three pounds of suet, and three pounds of pared and cored apples. Wash and dry three pounds of currants, stone and chop one pound of raisins, beat and sift one pound and a half of loaf sugar, cut small twelve ounces of candied orange peel and six ounces of citron; mix all well together, with a quarter of an ounce of nutmeg, half an ounce of cinnamon, six or eight cloves, and half a pint of French brandy; put it into closed jar, and keep it for use.

548. MINCEMEAT (Hertfordshire)

Five pounds of suet, two pounds of raisins, two pounds of sultanas, two pounds of currants, three pounds of apples, three pounds of Demerara, two pounds of pears, two pounds of candied peel, one and a half pounds of almonds, half an ounce of mixed spice, four pounds of lemons, four pounds of oranges, two pints of brandy, one pint of sherry, four wineglassfuls of maraschino or noyeau.

549. NEW ENGLAND MOLASSES PIE (American)

Line a deep pie-dish with an undercrust, mix half a pint of treacle with a tablespoonful of flour, add the juice of a lemon, and the rind and juicy pulp chopped fine, (do not use any of the white pith). Moisten the edges, and cover with a crust; bake, and eat while hot.

550.   ORANGE PIE (Surrey)

Take the juice and grated rind of one orange, one small cup of sugar, yolks of three eggs, one tablespoonful of corn-starch, made smooth with milk ; a piece of butter as large as a chestnut, and one cupful of milk. Beat the whites of the three eggs with four tablespoonfuls of sugar, and place on the top after the pie is baked, leaving it in the oven until browned.

551.   SWISS RHUBARB TART (Hertfordshire)

Make a tart in the usual way, sweeten the rhubarb and flavour it with some slices of lemon rind. When cold, cut off the top crust, and leave the edge quite neat. Beat up the juice with a fork. Take a gill of cream, or more if the tart be large, slightly sweeten it, and whip till stiff. Pile this roughly over the sweet ; garnish with strips of angelica and preserved cherries, and serve.

552.   TART OF ROSE-HIPS (Seventeenth Century)

Take some hips, cut them and take out the seeds very clean. Wash them, season with sugar, cinnamon, and ginger. Cover the tart and bake it, ice it, sprinkle sugar on, and serve it. (Water has been omitted. I should advise giving the hips a preliminary cooking and pulping through a sieve. Rose-hips need very careful removal of the irritating hair in which the seeds are enveloped ; but this should come out as a whole if they are ripe. Ed.)

553. SULTANA PUFFS (Surrey)

Excellent and wholesome puffs can be made, to use up any short crust left over from a pie, by rolling out the paste a quarter of an inch thick, cutting it in rounds, and placing about one heaped table-spoonful of picked sultanas in the centre of each. Moisten the edges and turn over in three flaps, to make a three-cornered puff. Bake in moderate oven.

554. SUSSEX PANCAKES (Seventeenth Century)

Take some very good pie paste made with hot lard and roll it thin; fry it in butter, and serve it with beaten spice and sugar as hot as you can.

555. TREACLE-GEORGE (Devonshire)

Take a shallow cake-tin, or a deep plate, or a pie-dish ; butter it.   Place at the bottom a layer of pastry (short-crust) about a quarter of an inch thick. Over this put a layer of treacle ; over this a layer of fine bread crumbs, sufficient to hide the treacle ; over this squeeze a little lemon-juice ; then put a layer of pastry, and go on in the same rotation till the tin is filled up to the height of three or four inches or so.   Bake in a fairly quick oven, and remove from tin, and serve either hot or cold.   This is a whole-some and attractive dish for children.

556. TO MAKE CRISP PASTE FOR TARTS
(Eighteenth Century)

Take one pound of fine flour, mixed with one ounce of sifted sugar, make it into a stiff paste, with a gill of boiling cream and three ounces of butter; work it well, and roll it very thin. When you have made your tarts, beat the white of an egg a little, rub it over them with a feather, sift a little sugar over them, and bake in a moderate oven.

For icing : Beat the white of an egg to a strong froth, put in by degrees four ounces of sifted sugar, with as much powdered gum as will lie on sixpence, beat it half an hour, then lay it over your tarts the thickness of a straw.

557. VEGETABLE-MARROW TART (Sussex)

Take a small marrow, stew it quite tender, mash it up with butter and sugar to taste, add a little flavouring of lemon, spice, and ginger, and beat an egg-yolk well in. Make tartlets of puff paste in patty pans, or line a dish with puff-paste, and when the pastry is baked and has gone cool, fill it with above mixture, and put it back for a minute in the oven. The whipped white of egg can be laid on top, if liked.

FRUIT DISHES

558. SCRAPED APPLES (Surrey)

Take one pound of good *eating* apples, peel them, and scrape or shred them finely with a sharp knife into a glass dish. Have ready, not too hot, a nice two-egg custard, flavoured with sugar and vanilla, and pour this at once over the apples, as they discolour while exposed to the air. Let them be well covered with the custard. This is a most delicious and wholesome dish, and will suit invalids.

559. SIMPLE RECIPES FOR COOKING JAMAICA BANANAS

By a Black Lady

1. As a *Vegetable*, wholesome, and filling. Peel green bananas, boil them in salt and water until soft like potatoes. Are good mashed with butter and peppernut.

2. *Fried Bananas*. These are what children like. Ripe bananas, sliced lengthways, and fried in lard. Eaten either with meat, or served with sugar sprinkled on them. A squeeze of lemon is an improvement.

3. *Baked Bananas*. Fit for the gods! Peel ripe bananas and place in a pie-dish. Sprinkle a little lemon juice over them (also sugar), half cover with water, bake for twenty minutes. When cool, serve with custard, cream, or milk.

4. *Banana Fritters*. If well made are tip-top. Dip them whole or sliced in batter. Fry until crisp and light brown.

560. DATE CAKE (Somerset)

One pound of cheap dates, 3*d.* per pound, two ounces (sweet) almonds, blanched. Grease a small pudding basin with cooking butter (basin should be a little larger than a breakfastcup). Make a cross in it with split blanched almonds, thus, +. Take out the stones of the dates, and in place of each insert half a blanched almond. Then pack the dates in the basin (one at a time) as closely as possible—pressing them in tightly. When full, put a *heavy* weight on the dates—the size of the top of

the basin—and let it stand for twenty-four hours;
then turn out of the basin (by slipping a thin
knife round the sides of the basin) on to a plate
(a green plate looks best), and when wanted, cut
it in thin slices (as you would a round cake).
To be eaten for breakfast, tea, or supper, with a
knife and fork and bread and butter—a perfect meal.

561. DATES IN CUSTARD (Hampshire)

Stone enough dates to cover the bottom of a glass
dish, and put half a blanched almond in each ; pour
over them one pint of custard and serve cold.

562. DATE MOULD (Middlesex)

Remove the stones from one pound of dates;
chop up the fruit and put it into a lined pan, with
the grated rind and the juice of a good-sized lemon.
Just cover it with water, and set it to simmer. If
the water simmers away, you must put a little more.
Stir gently now and then, as it may stick and burn.
When it becomes a thick paste, turn it into a wet
mould, and when quite cold, turn it out and serve
with custard or whipped cream.

Prunes may be treated in the same way, using
half a pint of water to one pound of prunes, but
you will want seven or eight lumps of sugar to one
pound of prunes, and half an ounce of gelatine,
previously melted in half a pint of water and added
to the rest.

563. GREEN FIGS (Hertfordshire)

Stew in a pint of compôte syrup for three minutes
a dozen small green figs, and serve with whipped
cream.

564. FIG JELLY (Surrey)

Take one pound of small cooking figs, remove the stems, and pour them over some very hot water, but it should not be boiling. Leave them for a minute or two, then drain off the water. Then cut each fig in pieces, and to each pound of figs put one pound of sugar, a little grated lemon-peel, and the juice of one lemon. Put them into a pan and let them cook very slowly, until the syrup thickens and the figs become clear : stir carefully, and if it gets too thick add a little water. When cold, pour off into jars and cover tightly.

565. STEWED FIGS (Surrey)

Pulled figs are the best for this. They should be cooked very slowly, in as little water as possible, with a very little sugar, to taste, and a thin lemon-rind, in the proportion of one lemon to the pound. They should not swell out so as to assume a bloated appearance, which shows that they have *boiled* instead of stewing. Test with a silver fork when they are soft enough, and add about two teaspoon-fuls of lemon-juice before taking them out of the stewpan.

566. PEAR COMPÔTE (Sussex)

Pare and core your pears, slice them into quarters, put them in a lined pan to a little sugar, and just cover them with claret. Let them cook very gently till they are quite tender. No cochineal will be required. The amount of sugar depends upon the kind of pears.

567. TO STEW PEARS (Eighteenth Century)

Pare the largest stewing pears, and stick a clove in the blossom end ; then put them in a well-lined saucepan, fill it with hard water, and set it over a slow fire for three or four hours till the pears are soft, and the water reduced to a small quantity. Then put in as much loaf sugar as will make a thick syrup, and give the pears a boil in it. Cut some lemon peel in straws and hang them about your pears, and serve them up with the syrup in a deep dish.

568. TO STEW PIPPINS WHOLE (Eighteenth Century)

Pare and core your pippins, and throw them into cold water as you pare them. Take the weight of the fruit in fine sugar, and dissolve it in a quart of water ; then boil it up, skim it clear, and put in the fruit. Let them steam gently till they are tender and look clear. Then take them out, and squeeze into the syrup the juice of a large lemon. Let it boil, skim it, and run it through a jelly-bag upon the fruit. You may stick the pippins with strips of candied fruits if you please.

569. RASPBERRY SPONGE (Essex)

Take the whites of four eggs and beat them to a firm froth. Take about one pound of good fresh ripe raspberries, stalk them, mash them thoroughly, and sweeten them to taste with sifted sugar. Then gradually beat them into the whisked whites, a little at a time, so that the sponge keeps stiff. Pile it up in a glass dish.

15

570. SAGO FRUIT (Kent, 1809)

Put five tablepoonsfuls of sago into cold water
and let it stand all night, then strain it and mix it
with one quart of currants and raspberries. Stew
it till quite a jelly, and stir into it some white sugar
to sweeten it, then put it into a mould.

VARIOUS

571. FRENCH BANCES (Eighteenth Century)

Take half a pint of water, a bit of lemon peel, a
bit of butter the bigness of a walnut, a little orange-
flower water ; let these boil three or four minutes ;
then take out the lemon peel, and add to it a pint of
flour; keep the water boiling and stirring all the
while till it is stiff, then take it off the fire, and put
in six eggs, leaving out the whites of three ; beat
these well for about half an hour, till they come to
a stiff paste. Drop small pieces of this into a pan
of boiling lard, with a teaspoon ; if they are of a
right lightness they will be very nice ; keep shaking
the pan all the time till they are a light brown. A
large dish will take six or seven minutes to cook ;
when done enough, put them into a dish that will
drain them, set them by the fire, and strew fine
sugar over them.

572. BENITA SHAPE (Devonshire)

Two eggs, juice of two lemons, half a pound of
castor sugar, grated rind of one lemon, five sheets
of gelatine. Melt the gelatine in a tumbler of warm
water ; slightly whip the yolks of the eggs and

castor sugar gradually together, add the lemon rind
and juice and gelatine whilst warm. When almost
cold, stir in lightly the whites of eggs well whipped.
Pour into a wet mould and put into a cool place to
set. This can be made with oranges instead of
lemons, and the rind can be left out if not liked.

573. BROWN BREAD-CRUMB TRIFLE (Surrey)

Put through a fine sieve any stale brown bread,
till you have two breakfastcupfuls of fine crumbs,
which pile on a dish. Put over about a breakfastcupful of some moist juicy jam, such as strawberry,
which will soak into the crumbs. When it has fairly
soaked in, mask the whole in whipped cream. This
is exceedingly good if the crumbs are well saturated.

574. COLDHARBOUR BALLS (Surrey)

Dissolve an ounce of butter in a quart of warm
milk, and use as much fine flour as will make a stiff
paste; add, in making the paste, about half a teaspoonful of salt, and two eggs beaten up with a tablespoonful of yeast; cover with a cloth and keep it
before the fire for half an hour, then roll into balls or
in pieces of the size and length of the little finger,
and bake in a quick oven.

575. APPLE FRITTERS (Cheshire)

Take some *large* apples, peel, and slice them
through in rounds a quarter to half an inch
thick. Lay some slices for two hours in a basin
with brandy and powdered white sugar. Then
make a stiff batter, and stir into it just before using

the whites of two eggs beaten to a stiff froth. Drain
the apples, cover well with the batter, and fry in
hot lard or butter. Drain on blotting paper before
the fire. Pile high on a dish, and sprinkle with
sifted sugar.

576. COMMON FRITTERS (Eighteenth Century)

Take half a pint of ale and two eggs, beat in as
much flour as will make it rather thicker than a
common pudding, with nutmeg and sugar to your
taste, let it stand three or four minutes to rise, then
drop it in tablespoonfuls into a pan of boiling lard ;
fry them a light brown, drain them on a sieve ; serve
them up with sugar grated over them, and wine
sauce in a boat.

577. PLAIN FRITTERS WITH RICE
(Eighteenth Century)

Grate the crumb of a penny loaf, pour over it a
pint of boiling cream, or good milk, let it stand four
or five hours, then beat it exceedingly fine. Put to
it the yolks of five eggs, four ounces of sugar, and
a nutmeg grated, beat them well together, and fry
them in hog's lard ; drain them on a sieve, and
serve them up with wine sauce under them. *N.B.*
You may put currants in if you please.

578. WATER FRITTERS (Eighteenth Century)

Take a quart of water, five or six tablespoonfuls
of flour (the batter must be very thick) and a little
salt, mix all these together and beat the yolks and
whites of eight eggs with a little brandy, then strain

them, through a hair sieve, and put them to the other things ; the longer they stand before you fry them the better. Just before you fry them, melt about half a pound of butter very thick, and beat it well in ; you must not turn them, and take care not to burn them. The best thing to fry them in is fine lard.

579. FRENCH PANCAKES (Cumberland)

Two eggs, a gill of milk, the weight of the two eggs in butter, flour and castor sugar, jam. Beat the butter to a cream, then beat in the sugar and flour. Beat up the eggs with the milk, add them to the other ingredients ; beat all very well. Butter some saucers, put in the mixture, and bake in a quick oven for twenty minutes. Warm some jam, put a little on each pancake, double them over, sprinkle with sugar and serve.

580. FRENCH PANCAKES (Ireland)

Beat two ounces of butter to a cream, add two beaten eggs, stir in two ounces of flour and two ounces of sifted sugar. When well mixed, add half a pint of new milk. Beat mixture. Put on two buttered plates. Bake twenty minutes and serve with jam. Very light and nice when well made with fresh eggs.

581. MADRAS PANCAKES

To six eggs, well beaten, add two tablespoonfuls of boiled rice, sugar to taste, a little pounded cinnamon, and a little orange-flower water ; mix all well together, and fry it in butter to a good colour. When served, divide it into quarters, and strew with powdered sugar.

582. PINK PANCAKES (Eighteenth Century)

Boil a large beetroot tender, and beat it fine in a marble mortar, then add the yolks of four eggs, two spoonfuls of flour, and three spoonfuls of good cream; sweeten it to your taste, grate in half a nutmeg, and put in a glass of brandy; beat all together half an hour. Fry the pancakes in butter, and garnish them with green sweetmeats, preserved apricots, or green sprigs of myrtle. It is a pretty corner dish for either dinner or supper.

583. RUSSIAN PANCAKES (Hertfordshire)

Make some very small thin pancakes, fill them with thick jam, or (if desired as a savoury) with quenelle forcemeat, fish, or fowl; roll up the pancakes, trim them evenly, dip in egg and bread crumbs, and fry. Serve quickly.

584. A DELICIOUS COLD SWEET (Kent)

Take twelve almond cakes (soak six in sherry and the other six in the custard when it is *hot*). Make a custard of four eggs, and one and a half pints of milk, sugar, and half an ounce of gelatine. Put in the mould a few dried cherries. Pour a little custard into the mould, then the cakes, and then the remainder of the custard.

585. AN EXCELLENT SWEET (Staffordshire)

Take twelve yolks of eggs, a gill of sherry; place them over a slow fire with sugar to your taste. Whisk the mixture until it becomes thick. Pour it into a glass dish, and when cold ornament with ratafia cakes, or anything else you may fancy. Half the quantity makes a nice small dish.

586. TAPIOCA CREAM (Essex)

Three ounces of tapioca, one pint of milk, half a pint of cream, sugar, lemon juice or sherry, essence of almond, four penny sponge cakes, one ounce of sweet almonds. Wash the tapioca and put it to soak in the milk the evening before it is required. Cook slowly till tender. Add sugar to taste, and let cool. Put the sponge cakes into a glass dish and pour over enough lemon juice or sherry to soak them. Pile the tapioca roughly over, whip the cream, heap it on top, and decorate with the almonds blanched and cut into spikes.

587. TAPIOCA SNOW (Lancashire)

Three tablespoonfuls of tapioca, one pint of new milk, essence of vanilla, two tablespoonfuls of sugar, two eggs. Boil tapioca in milk till quite soft, sweeten with sugar, stir in the yolks of both eggs, and cook gently over slow fire for about six minutes. When cool, flavour with fifteen drops of essence of vanilla, and turn into a glass dish. When quite cold, place the whites of the eggs (beaten to a stiff froth with a little sugar and five drops of vanilla) on the top.

CHAPTER XV

CREAMS, CUSTARDS, JUNKETS, SYLLABUBS, ETC.

NOTE.—In the making of creams and custards, and of all those fluffy, frothy, delightful festival dishes which are much " too bright and good for human nature's daily food," our grandmothers undoubtedly excelled.

The very recipes make one's mouth water, and although we cannot usually command the warm and foamy milk fresh from the cow, or the unlimited quarts of rich cream, in which they seem to have rejoiced—yet we can at any rate adapt to our narrower conditions some of the admirable concoctions here collected and presented. She is no good cook who cannot make the best of what she already has. The junkets and custards are in particular worthy of attention; for all the multiplicity of custard powders, egg powders, pudding powders, of to-day, shall never equal the hand-made, home-made delicacy. The " Everlasting Syllabub " on page 241 is a singularly admirable dish.

CREAMS

588. BURNT CREAM (Middlesex)

Beat and mix well together the yolks of six eggs, two tablespoonfuls of flour, the peel of a lemon

grated, and four or five bitter almonds ; sweeten
with lump sugar, and stir over the fire till it comes
to a good thickness, and pour it into the dish in
which it is to be served ; boil some pounded loaf
sugar in water until it turns brown, and then pour
it over the cream in fantastic figures.

589. COFFEE CREAM (Middlesex)

Having dissolved one ounce of isinglass, boil it
with two quarts of cream, and mix it with one and
a half pints of very strong coffee ; sweeten well,
whisk it for ten minutes, put it into custard cups,
and let them stand in a pan of boiling water till
they become firm.

590. COFFEE CREAM (Berkshire)

One pint of milk and cream mixed, half a cup of
strong coffee added, sweeten to taste. Dissolve one
ounce of gelatine (previously soaked). Beat all
together and turn into a wet mould.

591. CREAM FOR FRUIT PIES (Middlesex)

This is made by boiling new milk with grated nutmeg or cinnamon, two or three peach leaves, or a
few bitter almonds, and a sufficient quantity of sugar
to sweeten it ; then straining the cream and, when
cold, beating up with it the yolks of eggs in the
proportion of four to a quart, and warming the
whole over the fire until it thickens. This is eaten
cold with fruit tarts, or with any fresh fruits at
dessert. If one-quarter of the quantity be rich
cream, instead of the whole being milk, it will be
improved.

592. TO MAKE DEVONSHIRE CREAM (Sussex)

Place new milk in a clean jug or can, and stand it in a saucepan of warm water. Bring the water to the boil, and let it boil for half an hour. Then pour the milk into a shallow basin or dish, and let it stand until quite cold. The cream will be found quite thick and clotted, like Devonshire cream; and if it is required still thicker, it can be whipped in the same manner as unscalded cream.

593. FROTHED CREAM (Kent)

Rub a lump of loaf sugar on the rind of a lemon ; put it into a pint of cream, and sweeten it to your taste, then put in a glass of Madeira wine, or French brandy. Mill it to a froth in a chocolate mill ; take it off as it rises, and lay it on your dish.

594. ITALIAN CREAM (Middlesex)

Having sweetened a pint of cream, boil it with a lemon, cut very thin, and a small stick of cinnamon ; strain and mix with it a little dissolved isinglass : while hot, add to it the yolks of eight eggs well beaten, and stir it till quite cold.

595. KING WILLIAM'S CREAM (Eighteenth Century)

Beat the whites of three eggs very well. Squeeze out the juice of two large, or three small lemons : take two ounces more than the weight of the juices in sifted sugar, and mix it with two or three drops of orange-flower water, and five or six spoonfuls of cold water. Melt this in a pan, and when all the sugar is melted, put in the whites of eggs, and

the juice. Set it over a slow fire, and keep stirring
till you find it thicken : then strain it through a
coarse cloth quick into a dish.

596. LEMON CREAM (Ireland)

Take a pint of thick cream, and put to it the yolk
of two eggs well beaten, four ounces of white sugar,
and the rind of a lemon. Boil it up ; stir it till
almost cold. Put the juice of a lemon into a bowl,
and pour the cream upon it, stirring it till cold.

597. MADEIRA CREAMS (Hertfordshire)

Cut some bananas and rub them through a coarse
sieve ; add as much cream as you have fruit, and
a pinch of salt. To every pint of this mixture add
two ounces of sugar, and a dessertspoonful of brandy
or liquor. Beat this very stiff and light, and, just
before serving, place in custard glasses.

598. LEMON CREAM (Middlesex)

Required : two lemons, two eggs, two ounces of
cornflour, six ounces of castor sugar, one pint of
water. Pare the lemons thinly, and boil the rind
well in the water for five minutes, mix the cornflour with the strained juice of lemons, add the
liquid from the rinds, return to the saucepan and
boil for three minutes, stirring all the time. Add
the sugar and cook slightly, mix in the yolks of
eggs well-beaten, and stir over a gentle heat, until
they thicken. Whip the whites into a stiff froth,
and stir lightly into the mixture. Pour into a wet
mould ; when cold, turn out.

599. RATAFIA CREAM (Hampshire)

Take one lemon, half a pint of fresh cream, two penny sponge cakes, one wineglassful of sherry, fifteen lumps of sugar, a few ratafias. Peel the lemon very thinly, and allow the rind to soak some hours in the juice and wine, to which also add the sugar. Cut your sponge cakes in slices, and place them in a glass dish. Now whip the cream as stiff as possible, and put it on the cake. Decorate with the ratafias, and the dish is ready. This cream is very nice used without the sponge cakes, and served in custard glasses ; it is then called Everlasting Syllabub.

600. SNOW CREAM (Kent)

Put to a quart of cream the whites of three eggs beaten, four dessertspoonfuls of white wine, sugar to your taste, add a piece of lemon peel, and whip to a froth. Remove the peel, and serve in a dish.

601. SPANISH CREAM (Seventeenth Century)

Take three dessertspoonfuls of rice flour sifted very fine, the yolk of three eggs, three dessertspoonfuls of water and two of orange-flower water. Put to them one pint of cream. Set the mixture over a good fire and stir till it be of a proper thickness, then pour it into cups.

602. SPANISH CREAM (Surrey)

Boil two ounces of isinglass in a pint of water till quite dissolved, and mix with it two quarts of good milk ; stir it over the fire till it begins to boil, then let it cool a little, and add gradually the yolks of twelve eggs well beaten, a large glass of white wine, and a little ratafia ; pour it into a dish, sweeten to taste, and when cold put it into shapes.

603. STONE CREAM (Middlesex)

This is made by boiling a quarter of an ounce of isinglass in a little water, and boiling it with a pint of sweetened cream, stirring it well ; pour this into a dish in which have been placed preserved fruit, such as apricots, cherries, etc., with some lemon juice (say two or three tablespoonfuls) and some grated lemon peel.

604. STRAWBERRY CREAM (Middlesex)

Boil some good cream with a sufficient quantity of sugar to sweeten it, and reduce it to one half its bulk : then add a little rennet, and the juice of strawberries, sufficient to give a good flavour ; and bake in a slow oven.

605. SWISS CREAM (Surrey)

Boil the grated peel of a good-sized lemon, and rather more than half a pound of white loaf sugar in a pint of cream, thickening with a spoonful of flour previously mixed up with a tablespoonful of lemon juice ; this is to be added very gradually as the cream warms, and the whole is to be carefully stirred ; when it is taken from the fire, stir till nearly cold, and serve in a glass dish garnished with preserved fruits, or candied orange and lemon peel. There is another dish called Swiss Cream which is

eaten hot ; it is made by whisking up in a basin or
deep dish, previously made very hot, the yolks of
eight eggs with half a pound of pounded loaf sugar,
the grated rind of a lemon, and half a pint of white
French wine.

CUSTARDS

606. CUSTARD (Kent)

To one quart of good milk add the yolks of ten
eggs. First boil the milk with some cinnamon and
sugar ; when nearly cold add it to the eggs, and
keep constantly stirring. Put it into a large jug,
and put the jug into a pot of boiling water. Do
not allow the custard to boil ; and before taking it
out of the jug, add some bitter and some sweet
almonds ; then put into glasses.

607. BAKED CUSTARD (Berkshire)

To one quart of new milk allow four or five eggs,
a quarter of a pound loaf sugar, one lemon peel
grated, eight to ten bitter almonds pounded, or a
few drops of essence of bitter almonds, and a tablespoonful of brandy. Bake in a slow oven, but don't
allow it to boil, or the custard will "break" and
curdle.

608. CHEAP CUSTARD (Yorkshire)

Boil one pint of milk, sweeten it with any spice
you like. Rub smooth two tablepoonfuls of ground
rice in a little cold milk, then put into it two yolks
of eggs well beaten. Afterwards add the boiled

milk, and stir them well together. Then stir it over a slow fire till it thickens, but it must not boil.

609. CHOCOLATE CUSTARDS (Surrey)

Take one and a half ounces of best chocolate, dissolve it gently by the side of the fire in rather over one wineglassful of water, then let it boil till quite smooth. Add one pint of new milk, (flavoured with lemon peel or vanilla) and two ounces of fine sugar, and let all come to the boil. Then stir it into five well-beaten and strained eggs. Put the custard into a jar and set this in a pan of boiling water ; stir continually until it thickens, and then take it off. When nearly cold, pour it into glasses. This is much richer when made with yolks only ; but in that case you must use the following proportions : two ounces of chocolate, one pint of milk, half a pint of cream, two to three ounces of sugar, and eight yolks.

610. COUNTESS CUSTARD (Sussex)

Cut five sponge-cakes in half. Place on a dish with alternate layers of fruit, the last layer being fruit. Make a nice thick custard and flavour with orange-flower water, sweeten to taste, and when nearly cold, pour it over the fruit.

611. WASSAIL CUSTARD (Hertfordshire)

Line a dish with slices of stale sponge cakes, ratafia biscuits, and macaroons. Mix the juice of a lemon with a little raisin wine and pour it over the cakes. When these have quite absorbed the

liquor, pour a pint of good custard over, and decorate
the top with angelica, chopped cherries, and a little
chopped pistachio nut.

JUNKETS

612. JUNKET (Somerset)

Take one quart of new milk. Warm some of it
with five knobs of loaf sugar, then pour the hot and
cold milk together into a deep bowl. Add one good
tablespoonful of brandy and one of rennet. Stir
it well round together. Let it stand in a warm place
to set, say on a dish on a cool part of the stove.
Then remove it, and cover the top with Devonshire
clotted cream. Throw over it a tablespoonful of
brandy, then grate a little nutmeg on it and scatter
sifted sugar. Walnuts are a welcome addition. Send
to table with plain biscuits or bread.

613. JUNKET (Surrey)

One quart of milk, *lukewarm* (not scalded or even
hot); two tablespoonfuls of soft white sugar; two
tablespoonfuls of rum; one dessertspoonful of
essence of rennet. Put the milk to stand on the
stove for five or ten minutes to get slightly warm,
then stir in the sugar and rum and mix them well,
then add the rennet; stir it well, and then stir again
in a few minutes. Leave the junket in a corner of
the stove, *not too hot*, until it is solid, then grate a
little nutmeg over it and put it to cool.

(*N.B.* Sherry may be advantageously substituted
for the rum.)

614. COFFEE JUNKET (Surrey)

To one pint of new milk add half a teacupful of strong coffee, and one dessertspoonful of castor sugar. Make this as you would ordinary junket, using one teaspoonful of essence of rennet or one rennet tablet. Pour into the bowl it will be served in, and let it stand in a moderately cool place till set. Whip two-pennyworth of cream, add a little sugar, and arrange little dobs of cream on the top of the junket, just before it is sent to table.

SYLLABUBS

615. SYLLABUB (Kent, 1809)

The whites of four eggs beaten to a froth ; add half a pound of fine sugar, a little at a time, beating till the sugar is melted. Put in the juice of a good lemon and half a pint of sweet white wine. Keep beating it with a whisk that it may be well mixed. Put to it a pint of very sweet thick cream, beat it well together. Then fill your glasses. They should stand six or seven hours.

616. SYLLABUB (Surrey)

Half a pint of scalded cream, half a pint of raw cream, one dessertspoonful of white sifted sugar, two wineglassfuls of sherry, two tablepoonfuls of brandy, a little grated nutmeg, the juice of one and a half lemons. Whip it to a froth and fill the glasses.

617. EVERLASTING SYLLABUB (Isle of Wight)

Steep the peel and juice of one lemon overnight in a wineglassful of white wine. Next morning, pour

16

this into a deep pan, and stir in gradually half a pint of thick cream, with sugar to taste : whip for a quarter of an hour, and put into glasses. This is better made the day before using, and will keep for several days.

618. SYLLABUB WITH CAKES (Middlesex)

Steep sponge biscuits, or any other cakes, in equal quantities of port, claret, and brandy ; mash them up with a spoon, and add grated nutmeg, and lemon peel, lemon juice, sweet almonds, blanched and pounded to paste, and sufficient sugar to make the whole sweet ; the quantity of the above will depend on the size of the syllabub required. Put all these ingredients into a bowl, and let the milk of a cow. be milked upon them, adding a little good cream and sifted loaf sugar. A very good syllabub may be made by mixing half a pint of sherry, half a pint of Burgundy, a wineglass of any ratafia, half a pound of pounded white sugar, some grated nutmeg, the grated peel of a lemon, and the juice of a lemon ; when these have been well stirred together, and the sugar is dissolved, add one quart of rich cream, and whisk it up until it froths well ; put some macaroons, or sponge biscuits, into a dish, and pile the froth upon them ; or the syllabub may be served in glasses. If the whites of six eggs be whipped up with the syllabub, it may be served up differently, but the whipping must be continued for a long time ; as the froth rises, put it on a sieve to dry, and having half filled wineglasses with wine, fill them up with the froth. The common syllabub is generally served without cream or whipping ; wine, nutmeg, sugar, grated lemon peel, with or without a little brandy or liqueur, are mixed in a basin, and the milk of the cow is milked upon them. The quantity of milk is generally in the proportion of three pints to one pint of wine ; but this may be reduced, or increased, according to taste.

619. WHIPPED SYLLABUB (Yorkshire, 1769)

Take two porringers of cream and one of white wine, grate in the rind of a lemon. Take the whites of three eggs, sweeten to your taste, then whip it with a whisk. Take off the froth as it rises, and put it into your syllabub glasses.

620. LEMON POSSET (Yorkshire, 1769)

Take one pint of good thick cream, grate into it the outer rind of two lemons, and squeeze the juice into half a gill of white wine, and sweeten it to your taste. Take the whites of two eggs and beat them to a froth, then beat all together in a bowl, then put it into the glasses for use.

TRIFLES

621. TRIFLE (Isle of Wight)

Take three penny sponge cakes, three tablespoonfuls of raspberry or apricot jam, two eggs with whites and yolks separated, a quarter of a pint of milk, one tablespoonful of castor sugar, three drops ratafia essence. Cut the sponge cakes into slices and spread with the jam ; lay them in a glass dish. Make a custard of the yolk, milk, and essence, and half the sugar. Pour it over the sponge cakes and

allow them to soak for a quarter of an hour. Mix
the rest of the sugar with the whites, which must
be whipped to a stiff froth and then piled lightly on
the top. Cost 7*d*.

622. TRIFLE (Kent)

Cover the bottom of a dish with Naples biscuits,
macaroons, and ratafia cakes. Wet them with
sweet wine ; put over them a thick custard, then a
small quantity of raspberry jam, and cover the whole
with a frothed cream.

623. TRIFLE (Middlesex)

To prepare this, take two ounces of blanched sweet
almonds, and one ounce of blanched bitter almonds,
and pound them to a smooth paste, adding as you
pound them, a little rose-water ; take two lemons,
and grate the peels, and squeeze the juice into a
saucer ; four small sponge cakes, or Naples biscuits,
and eight, or more, macaroons must next be broken
into small pieces, and mixed with the almonds,
and the mixture be laid at the bottom of a glass
bowl ; grate a nutmeg over this, and throw in the
peel and the juice of the lemons ; to the whole add
half a pint of white wine mixed with half a gill of
brandy, and let the mixture remain until the cakes
are dissolved, when it may be stirred a little. To a
quart of cream, add a quarter of a pound of powdered
loaf sugar, and a glass of noyeau, and beat with a
whisk till it stands alone ; as the froth rises, take it
off with a spoon, and lay on a sieve, with a large dish
under it, to drain ; then take the cream that has
been drained into the dish, and pour it back into

the pan with the rest, the whole being beaten over
again ; this being done, set the cream in a cool place.
Have now a pint of rich baked custard, made of the
yolks of eggs, cold, and pour into the bowl upon the
dissolved cakes, and when the cream is cold, pour
that in also, heaping it high in the centre ; a layer
of fruit, jelly, or of well-preserved fruit, may be
put in between the custard and the frothed cream,
if that be preferred.

624. TINNED APRICOTS AND TRIFLE (Surrey)

Warm the syrup, add sugar if necessary, then
put in the apricots and cook a few minutes. Cut
stale sponge cakes into slices, place in glass dish ;
pour a little warm apricot syrup over them, leave
quite an hour. Put apricots (or peaches, or pears,
half a tin) on the sponge cakes, then a custard.
Finish the top with whipped cream, sweetened and
flavoured (a whipped white of egg may be added to
make more of it), decorate with pistachio nuts,
cherries, or angelica. For one pint of custard it will
be necessary to take half a pint of milk, one egg (a
yolk of another egg may be added), one ounce of
loaf sugar, and one teaspoonful of cornflour.

CHAPTER XVI

JAMS, JELLIES, PRESERVES, FRUIT PASTES, ETC.

NOTE.—The great pre-eminence of the home jam over the factory article, is that, in the words of Sam Weller, one " knows the lady wot made it." One also is assured that she did not put in carrots, seeds, glucose, or any alien matter in the way of coloratives, preservatives, or sweeteners unknown to the " home-farm." Of home-made jam one may partake freely with pleasant and beneficial results ; shop jam frequently leaves an acid taste in the mouth and a most undesirable effect upon the whole of the mucous membrane. Jams and preserves, more-over, can be so easily achieved, and in most cases so cheaply, that one is hardly justified in denying one's family these inexpensive and invaluable com-modities. It is especially advisable to attempt those concoctions which *cannot*, as a rule, be bought—apple jam, for instance, and rhubarb, and vegetable marrow—grape-jelly (a charming affair), —preparations of quince, mulberry, cucumber, etc. Not so many recipes as you might expect are to be found in the ensuing selection ; the reason being, I imagine, that people were so accustomed to jam-making as a matter of ordinary annual occurrence,

246

they never thought of writing down any formulas for what everybody knew quite well. Be that as it may, the everyday jams are to be found in any cookery-book; you can hardly go wrong in them. Those here presented are of a somewhat more unwonted character.

JAMS, JELLIES, MARMALADES

625. APPLE GINGER (Yorkshire)

Four pounds of apples, four pounds of sugar, one quart of water, two ounces of essence of ginger. Pare the fruit, take out the core, and cut in shapes as like ginger-root as possible. Boil the sugar and water for twenty-five minutes, till it is a nice syrup, then put in the apples, the syrup boiling *quickly* all the time, stirring it as little as possible; add the ginger; it will take about an hour to clear and become yellow. Skim it well. Be sure to have your apples all one kind, either all green or all yellow ones.

626. APPLE JAM (Cheshire)

Four pounds of apples peeled and cut as for a pie; an equal quantity of lump sugar; the rind and juice of two lemons, or rather more, and rather better than three-quarters of an ounce of beaten ground ginger; also a few cloves. Boil slowly for an hour and a half, or nearer two hours, without adding water. About five minutes before taking off the fire add a large wineglassful of spirits. This is to ensure the keeping well.

627.   APPLE JELLY (Essex)

To every three pounds of apples add *about* a quart
of cold water. Simmer gently till tender and just on
the point of mashing. Strain, without squeezing,
through a jelly bag or hair sieve. Measure the
juice which comes through, and boil it for fifteen
minutes alone, then add a pound of preserving
sugar to every pint, and boil sugar and juice together
for twenty-five minutes. (The sugar should be
made hot in the oven before using.) Pour into jars
or jelly glasses, and cover over when cold.

628.   APPLE JELLY (Ireland)
(For dessert use, not for keeping)

Take the amount you wish of codlings, or other
good English cooking apples ; pare, core, and cut
them into thin slices into a deep earthenware pan,
with as much water as will just cover them. When
soft, strain them through a jelly-bag. To every
pound of liquor, add one pound of crushed or (better)
powdered sugar. Boil it very fast for ten minutes.
Put some thinly sliced lemon peel in your moulds,
and pour in the jelly. Do not boil much at a time.

629.   APPLE JELLY (Kent)

Three pounds of white sugar, four pounds of
apples (peeled and cored), a teaspoonful of cayenne
pepper, two lemons, rind and juice.

630.   APPLE JELLY (Lancashire)

Pare, core, and quarter the fruit, and weigh it
quickly that it may not lose its colour. To each

pound pour a pint of cold water, and boil it until it is
well broken without being reduced to a white thick
pulp, as it would then be difficult to render the juice
perfectly clear, which it ought to be. Drain the
juice well from the apples, either through a fine sieve,
or a folded muslin strainer, and pass it afterwards
through a jelly-bag, or turn the fruit at once into the
last of these, and pour the liquid through a second
time if needed. When it appears quite transparent,
weigh, and reduce it by quick boiling for twenty
minutes. Add two pounds of sugar for three of
juice, then boil it for ten minutes. Put in the strained
juice of a small lemon for every two pounds of jelly,
a couple of minutes before it is taken from the fire.

631. APPLE MARMALADE (Middlesex)

Take six pounds of good cooking apples, peel and
core them and cut them into small pieces, as for a
pie, as evenly as possible. Put them into a basin
of cold water that they may keep their colour white,
while you do the rest. When ready, take them out
and weigh them, put them into a deep bowl, and
lay over them an equal amount of sugar, and to
every three pounds of apples add one tablespoonful
of ground ginger (this is better freshly grated, not
in the bought powder). Leave all to stand for three
days. The cores and peels should now be put in a lined
preserving pan, with enough water to cover them,
and boiled for half an hour, then strained off. At the
end of the three days, strain off the syrup from the
apples, add the juice from the peels, and boil for ten
minutes. Then put in the slices of apple, and let
them boil for half or three-quarters of an hour,

till they are quite clear, taking care that they do
not break.

632. APPLE MARMALADE (Surrey)

Take two pounds of good sound cooking apples,
and put them in a lined saucepan with one pound of
castor sugar and one pint of sweet cider. Let them
cook quietly for three hours or so, until the fruit
is so soft it can be put through a sieve. If it is not
sweet enough, more castor sugar can be now added.
Put it into jars or pots, like ordinary jam.

633. BARBERRY JAM (1815)

Pick your barberries from the stalks, and put them
into an earthen pan, then into the oven to bake ;
when baked, pass them through a sieve with a large
wooden spoon, taking care there are no skins of the
barberries left in ; weigh the barberries and to every
two pounds allow two pounds and a half of powdered
sugar ; mix the sugar and the fruit together, put
it in your pots and cover it up ; set it in a dry
place ; when you have filled your pots with it, sift a
little powdered sugar over the tops of them.

634. BLACKBERRY JAM (Yorkshire)

Half a pound of good brown sugar to every pound
of fruit ; boil the whole together gently for one hour,
or till the blackberries are soft, stirring and mashing
them well.

635. CELERY IN IMITATION OF PRESERVED GINGER (Middlesex)

Cut the blanched part of the celery in pieces, and
boil it in water with a large quantity of ginger until

it is quite tender, then throw it into cold water and allow it to remain an hour.   At the end of this time put it over a slow fire in good syrup, with some pieces of ginger, and let it remain simmering for an hour. Cool it again, and in the meantime, thicken the syrup by further evaporation.   Put the celery in again, and repeat the same process.   After a third simmering in this way, taking care to keep the syrup thick, put the celery into pots, and cover with syrup.   The stalks of lettuce, taking off the outside, prepared in the same way, make a very nice dessert sweet.

636. TO DRY CHERRIES WITHOUT SUGAR
(Seventeenth Century)

Stone the cherries and set them in a pan over the fire, with only what liquor comes out of them. Shake them as they boil, then put them in an earthen pot.   The next day scald them, and when they are cold, lay them on sieves to dry in an oven not too hot.   Twice heating in an oven will dry any sort of cherries.

637. PRESERVED CITRONS (Kent)

Put them into water overnight ; boil them till quite tender, cut them in halves, and to every pound of citrons add a pound of sugar.   Put about a table-spoonful of water to every pound of sugar ; when all is dissolved, pour it on the citrons, then put all on the fire and let them boil about half an hour.   Soak a few races of ginger in water three or four days— boil them first with a thin syrup, and afterwards with the citrons.

638. TO PRESERVE SIBERIAN CRABS (Cheshire)

A pound of loaf sugar to half a pint of water.
Simmer till clear. Then boil the crabs in this, very
gently till done, having first pricked them all over
to keep them from bursting. A little ginger, lemon,
and cochineal to be added before boiling. The
stalks are to be left on.

639. CRAB-APPLE JELLY (Kent)

Cut the crab-apples in halves, and put them in
a preserving pan with enough water to cover them.
Let them come to the boil but not to a pulp ; then
strain, and to every pint of juice add three-quarters
of a pound of white sugar. Boil three-quarters of
an hour.

640. PRESERVED CRANBERRIES (Middlesex)

For every pound of the fruit use two pounds of
sugar : pour a little water into the preserving pan,
then a layer of sugar, and then a layer of fruit :
boil gently for twenty minutes, and skim.

641. PRESERVED CUCUMBER (Ireland)

Take large and small cucumbers free from seeds ;
put them into salt and water, with cabbage leaves
on the top to keep them down. Tie a paper over,
and put them in a warm place till they are yellow ;
then wash them out and put them into fresh salt
water. Continue to change the water till they are a
good green ; then take them out, and cut out all
the pulp, and put them into cold water to take out
the salt. Let them so remain two or three days,

changing the water twice a day. Take one pound
of fine sugar, and half a pint of water, put on the fire
and skim it clear. Add the rind of a lemon, cut very
thin, and one ounce of ginger. When the syrup is
cold, wipe the cucumbers, and put them in. Boil
up the preserve three times a week for three weeks.

642. QUIDDANY OF RED CURRANTS
(Yorkshire, 1769)

Put your red currant berries into a jar, with a
spoonful or two of water, and cover it close, and
stand it in boiling water. When you think they are
done enough, strain them, and put to every pint
of juice a pound of loaf sugar. Boil it up jelly
height, and put it into glasses for use.

643. DAMSONS FOR WINTER USE (Kent)

To every pound of fruit allow half a pound of preserving sugar ; fruit to be sound and not too ripe.
Put the fruit into large jars ; sprinkle the sugar
over the fruit. Lay saucers over the jars and place
them in a moderately cool oven for an hour or two,
until the fruit is tender. When cold, cover the top
of the jars with white paper cut to the size of the
jar. Pour over this melted mutton fat, about two
inches thick ; cover over with brown paper, and
keep in dry place. As a rule they keep till February ;
but the fruit must not be too ripe.

644. GOOSEBERRY JELLY (Lincolnshire)

Make gooseberry jelly the ordinary way, and when
it is ready to take off the fire, have ready a bunch
of elder-flowers tied up in a piece of muslin, which

turn round and round in the jelly until it has the desired flavour ; it is really like a most delicious grape.

645. GRAPE CONSERVE (American)

One basket of grapes, one and a half pints of sugar, one and a half pounds of seeded raisins, half a pound of walnut kernels. Remove pulp from grapes, boil five minutes, put through a colander, to remove seeds. Add raisins, sugar, and nuts chopped fine, and boil thirty minutes till thick.

646. GRAPE JELLY (American)

Free the grapes from stems and leaves. Put in preserving kettle, mash, and heat slowly. After reaching boiling-point, simmer for half an hour. Put them in a jelly-bag—I let mine drip all night. Measure juice, put in kettle, boil for twenty minutes. Measure equal quantity of sugar, add to juice, and stir till dissolved. Put into jelly glasses.

647. GRAPE MARMALADE (American)

Pulp the grapes ; cook pulps till tender. Press through sieve and add skins, allowing three-quarters of a pound of sugar to half a pound of fruit. Cook. slowly.

648. LEMON MARMALADE (Surrey)

For this you want twelve lemons, and an equal weight in preserving sugar. Wash and wipe the lemons, then halve them, strain out the juice, and put the pips by themselves into a bowl with a tumblerful of cold water. The peels must be put into cold water in a lined pan, and boiled till thoroughly tender. Then take them out, and having removed all the white pith you can, cut the rinds into the thinnest possible shreds or strips, about half an inch long. Next put the lemon juice, the water from the pips, and the sugar into a preserving pan, and let it boil to a syrup. Add the rinds, and boil till the marmalade will " set."

649. MOUNTAIN ASH JELLY (Surrey)

Pick the mountain-ash berries clean from the stalks, and stew them down to as near a pulp as you can, with enough water to cover them and a very little " race " ginger. Crush and strain the pulp, and boil it up again for half an hour, with two-thirds of its weight in sugar. (Mountain ash is known in Ireland as " quicken " and in Scotland as " rowan." It is credited with wonderfully restorative properties, and is, I believe, largely used in the jelly form upon the Continent, especially in Switzerland. Ed.)

650. ANOTHER WAY (Middlesex)

Pare, core, and slice two pounds of good preserving apples of the juiciest kind, and boil them for twenty minutes or more in one quart of water, till they are well to pieces. Strain off the water, and add to the apples in the preserving pan three pounds of mountain ash berries. Let all simmer gently until quite pulped : then strain off the juice, and to every pint measure one pound of sugar. Let the juice boil fast for twenty minutes, then put in the sugar, which

should be warmed and crushed. Boil for fifteen
minutes more, skimming well, and then pour off the
jelly into heated pots. Some people put a leaf of
scented geranium, such as oakleaf, into every pot.

651. PRESERVED MELONS OR CUCUMBERS (Kent)

Gather the melons when fresh and green ; rub
them smooth with a coarse cloth ; put them in strong
salt and water ; tie them down close and set them
by the fire ; change them from top to bottom till
quite yellow, then put them in a skillet with layers
of vine leaves and strong salt and water, a small
piece of soda and the same of alum. Put it over the
fire at some distance till quite scalding hot, but not
boiling. If not green in a few hours, change the
water and leaves, and put them on again ; when
green, drain them on a sieve, and throw them in
fresh water for three days, changing it every day.
Make a thin syrup with one pound of sugar and a
gallon of water boiled an hour and cleared with the
white of an egg. When nearly cold, pour it over
them, repeating the same for a week, each day a
little warmer ; the last day let them boil five minutes.

652. TO PRESERVE MULBERRIES IN SUGAR
(Middlesex)

Choose large and very ripe mulberries ; put them
gently into some strong syrup, and let them boil,
covering over the pan, and shaking it gently from
time to time ; then take off the fire, skim the syrup,
and let them stand for two hours. They are then
to be put on again, and boiled until the syrup is
exceedingly thick. Pour into glasses and pots, and
keep by for use.

653. TO PRESERVE MULBERRIES IN A DRY
STATE (Middlesex)

Gather them when not quite ripe, and give them
a boil in syrup; then let them stand for twenty-four
hours near the fire, so as just to keep warm. At
the end of this time, take them out, drain them, and
put them upon tins, powdering them well with dry
sugar, and exposing them to the sun. When they
are dry on one side, turn them, powder them in the
same way, and finish the drying.

654. ORANGE JELLY (Kent)

One ounce of isinglass, one pint of hot water.
Rub some loaf sugar on the rinds of six oranges and
four lemons until they appear white. Put the sugar
into the water, and let it remain until the isinglass
is dissolved, then add the juice of the fruit and let
it just boil, then strain into moulds.

655. ORANGE MARMALADE CONSERVE
(Devonshire)

Take three Seville oranges, one sweet orange, one
lemon, five pounds of sugar, five pints of water. Cut
fruit in half, squeeze all the juice out, put straight in
preserving pan. Cut up the peel as finely as possible
with very sharp knives, put into the pan also and
five pints of water. Leave to soak for twenty-four
hours. Put the pips to soak in a little water separately; boil them for some time and strain off into the
other pan. Boil all for one hour without sugar,
and then, without letting it cool, for two hours with
sugar. When the juice begins to jellify on a cold
saucer, it is done.

17

656.   SMOOTH ORANGE MARMALADE (Kent, 1809)

Weigh the oranges, take the same weight of sugar as of fruit, wipe all the oranges with a wet cloth and grate the rind, cut the fruit in quarters longways, strip off the skin with a knife and pick out the seeds clean from them, then put on the skins to boil until they are so tender that they will beat to a mash. When you take the skins off the fire, squeeze the water out of them, and take away all the strings. Pound them in a marble mortar, clarify the sugar, then take the pounded skins and mix them by degrees with the syrup. When it is well mixed put it into the pan and let it boil until the sugar is incorporated with it, then put in the pulp, which must be carefully scraped with a knife off the skins before they are put on to boil. Let the marmalade boil till it is of an equal thickness, you will know when it is done enough by its turning heavier in stirring, and of a finer colour. Whenever it begins to sparkle it is done enough. Pound the grated rind in a mortar, take off the marmalade and stir in the grated rind carefully; when it is all in, put on the pan again, and let it boil until it is thoroughly mixed. You may keep out some of the rind, unless you like it very bitter and thick. If you keep it out, use it for seasoning. In making Chip Marmalade only a small part of the skins are to be pounded, the remainder cut in strips.

657.   TO PRESERVE PEARS (Devonshire)

Take the largest stewing pears when they are on the turn. Pare them nicely, cut them in halves, leaving the stem on. To every pound of pears add three-quarters of a pound of loaf sugar, and to about fifty pears put a pint of water, the juice and peel of four lemons (the peel to be pared thin and cut in long strips), a small cup of cloves, and a little cochineal to colour them. Let them stew very gently over a slow fire, turning them constantly until you can pass a straw through them, then add a teacupful of brandy and let them boil two or three minutes longer. Put them in jars and tie down as other preserves ; they will keep good for twelve months.

658. PEAR MARMALADE (Yorkshire)

You require six pounds of small pears, and four pounds of sugar. Put the pears into a saucepan with cold water ; cover it and set it over the fire till the fruit is soft ; then put the pears into cold water ; pare, quarter and core them, put to them three teacups of water, set them over the fire. Roll the sugar fine, mash the fruit fine and smooth, put the sugar to it, stir it well together till it is thick, like jelly. Then put it into tumblers or jars, and when it is quite cold serve it in the same way as jelly.

659. TO PRESERVE JARGONEL PEARS (Ireland)

Pare very thin, and simmer for ten minutes in a syrup of one pint of water and one pound of sugar. Let them lie a day or two. Make the syrup richer, and simmer again. Repeat this till they are clear, and the syrup the thickness of honey.

660. PRESERVED PEACHES (Kent)

Take an equal weight of fruit and sugar ; lay the fruit in a large dish, and sprinkle half the sugar over, in fine powder ; give them a gentle shaking ; the next day make a thin syrup with the remainder of the sugar, and instead of water, if you have it, allow one pint of red currant juice to every pound of peaches ; simmer them in this till sufficiently clear.

N.B.—Pick them when not dead ripe.

661. QUINCE JAM (Kent)

Half a pound of sugar to one pound of fruit ; about a large teacupful of water to five or six pounds of fruit. Cover the stewpan close during the last ten minutes to improve the colour. The hard, dry quinces are better if peeled and put into a jar with a small quantity of sugar ; the peelings can be put on the top and covered with paper and put into the oven after the bread is out, and then preserved in the usual way.

662. QUINCE MARMALADE (Kent)

Peel the quinces and cut them into quarters, and to every pound of fruit allow three-quarters of a pound of loaf sugar with a little water. Boil them gently for three hours and put it into jars ; simmer the seeds in water to a jelly, and add to the above while boiling.

663. UNBOILED RASPBERRY JAM (Gloucestershire)

One and a quarter pounds of best lump sugar to each pound of raspberries. Put on the fruit, bring it to boiling point, but do not let it boil more than two or three minutes. Add the sugar—stir till quite dissolved. Again bring to boiling point. Dish it at once into warm jam pots and cover while hot. Keeps well. Is of splendid colour and retains the flavour of fresh fruit.

664. RHUBARB JAM (Essex)

Required : eight pounds of rhubarb, eight pounds of sugar, four level teaspoonfuls of ginger, one pound of candied peel. Wipe the rhubarb and cut into pieces about one inch long. Put in a pan, slightly crush the sugar and spread this over it. Leave it till next day. Then cut the lemon peel up thinly, add the ginger, and boil the whole till it turns a nice red colour, probably one and a half hours. Pour into dry scalded jars and cover down at once. It will not need any brandied paper. The easiest way to cover jam is to cut pieces of tissue paper to the desired size, dip in cold milk, and use, pressing carefully against the jar so that the covering shall be all tight. Unless carefully done, the paper will tear.

665. PRESERVED RHUBARB (Lincolnshire)

Weight for weight of fruit and sugar. Pare the rhubarb and cut in three-inch pieces ; pound one third of sugar, and put it over rhubarb. Let it stand all night. Pour off the juice in the morning, and boil it with the remainder of sugar. Then pour it over the fruit and let it stand till cold. Then put it through a hair sieve, and boil the juice again for fifteen minutes. Add the fruit and let it boil till tender. Some essence of ginger to be put in a little before it is taken off the fire.

666. CONSERVE OF RED ROSES

(Seventeenth Century)

Take a quart of red rose-water, and a quart of
fair (fresh) water, and boil in it a pound of red rose-
leaves, the whites cut off. The leaves must be boiled
very tender ; then take three pounds of sugar,
and put it to the roses, a pound at a time, and let
it boil a little between every pound : and so put it up
in your pots.

667. ROSE-PETAL JAM (Surrey)

Make a syrup of one pound of loaf sugar and as
little rose-water as you can do with. Take a pound
of rose-petals (cabbage roses are best) and dry them
in a shady place. Scald them for a moment in
boiling water, then drain and dry them, and add
them, with a spoonful of orange-flower water, to
the syrup. Boil in a preserving-pan until the jam
will " set " or " jell " when dropped upon a plate.
When it has cooled off a little, pour it into pots, and
cover up well, the usual way.

668. COMPÔTE OF WILD ROSE-BERRIES (Surrey)

Collect wild rose-berries, cut off the tops, cut them
open and carefully remove all seeds and hairs (it
is well to wear gloves while doing this, as the hairs get
under the nails and are curiously irritating). Then
boil down the berries in a preserving-pan, with as
little water as possible ; and when they are quite
tender, pulp them through a sieve. Add sugar, the
proportion being at least three-quarters of a pound
to each pound of pulped berries, and let the mixture

boil up quickly till the sugar is dissolved, then remove it from the fire and bottle it as soon as coolish. (This compôte, under the name of *Hagenmarken*, is largely made and sold in Germany. The difference between a compôte and a jam is stated variously by various authors ; but I take it that the latter term applies to " wet " fruits, such as strawberries, raspberries, etc., and that the sugar is put in along with the fruit to boil. In a compôte, the material, being harder and drier, needs long preliminary cooking ; the sugar really requires none at all, so can be added at the last moment ; it is not essential that it should be either syrupped or candied. Ed.)

669. PRESERVED STEWED FRUIT (Somerset)

Take equal weight of fruit and sugar, put the sugar in the oven and let it get so hot that it will burn the hand, but be careful it does not brown. Bring the fruit to boiling point and allow it to boil for five minutes; add the melted sugar and let it boil for three minutes : it is then done. Raspberries done in this way will be a bright red colour, and taste like ripe fruit ; they will keep as well as a preserve done thus.

670. TO SUGAR ANY SORT OF SMALL FRUIT
(Seventeenth Century)

Beat the white of an egg, and dip the fruit in it ; let it lie on a dry cloth : take some fine sifted sugar and gently roll the fruit in it till it is quite covered and coated with sugar. Lay it in a sieve on the stove, or before a fire, to dry it well : it will keep well for a week.

671.   PRESERVED TOMATOES (Essex)

Put the tomatoes in wide-mouthed open jars,
cover them entirely with cold water, on the top of
which pour half an inch of salad oil. Cover them
closely and securely. (The correct placing of this
recipe, as regards chapter, is hardly possible ! Ed.)

672.   VEGETABLE MARROW JAM (Middlesex)

Procure a good sound well-ripened marrow, of
twelve pounds weight. Peel it and cut it into
cubes two inches square, add the juice and very
thinly cut rind of four lemons ; mix in one pound of
sugar to every pound of marrow, and place in an
enamelled preserving-pan or in a deep earthenware
jar, for twenty-four hours. Then add three ounces
of bruised race ginger, and a quarter of an ounce of
chillies (this is optional) in a muslin bag. Let the
mixture boil for one and a half hours in the preserving-pan (counting from the time that it comes
to the boil) and, just before it is done, add half a
pound of candied peel cut into very thin strips.

673.   PRESERVED VEGETABLE MARROW (Ireland)

Cut the marrow in long narrow strips ; peel and
weigh equal quantities of loaf sugar ; sprinkle a little
sugar on the fruit, and leave it for a night. Next
day, boil it with its own syrup, and the rest of the
sugar, and one lemon to every pound of fruit. Put
about thirty pepper pods to every four pounds ;
two wine-glasses of spirits to be added before taking
it off the fire. Before adding the spirits, it is well
to take out the fruit and boil the syrup with some

more sugar, then pour over the fruit. It should be quite clear. The lemons should be cut in circles ; only half the rinds. Tie the pepper in muslin.

674. DUTCH RECIPE FOR PRESERVING FRUIT
(Cape Colony)

Make a syrup to the proportion of two cups of sugar to four of water. Let it boil for a few minutes in a preserving pan. If it is not clear, strain through butter muslin. Then put two or three pounds of fruit in it at a time while the syrup is boiling, and simmer from ten to twenty minutes, according to the kind of fruit ; the latter should be soft and clear when done, and unbroken. Take the bottles, previously warmed, fill to the top with fruit and a little syrup. Screw them down tightly. Then add more fruit to the boiling syrup until it is used. Do not forget to screw the covers more tightly the following day. If you have no screw bottles, pour boiling mutton suet on the top of each bottle when cold, about a quarter of an inch thick. Any syrup over can be bottled and used as a fruit drink. Add vinegar and water to it at the table. Must be kept in a dry place. Will keep for months.

FRUIT CHEESES AND PASTES

675. ALMACKS (Kent, 1809)

Equal quantities of plums, pears, and apples, cut in slices, put into an earthen jar and baked. When thoroughly done, squeeze them through a colander. To three pounds of fruit, add one pound of moist sugar, and let it simmer gently for some time till it

becomes a thick jam, then put it into saucers or
shallow pans, and let it stand on the kitchen rack
for a day to stiffen and dry. When dried so, it will
keep in paper.

676. APPLE CHEESE (1815)

Pare and quarter your apples and take out the
cores, put them into a deep pot or jar, and put the
paring and cores at the top ; let them bake in a
moderate oven till quite soft ; take off the parings,
cores, and bits of apple which are at the top, if they
are dry or hard ; then put your apples into a stewpan, with fine powdered sugar to your taste, and
boil them four hours till it is quite stiff. Put the
cheese in moulds or cups, and lay paper over it
moistened with brandy ; set it in a dry place, and
in three weeks it will cut quite smooth. *N.B.*—
You may add a little of the rind of a lemon grated,
or a few drops of essence of lemon, before you put
it into the moulds; also a few blanched almonds
cut into small pieces and mixed with it.

677. APPLE PASTE (Middlesex)

Peel and core some fine apples and boil them in
water. When quite soft, take them out and put
them in cold water ; having drained them, press
them through a coarse cloth ; put this marmalade
into a pan on the fire, stir it frequently with a wooden
spoon, and when it is nearly dry, take it out and
add an equal weight of sugar, mixing them well
together. Press the mixture flat, of the thickness
of an ordinary piecrust ; put it upon tins and place
to dry in a slack oven.

678. APRICOT PASTE (Middlesex)

Set any quantity of the fruit you may require over the fire in a stewpan, and cook till they are quite soft ; then take out the stones, pass the fruit through a sieve, and dry. Then take clarified sugar equal in weight to the fruit, mix, and let them press well together. Turn out into shapes, and dry in a slow oven or in the sun.

679. BULLACE CHEESE (Eighteenth Century)

Take your bullaces when they are full ripe, and to every quart of fruit put a quarter of a pound of loaf sugar beaten small. Put them in a jar in moderate oven to bake till they are soft, then rub them through a hair sieve, and to every pound of pulp, add half a pound of loaf sugar crushed fine. Then boil it four and a half hours over a slow fire, and keep stirring it all the time. Put it into pots, and tie brandy papers over them, and keep them in a dry place. When it has stood a few months, it will cut out very bright and fine. You may make sloe cheese the same way.

680. CHERRY CHEESE (1815)

Stone some Kentish cherries, crack as many of the stones as you choose, blanch the kernels in boiling water, and mix them with the fruit ; to every twelve pounds of fruit add three pounds of Lisbon sugar ; boil it to a thick jam, and when the fruit no longer cleaves to the pan, it is done enough.

681.   BLACK CURRANT PASTE (Middlesex)

The best way of making black currant paste is to
dissolve an ounce of isinglass in about half a pint of
the filtered juice, and equal weight of sugar; put
them in a stewpan, and let them simmer for at
least an hour, then pour out the juice into a very
shallow tin mould, and when it is cold and quite
hard, cut it into pieces.

682.   DAMSON CHEESE (1815)

Pick the damsons free from stalks, leaves, etc.,
put them into a jar and tie white paper over them ;
bake them in a slow oven till quite soft, rub them
through a colander while hot ; put the pulp and
juice which has passed through the colander into
a stewpan, with fine powdered sugar to your taste ;
boil it over a moderate fire till it is as stiff as you
can possibly stir it, which will take three hours ;
keep stirring it to prevent it burning to the pan ;
and a few minutes before you take it off the fire,
put the kernels of the damsons into the pan, and
mix with it ; put it into cups or moulds, let it stand
a day, and cut some pieces of writing paper the size
of the tops of the cups or moulds, dip them in
brandy and put close over them : put them in a dry
place, and they will keep for several years.
You may make plum or bullace cheese the same
way.   It is necessary to take the skins off the kernels
before you put them into the pan.

683.   DAMSON CHEESE (Cheshire)

Put your damsons in a large stone jar, and tie
it over tight, and put it' in the oven till the fruit

is soft and the juice running out. Rub the fruit through the sieve till you have got the pulp out. Add three-quarters of a pound of sugar to every pound of pulp. Boil it well. Try a little in a saucer, and if it sets, it will be boiled enough. Break the stones and put in the kernels or some blanched bitter almonds while boiling. Stir all the time, as it soon burns.

684. GOOSEBERRY PASTE (Surrey)

Take some gooseberries from which you have extracted the juice for jelly, without drawing them very closely. Pass them through a sieve, weigh them, and boil the pulp for about one and a quarter hours, until it forms a dry paste in the pan. Lift it off the fire and stir in six ounces of good pounded sugar to each pound of fruit. When this is nearly dissolved, boil the mixture for twenty to twenty-five minutes ; stir it incessantly, or it will be likely to burn. Put it into moulds or shallow dishes, and use it as wanted for table.

685. CONSERVE OR PASTE OF PEACHES (Middlesex)

Make a marmalade of ripe peaches in an iron pot, with three-quarters of a pound of sugar to every pound of fruit; stir frequently, taking care they do not burn ; dry the marmalade carefully on a hot plate, or in a slack oven ; and when nearly dry, mix a quarter of a pound of the marmalade with a pound of very finely pounded sugar ; press it into the form of a cake, drying thoroughly, and it will keep for almost any length of time. It cannot be dried too slowly.

686. LOZENGES OF RED ROSES
(Seventeenth Century)

(Proportions not given.) Boil your sugar to sugar again (*i.e.* till it candies); then put in your red roses, being finely beaten and made moist with the juice of a lemon. Let it not boil after the roses are in, but pour it upon a pie plate and cut it into what form you please.

CHAPTER XVII

SWEETMEATS AND CANDIES

NOTE.—The home-made sweetmeat is so pure, so wholesome, and so attractive, as compared with the manufactured article, that one need hardly utter a syllable in its praise. It is its own praise. The old MS. books to which I have had access, did not deal with any great variety of confections : theirs are, as a rule, simple sugary affairs at best, with a modest flavouring or colouring.

Either the involved and artistic achievements of the present day, it would seem, were beyond the scope of our mothers, or they did not trouble to set down the secrets thereof. These, therefore, are more or less of a familiar nursery type : but such as they are, they are always a source of gratification : pure of glucose and of baneful colouring matters, safe and sound to eat.

A buttered dish is indispensable in sweetmaking, and a very sharp knife. " Lined " saucepans or copper preserving pans must be used : and it is hardly necessary to remark that all utensils should be exquisitely clean.

687. CANDIED ANGELICA (Middlesex)

When the stems are of a good size and before they run to seed, cut them into slices, and put them for

271

some time into cold water after having removed the
rind : then boil them until they become soft, and
wash them afterwards two or three times in cold
water ; boil them in strong syrup for an hour, then
let them stand for twenty-four hours ; now take
them out of the syrup, and drain them. In the
meantime, strengthen the syrup by the addition
of more sugar, and afterwards let the angelica
simmer in it for half an hour. It is then to be taken
out, placed upon tins, and dried in a slow oven, or
on a hot plate, powdering it well with white sugar.
Angelica preserved in this way will remain good for
several years.

688. BURNT ALMONDS (Eighteenth Century)

Take two pounds of loaf sugar, and two pounds
of almonds, put them in a stewpan with a pint of
water, set them over a clear coal fire, let them boil
till you hear the almonds crack. Take them off
and stir them about till they are quite dry; then
put them in a wire sieve and shake all the sugar from
them. Put the sugar into the pan again with a
little water, give it a boil, put four (tea ?) spoonfuls
of scraped cochineal to colour it. Put the almonds
into the pan; keep stirring them over the fire till
they are quite dry. They will keep twelve months
in a glass jar.

689. BURNT ALMONDS, RED (1815)

Take some of the finest Jordan almonds you can
get, sift all the dust from them, have some syrup
boiling in a pan, and let it boil till it comes almost

to caramel ; put half a (tea ?) cupful of cochineal
in ; put the almonds in as fast as you can, and
stir them till they are cold ; then put them in your
sieve, and break those that stick together; then
have another pan of syrup boiling, the same as
before, and when they are cold, pick them from
each other, for they must always have the coats of
sugar on them. See that your cochineal is properly
mixed to make them of a fine colour, as you must
put more cochineal in the last coat than you did in
the first.

690. BURNT ALMONDS, WHITE (1815)

Take some of the finest Jordan almonds you can
get, and sift all the dust from them ; then have some
syrup boiling in a pan, and let it boil till it comes
almost to a caramel ; put your almonds in, and stir
them till they are cold ; put them in your sieve,
break those that stick together, and then have
another pan of syrup boiling, the same as before,
and give them two coats of sugar ; when done, pick
them from each other.

691. ALMOND PASTE (Somerset)

Take one pound of ground almonds, one pound
of castor sugar, one tablespoonful of orange-flower
water, eight or nine drops of essence of almonds,
two whole eggs and one white of egg.   Mix sugar
and almonds well together ; add orange-flower water
and essence of almonds. Beat the eggs well and
knead them into it. If to be used on a cake, spread
the paste on with a knife dipped in hot water.

18

692. CANDIED APRICOTS (Surrey)

Take some apricots which are not quite ripe, and
remove the stones without entirely dividing the
fruit. Put them into cold water ; then blanch them
on the fire ; when they become soft, take them off,
and put them again into cold water. When they are
cold, drain them, and throw them into some clarified
sugar, which has been made into a thick syrup
while it is in a boiling state ; let the whole boil
again for a few minutes, and let them stand for
twenty-four hours. Take out the apricots, and give
the syrup another boil, then throw it boiling over
the fruit, and let all stand another twenty-four
hours ; after which take them out, drain them, put
them on dishes which have been well covered with
powdered sugar, dry them in a stove, and lay them
by in a box, placed in layers, with a sheet of paper
between each.

693. CANDIED BARBERRIES (Surrey)

Make a good strong syrup, and when it boils, put
in your barberries *in bunches* (the proportion of
syrup should be two pounds of sugar to three pounds
of barberries), and let them simmer a few minutes.
Then lift them out and let them get cold. The
next day boil them again in the sugar for about half
an hour. When cold, take them out and powder
them with sugar, and let them dry under glasses in
the sun.

694. BARLEY SUGAR (Middlesex)

Melt some sugar over the fire with a decoction of
barley, mixed with whites of eggs, well beaten into

a light froth : this is then passed through a jelly-bag, and again boiled till it forms large bubbles : then throw it out on a marble slab or flat dish, which has been lightly rubbed over with oil of sweet almonds : when the bubbles disappear, it is rolled into round sticks, and left to cool and harden.

695. BARLEY SUGAR (Surrey)

Put into a lined saucepan a good handful of fine barley, and the thinly pared rind of half a lemon. Pour in one quart of cold water, and let it simmer for two hours. Then let it stand and settle ; when it has settled, pour off the water carefully. Pour a pint of what is left, with two pounds of loaf sugar, into a pan, and stand it over a gentle heat until the sugar is melted, then let it boil. Add the juice of one lemon, and boil up again till it begins to crack. Pour it out on to a buttered dish, and when cool cut it into strips. When these are almost cold, hold them at either end and twist them in opposite directions.

696. BLACK CURRANT DROPS (1815)

Get half a sieve of black currants, put them in a pan ; mash them with your spaddle, and put them over the fire ; bring them just to a boil, and pass them through a sieve over an earthen pan. Put what jelly comes from them in an earthen pipkin, and put it over the fire and let it boil for two hours ; stir it all the time at bottom with your spaddle, or else it will burn ; put in two pounds and a half of powdered sugar, mix it with the jam and stir it over the fire half an hour.   Drop it on metal sheets or

plates, in little drops from your knife, and put them
in your hot stove ; let them be there till you find
they are quite dry, and then take them off with your
knife.

697. BUTTERSCOTCH (Middlesex)

Take one pound of lump sugar and half a pint of
milk, stir them together in a saucepan over the fire
until the sugar is thoroughly melted. Then add
half a pound of butter, dropping in little bits at a
time, and a pinch of cream-of-tartar. Mix well,
and boil the butterscotch until a piece will set into
a fairly hard ball on being dropped into cold water.
Pour it upon an oiled or buttered tin, and cut it into
small squares when sufficiently set.

698. CHOCOLATE ALMONDS (Surrey)

Blanch your almonds : melt some good chocolate
in a lined pan, thinning it if necessary with a very
little syrup. Dip the almonds in, one at a time,
upon a long pin, and lay them to dry upon a
buttered dish.

699. CHOCOLATE DROPS (1815)

Take one pound and a half of chocolate, and
put it in the oven just to warm the chocolate ; then
put it into a copper stewpan, with three-quarters
of a pound of powdered sugar ; mix it well over
the fire, take it off, and roll it in pieces the size of
small marbles ; put them on white paper, and when
they are all on, take the sheet of paper by each
corner, and lift it up and down, so that the paper
may touch the table each time, and by that means

you will see the drops come quite flat, about the size of a sixpence ; put some sugar nonpareils over them, and cover all that are on the paper, and then shake them off, and you will see all the chocolate drops covered with the sugar nonpareils. Let them stand till cold, and they will come off well, and then put them in a papered box.

700. COCONUT CANDY (Hampshire)

Take one and a half pounds of white sugar and put it with three-quarters of a pint of cold water to boil in a lined saucepan. When the sugar has dissolved, boil for five minutes, then strain it, and mix in, thoroughly well, one and a half pounds of grated coconut. Put the saucepan close to the fire and stir the mixture until it begins to candy. Then spread it on sheets of white paper which have been made warm, or on a warmed tin, well buttered. Before the candy is quite cold, take off the paper, and cut it into squares Let it get quite dry before being stored. If you wish any to be pink, divide the mixture into two pans (before putting in the coconut), and colour the syrup in one of these with a little cochineal.

701. COCONUT CANDY (Surrey)

Take a fresh coconut, rasp it very fine, spread it on a dish, and let it dry naturally for two or three days. To every four ounces of grated coconut add one pound of sugar (but you can add more coconut if you choose). Boil the sugar to a syrup; when it has boiled about ten minutes, and begins to be thick and white, stir in the nut, mix it well,

and do not leave it a moment till it is done. Stand
the pan *over*, not *on*, the fire, as this candy burns
very easily. For almond candy, proceed the same,
but first dry the almonds in a gentle oven, and do
not put them to the sugar till it approaches candying
point.

702. ANOTHER WAY

Take two pounds of powdered sugar, set it in a
lined saucepan, just covered with water. Let it
boil till it is brittle, then take it off the fire. Have
ready two whites of eggs well beaten, and beat them
as quick as you can into the sugar. When the
mixture is quite cool, add either a grated coconut
(fresh), or the same amount of desiccated coconut
and ten or twelve drops of lemon-juice. Then pour
off into a buttered dish or pan, and cut it in strips.
For pink candy, set half the mixture in a separate
saucepan, and colour it with a little cochineal.

703. COCONUT ICE (Hampshire)

Take one grated fresh coconut, two pounds of
loaf sugar, a small piece of butter, one tablespoonful
of cream, a little cochineal. (A very large nut will
require three pounds of sugar, and water in proportion.) Take the coconut milk, and add water
sufficient to make half a pint all together. Add the
sugar, and boil well for ten minutes, then stir in
the grated nut and boil another ten minutes. Take
it off the fire, add the cream, and beat the mixture
well until it begins to set. Pour half into a buttered
soup-plate ; add a little cochineal to the other half,
and pour this on top of the first when it is set enough
to bear it. When cold, cut it up into strips.

704. TO CANDY COWSLIPS OR ANY OTHER
FLOWERS IN BUNCHES (Seventeenth Century)

Steep gum arabic in water, wet the flowers with
it, and shake them in a cloth that they may dry.
Then dip them in fine sifted sugar, and hang them
on a string across a stove or chimney-piece when
there is a fire. They must hang for two or three
days, until the flowers are quite dry.

705. CANDIED FILBERTS (Middlesex)

Blanch them, and when the skins are removed, let
them simmer in very thin syrup for about an hour :
put them to cool, and then set them on the fire again,
adding more sugar, so as to thicken the syrup ;
simmer for another hour, and then let them cool.
Repeat this process a third time, adding more sugar,
until the syrup has become so thick as to candy
when cold : take out the filberts before the syrup
is cold, and cover them well with pounded loaf sugar :
then dry in the sun or in a slow oven. The syrup
may be used for any other preserve.

706. HARDBAKE (Surrey)

Put one pound of Demerara sugar into a saucepan
with enough water to make a strong syrup—half
a pint more or less. Boil the sugar until it sets when
dropped into cold water. Meanwhile have split
blanched almonds laid in rows, flat side down, upon
a buttered dish. Pour the syrup over the almonds,
and put the dish in a cool place. When the hardbake is quite dry and hard, cut it into pieces, and
keep it in a dry tin.

707. LEMON PRALINES (Hampshire)

Peel some lemons thinly, and cut the peels into small narrow strips about an inch long. Put one pound of powdered loaf sugar to boil in one teacupful of water, and when the sugar is dissolved put in a quarter of a pound of butter, beaten to a cream. Keep stirring it over the fire until it will nearly set if dropped upon a dish. At this point put in the lemon strips. Lift the pan from the fire, and stir the lemon strips about till it is nearly cold, with a wooden or silver spoon. Then put them in a sieve to drain. To be kept in a dry tin. Some people add six drops of essence of lemon just before putting in the strips.

708. LEMON PRAWLONGS (1815)

Take some lemons and peel the rind off in four quarters ; take all the white off from the inside of the rind ; cut the yellow rind in pieces, about one inch long and about the tenth part of an inch wide. Have a pan of boiling syrup on the fire, and let it boil till it comes almost to caramel ; then put the prawlongs in, and stir them very much with a large wooden spoon, till they are cold ; put them in a large sieve, and shake them just to let the sugar that does not stick to them go through the sieve ; lastly, put them in your box, and keep them in a dry place.

709. CANDIED LEMON OR ORANGE CHIPS (Kent)

Cut the fruit in halves : take out all the pulp and juice. Boil the rinds till quite tender, drain them on a cloth, and cut them into chips. Weigh an equal

quantity of white sugar, and to every pound of sugar
put a pint of water ; set it on the fire, and when
it is quite dissolved put on the chips. Boil quickly on
a clear fire, about half an hour, or till you perceive
it begin to candy, then take it off. When quite
cool, spread it upon a dish or slab, and continue
to move it about during two or three days, so as to
separate it. It will take a fortnight to dry in the
sun, or in a cool oven. When dry enough, put it
up in folds of paper.

710. MARZIPAN (Middlesex)

Mix a quarter of a pound of icing sugar with a
quarter of a pound of ground almonds. Add in
the white of one egg well beaten, and a pinch of salt.
Mix this well with a wooden spoon, and if it is too
stiff use a little orange-flower water (not more than
a teaspoonful) ; but on no account make it too wet.
Put it into a basin and let it stand for twenty-four
hours. It can then be rolled out about half an inch
thick and cut into shapes, or made into small balls
to imitate fruits, with a strip of angelica as stalk.
This is a cheap and wholesome sweet.

711. MARZIPAN POMME DE TERRE (American)

Take half a pound of ground almonds, half a
pound of icing sugar, one egg, and the yolk of
another, chocolate powder, and a few drops of
essence of almonds. Proceed as above.

712. MARZIPAN POTATOES (Hampshire)

To six ounces of ground almonds, add three-
quarters of a pound of sifted icing sugar, twelve

drops of orange-flower water (or a little brandy), and a few drops of almond essence. Mix to a stiff paste with the beaten white of an egg (sometimes two eggs are needed). Roll the paste into small pieces, potato shapes, and roll them in a mixture of castor sugar and grated chocolate.

713. NOUGAT (Middlesex)

Blanch a pound of sweet almonds, and, having sliced them lengthways, let them lie in the sun for a short time, until they become slightly discoloured. Now dissolve, in an iron stewpan slightly buttered, twelve ounces of sugar without water, stirring constantly, and when the sugar has melted, and begins to change colour, throw in the almonds, which are previously to be made thoroughly hot, in another vessel, over the fire, but without burning them. Mix them well with the sugar, and, as they mix, range them round the sides of the saucepan, leaving about the same thickness at the bottom as at the sides : now, let the saucepan become a little cool, and turn out the mixture upon a plate : having done this, press the contents well together in the form of a thick cake, and wrap up in writing paper. It should be kept in a dry tin.

714. ORANGE-FLOWER CANDY (Middlesex)

Throw some orange flowers into syrup (proportion not stated) when it has boiled about ten minutes ; and after they have simmered in it for five minutes more, pour the whole out, and leave them to infuse until the following day, or even longer if convenient.

Then bring the syrup to the boiling point again, strain it from the blossoms through a piece of muslin, and lay it quickly in cakes, with a large spoon, upon thick and very dry sheets of paper or tin. Take the candy off before it is quite cold, and lay it reversed upon dishes. This, kept secure against air, will be excellent for more than a year.

715. PEPPERMINT CREAMS (Hampshire)

Take the white of an egg (not beaten), add half its quantity of cold water. Stir well to mix the two together. Put in enough icing sugar to make it stiff enough to handle : mould into any shape desired. Flavour with essence of peppermint. Vanilla creams are prepared the same as above, only with vanilla flavouring instead of peppermint. Shape into balls, and put a piece of dried walnut at top and bottom.

716. CRYSTALLIZED ROSES OR VIOLETS (Surrey)

Select large sweet rose-petals, set them in rows before you on a pasteboard. Have a thoroughly good strong syrup boiling, and dip the rose-leaves in, one at a time—let them be thoroughly coated, then set them on a sieve to drain and dry.

717. SUGAR CANDY (Middlesex)

Clarify four pounds of lump sugar, which must be allowed to simmer with a little water, over the fire, until by taking up a little on a spoon, and blowing on it, you find it fly off in small flakes : then having skimmed it well, take it off the fire, throw into it a glass of good spirits of wine, and

pour the whole out into an earthen dish : cover it
over and put it into an oven for eight days, taking
care to keep it of an equal temperature : at the
end of that time, drain off the syrup, and the candy
will remain attached to the dish, which must be
warmed in order to allow the candy more readily
to be detached.

718. TO KNOW WHEN SUGAR IS AT CANDY HEIGHT (Yorkshire, 1769)

Take some sugar and clarify it, keep it boiling
till it becomes thick, then stir it with a stick *from* you,
and when it is at candy height, it will fly from your
stick like flakes of snow, or feathers flying in the air.
And till it comes to that height, it will not fly.
Then you may use it as you please.

719. TO MAKE SUGAR-PLUMS OF ANY SORT (Surrey)

Take a copper pan which has not only a handle
of some sort across the middle, but two side holes
or handles. Suspend it from a rack, or otherwise,
about four inches above a charcoal brazier or red-
hot fire. Put the articles which are to be sugar
coated—blanched almonds, nuts, walnuts, or whatever they are—into the pan with some strong syrup.
Shake the pan so that every part of the articles may
be covered, and keep on gently agitating it until
the sugar has dried on them. Then add more syrup,
and agitate till dry ; and so on until the coating is
as thick as you desire. The original shape of the
articles will in this way be preserved, and they
will be covered with any thickness of sugar required.
The same applies to any paste of fruit and sugar;
but this must be dry before going into the pan.

720. FRUIT PASTES FOR SUGAR PLUMS (Surrey)

You take the fruit—black currants, damsons, quinces, etc.—whatever it may be, and boil it till it is so soft it can be put through a sieve, all except the skins and stones. Then put the pulp back again in the pan and boil it again till the moisture is evaporated. Then put in three-quarters of a pound of sugar to every pound of pulp, mix it in well, and let it go on boiling slowly till it becomes a firm, . smooth paste. It must be put into pots and well covered with brandied paper and butter paper.

721. TOFFEE (Kent)

Take half a pound of coarse sugar, two ounces of butter, one tablespoonful of vinegar, a piece of lemon peel. Boil them together for half an hour. Butter a large dish all over, and pour on thinly.

722. DEVONSHIRE TOFFEE

Mix granulated sugar with cream just beginning to "turn," until it assumes the consistency of a very thick batter. Put it into a lined saucepan and keep on stirring until it is smooth and white and thoroughly cooked. Then add a spoonful of jam, raspberry for preference : give it another stir-up, pour it into a buttered tin, and cut it into squares before it has set hard.

723. EVERTON TOFFEE (Lancashire)

Take one pound of butter, quarter of a pound of treacle, one pound of sugar (two tablespoonfuls of water to be first put in the pan). All to be boiled together for three-quarters of an hour.

724. RUSSIAN TOFFEE (Surrey)

This is much richer and better than ordinary toffee. Take half a pint of thick sour cream (or, if this cannot be had, condensed milk), and stir into it one pound of castor sugar. Boil it slowly over a clear fire till it is all dissolved and begins to thicken. Then add two teaspoonfuls of vanilla essence and one tablespoonful of whisky. Boil it up again until it froths and leaves the sides of the pan clear ; then turn it out on to a buttered dish slab, and when it sets, cut it into squares. If made with condensed milk, one small tin will suffice for the same amount of sugar ; boil until it hardens when dropped into cold water ; then add one teaspoonful of vanilla essence and the juice of half a lemon, and boil up as mentioned above.

725. TURKISH DELIGHT (Hertfordshire)

Soak one ounce of gelatine in half a pint of cold water for two or three hours ; put into a stewpan with two pounds of loaf sugar, and when it boils stir for twenty minutes ; take off the fire and add two teaspoonfuls of vanilla essence, and one of lemon essence ; pour into a wet soup plate and let it stand for twenty-four hours, then cut into squares and cover with icing sugar.

726. TURKISH DELIGHT (Surrey)

Boil two breakfastcupfuls of water in a lined saucepan, add two ounces of French leaf gelatine, and stir it with a wooden spoon. Add two pounds of loaf sugar, and go on stirring the mixure till it boils : let it boil for twenty minutes, and stir it all the time. Then add a small eggcupful of citric acid, and two good tablespoonfuls of rose-water. Wet two china pie-dishes with cold water, and pour half the mixture into one dish (through a strainer); put a few drops of cochineal into the other half, and pour into the second dish. Before the mixture cools, add (if liked) a few chopped nuts or almonds. Let it stand twenty-four hours, and then cut it into cubes, rolling it well in smooth sifted icing sugar.

CHAPTER XVIII

CAKES

NOTE.—Our mothers, grandmothers, and great-grandmothers were what we should consider extravagant in the matter of eggs. They used eight where we should hesitate over four. They liked their cakes rich, sweet, and highly flavoured ; and they liked them in great variety and plenty. That happy institution " high tea," previously mentioned, supplied an excellent opportunity for showing what the skilful housewife could turn out in this respect. Moreover, all important occasions—birth, christening, wedding, funeral, re-union of the family (as on Simnel or Mothering Sunday), and a host of other family functions, now only traditional, demanded each its own particular cake.

Hence it is that not only every county has its celebrated specialities, as have also a great many provincial towns, but families innumerable still possess certain favourite cake-recipes, whose sweetness custom cannot stale. Among those following will be found the most interesting and delightful concoctions ; and especially the reader is desired to note the large number of suggestions regarding ginger-bread and ginger-cake. For cheapness, wholesomeness, and toothsomeness, this nursery desideratum can hardly be bettered. The (salt) Irish potato-cakes are also extremely good.

The superiority of home-made cakes to " shop 'uns " is so self-evident, that no attention need be called to the fact. A hostess, with a reputation for dainty little cakes of private manufacture, has the first claim upon the gratitude of those guests who are weary of being regaled with the stereotyped productions of the local confectioner. Moreover, the saving in cost is enormous, and the doubling in excellence undeniable. The revelations of margarine and egg-powder—to say the least of it— which shop cakes afford, may well be abandoned in favour of the very little extra trouble involved in turning out one's own. A good oven is very desirable—neither spasmodically hot, nor irritatingly slow. But careful attention will obviate many of the faults of a bad one. The baking of a cake is at least as important as the making.

I have found that good beef-dripping (not bought dripping) is an excellent substitute for butter, and makes a large cake lighter as a rule. It is a good plan to warm the flour slightly first, and to mix your sugar with the flour, before rubbing in the butter or dripping : the work is thus performed much more quickly, because the grittiness of the sugar helps to break up the fat, especially in cold weather. Sour milk or buttermilk is invaluable for mixing cakes, rendering them much lighter. Always beat the mixture with a *fork*, unless specially otherwise directed.

Cakes and biscuits, whether stored or in daily use, should be kept in closed tins.

19

727. GENERAL RULES FOR MIXING CAKES
(Gloucestershire)

1. Beat butter to a cream.
2. Add sugar (castor, granulated, or Demerara).
3. Add eggs well beaten ; work in one at a time if possible.
4. Add flour, well sifted, and other ingredients. Lastly, add the baking powder.

728. BAKING POWDER (Somerset)

Twelve ounces of ground rice.
Six and a half ounces of bicarb. soda.
Five and a half ounces of tartaric acid.
Get chemist to mix well together.

729. GOOD BAKING POWDER (Kent)

Ground rice six ounces.
Tartaric acid, three ounces.
Carbonate of soda, five ounces.
Cream of tartar, three ounces.
One dessertspoonful to a pound of flour.

Mix the above ingredients well together, taking care there are no small lumps left in it, and keep it in a glass bottle.

730. AN EXCELLENT CHOCOLATE FILLING
(Hertfordshire)

This is for putting into cakes. Take one cupful of powdered sugar, four large spoonfuls of grated chocolate, and the whites of two eggs. Whisk the eggs to a stiff froth, then add the sugar, and then the chocolate. A few drops of essence of vanilla is an improvement to the mixture. Beat all together smartly for five or ten minutes.

731. ICING (Kent)

Beat and sift eight ounces of fine sugar ; put into a mortar with four tablespoonfuls of rose-water and the whites of two eggs beaten and strained. Whisk it well, and when the cake is nearly cold, dip a feather in the icing, and cover the cake well. Set it in the oven to harden but not discolour. Keep in a dry place.

732. TO ICE A CAKE (Yorkshire)

Beat up the whites of five eggs to a froth, and put to them one pound of double-refined sugar, powdered and sifted, and three spoonfuls of orange-flower water and lemon-juice. Keep beating this all the time the cake is in the oven, and the moment it comes out of the oven, ice it over the top with a spoon. Be careful to keep the sugar clean.

733. ALMOND ICING (Somerset)

To half a pound of castor sugar, allow six ounces of ground sweet almonds ; mix with one or two yolks of eggs, and a little rose or orange-flower water.

734. CHOCOLATE ICING (Cheshire)

Put into a saucepan half a pound of castor sugar, two ounces of grated chocolate, and about a gill of water. Stir it over the fire till the mixture is about as thick as cream, then dip in your almonds, or pour it over your cakes.

735. CHOCOLATE ICING (Surrey)

Half a pound of icing sugar, one white of egg, one
heaped up tablespoon of powdered chocolate, a few
drops of essence of vanilla. Decorate the cake
with blanched sweet almonds, or split walnuts.

736. ALMOND CAKE (Middlesex)

Put a quartern of flour upon a pie-board, and
make a hole in the middle to receive a piece of butter
the size of an egg, a little salt, a quarter of a pound
of fine sugar, and half a pound of sweet almonds
pounded very fine. Knead the whole, and form it
into a cake. When baked, cover it with sugar,
and glaze with a salamander.

737. AMERICAN CAKES (Kent)

Mix three ounces of cornflour, quarter of a pound
of sifted sugar, quarter of a pound of butter, three
eggs, one teaspoonful of baking powder, a little
citron peel. Bake in patty tins.

738. AMERICAN CAKE

One teacupful of currants, same of sultanas, lard
or dripping, candied peel, one teacupful of strong
coffee (as made for drinking), six teacupfuls of
flour, half of golden syrup, a little nutmeg, salt,
and one teaspoonful of carbonate of soda. Mix
together lard, treacle, and coffee, all hot in oven,
then add currants and peel. Stir the flour in
gradually, lastly the soda. Bake in a moderate
oven.

739. ARBETH CAKE (Hertfordshire)

Half a pound of brown sugar, three teaspoonfuls of baking powder, two of ground ginger, one-third ounce of grated nutmeg, half a teaspoonful of cinnamon, one teaspoonful of caraway seeds, a grated lemon, half a pound of fresh butter, with half a pound of flour, half a pound of raisins, half a pound of currants, one pint of butter-milk, all mixed well together ; this will make a three-pound cake.

740. AUNT-MARY CAKE (Ireland)

One and a half pounds of flour, half a pound of butter, one and a half pounds of sultanas, one and a half pounds of currants, one dessertspoonful of bread-soda (bi-carbonate ?), one pint of sour milk. Rub butter thoroughly into flour and mix all the dry ingredients, putting the bread-soda in last and mixing it well in. Last of all, put the milk. Mix all well, and bake in a greased tin for two and a half to three hours, in a hot oven to start with. When the cake has risen, the heat should be less.

741. AUSTRIAN CAKE (Hertfordshire)

Six ounces of ground rice, six ounces of sugar, eight eggs, fifteen drops of essence of almonds, glass of brandy. Mix rice and sugar together ; add yolks of eggs well beaten ; add essence of almonds, stir in stiffly the whites of five eggs, beat twenty minutes and bake in a quick oven an hour.

742. BANBURY CAKES (Oxfordshire)

Having made some puff-paste, strew some well-cleaned currants over it, and roll it out to a moderate thickness. Cut it into round cakes, and bake upon floured tins. When taken out of the oven, strew finely powdered sugar over them, and set them by to cool.

743. BARM-BRACK (Ireland)

One and a half pounds of flour, four ounces of butter, sugar to taste, half a breakfastcupful of currants, one dessertspoonful of caraway seeds. Rub the butter well into the flour, then the sugar, currants, and seeds. It must then be wetted with enough buttermilk to drop into shape, and not be in a solid lump. Bake in rather a slow oven for two hours, with paper on the top of shape. (Evidently the yeast or baking powder has been omitted here. By using self-raising flour and buttermilk or sour milk, this may be remedied. *Ed.*)

744. ANOTHER WAY

Quarter of a stone of flour, four eggs beaten up separately ; a breakfast-cupful of brown sugar, and the same of barm (yeast) ; one pound of currants, and a glass of spirits.

745. BORDEAUX CAKES (French)

Make a paste, with the white of egg well beaten, and powdered lump sugar, to a consistency proper to cut into shapes. Flavour with oil of cinnamon and bake in tins in a slow oven.

746. SMALL BRANDY SNAPS (Hertfordshire)

A quarter of a pound of butter, half a pound of treacle, a quarter of a pound of Demerara sugar : bring to the boil, add the juice of one lemon and rind, one ounce of ginger, a quarter of a pound of flour. Let the whole be well mixed and kept warm. Drop in teaspoonfuls on a baking sheet, bake in a quick oven, hang on a spoon until crisp.

747. CARAWAY CAKES (Middlesex)

Mix a pound of pounded loaf sugar with two pounds of flour, half a pound of butter, and a small handful of caraway seeds : make them into a paste with five eggs well beaten, a little orange-water, and a small glass of ratafia : roll it to the thickness of a crown, cut them into shape, and bake on floured tins in a quick oven.

748. CHARLIE'S CAKE (Gloucestershire)

One pound of sifted flour, half a pound each of currants and sultanas, half a pound of salt butter, half a pound of castor sugar, two ounces of grated mixed peel, two teaspoonfuls of baking powder, three eggs, half a pint of milk. A handful of ground almonds is sufficient for two medium-sized cakes. Takes about one hour in moderate oven to cook.

749. CHERRY CAKE (Hertfordshire)

Beat a quarter of a pound of butter to a cream with a quarter of a pound of castor sugar ; when

perfectly smooth and white, add, one by one, four
eggs, beating the mixture well before adding each
one ; sprinkle in lastly a quarter of a pound of flour
with a teaspoonful of baking powder, and a quarter
of a pound of cherries cut in halves. Bake for about
one and a quarter hours, and let the oven be rather
hot at first.

750. CHOCOLATE CAKE (Somerset)

Four ounces of butter, six ounces of sugar, eight
ounces of flour, two ounces of ground chocolate,
two large eggs or three small ones, half a teacupful
of milk, one teaspoonful of baking powder, half a
teaspoonful of ground cinnamon, a few drops of
vanilla. Beat the butter and sugar to a cream, add
the eggs well beaten, with a little flour, mix thoroughly; dissolve the chocolate in the milk on the
fire, add to the other ingredients. Bake one hour,
or until quite firm. This cake is much improved
if iced with almond or chocolate icing.

751. CHOCOLATE CAKE (Sussex)

Quarter of a pound of chocolate powder, quarter
of a pound of flour, quarter of a pound of sugar,
quarter of a pound of butter, one egg.

Or, *another way*—One pound of grated chocolate,
six ounces of white sugar, three or four pounded
almonds ; mix well, add a quarter of a pound of flour,
four whites of eggs, pour in a cake tin and bake till
done.

752. CHOCOLATE PUFFS (Eighteenth Century)

Take half a pound of sifted sugar, scrape into it one ounce of chocolate very fine, mix them together. Beat the white of an egg to a very high froth, then strew in your sugar and chocolate, keep beating it till it is as stiff as paste : sugar your baking paper, and drop the mixture on in pieces about the size of a sixpence, and bake them in a very slow oven.

753. CHRISTMAS CAKE (Hertfordshire)

Two pounds of butter, two pounds of sugar, two pounds of flour, two pounds of currants, one and a half pounds of raisins, two pounds of sultanas, half a pound of peel, half a pound of ground or chopped almonds, one ounce of baking powder, one teacupful of brandy or maraschino, sixteen eggs. Bake six hours.

754. CHRISTMAS CAKE (Yorkshire)

Four pounds of flour, three pounds of currants, two pounds of raisins, two pounds of sugar, six eggs, twelve ounces of butter in a pint of new milk, four ounces of candied lemon, two ounces of candied citron, two ounces of candied orange. Cinnamon and nutmeg to taste : flavour with almonds or an almond flavouring, add rather better than a pint of yeast, and a little wine or brandy.

755. CINNAMON BISCUITS (Kent)

Two pounds of flour, half a pound of butter, half a pound of lump sugar, half a pint of milk, a little volatile salts. Bake on tins in a slow oven.

756. COCONUT BISCUITS (Gloucestershire)

Twelve ounces of flour, four ounces of desiccated coconut, two ounces of lard, two ounces of butter, six ounces of sugar, three teaspoonfuls of baking powder, half teaspoonful carbonate of soda (in milk), pinch of salt. Make into stiff dough, roll out, and bake. (Should not be allowed to get too dark in colour.)

757. COOMBER CAKE (Sussex)

One pound of flour, half a pound of butter, ditto sugar and currants, three ounces of almonds, three eggs, half a pint of milk.

758. CORNFLOUR CAKES (Hertfordshire)

Six ounces of butter, beaten to a cream; add two yolks of eggs, then a quarter of a pound of sugar, a quarter of a pound of cornflour, one teaspoonful of baking powder, mix all together; then add the whipped whites of the eggs. Bake in small moulds.

759. CORNFLOUR CAKE (Gloucestershire)

Half a pound of cornflour, two ounces of butter, quarter of a pound of castor sugar, one teaspoonful of baking powder, two teaspoonfuls of plain flour, two eggs. Beat butter to a cream (must not be oily), add sugar, mix well. Break in eggs one at a time and work well together. Stir in lightly the cornflour, flour, and baking powder; beat for a few minutes. Pour into a well-greased tin and bake in a moderate oven. Be careful not to open oven for about thirty minutes, or the cake will fall in the middle.

760. CORNISH HEAVY CAKE (Cornwall)

About half a pound of flour, four ounces of fat
(two ounces of butter, two ounces of lard), four
ounces of chopped raisins, four ounces of currants
or sultanas, half an ounce of nutmeg, half a teaspoonful of mixed spice, two ounces of lemon peel,
three ounces of castor sugar, two eggs, salt. Mix
all well together, making it pretty stiff ; can be
moistened with milk, if necessary. Roll out to about
one or one and a half inches in thickness, put on a
greased flat tin, bake in moderate oven for about
half an hour.

761. CRACKNELS (Yorkshire, 1769)

Take half a pound of fine flour, half a pound of
sugar, two ounces of butter, two eggs, and a few
caraway seeds. You must beat and sift the sugar,
and put it to your flour and work it to paste. Roll
this as thin as you can, and cut out the cracknels
with queen-cake tins. Lay them on paper and bake
them in a slow oven. They are proper to eat with
chocolate.

762. CUP CAKE (Kent)

One cup of butter, one cup of sugar, three cups of
flour, four eggs, one cup of milk, two teaspoonfuls
of baking powder, two cups of sultanas. (Presumably breakfast-cups. Ed.)

763. ISLE OF WIGHT DOUGHNUTS
(Farmhouse recipe)

One gallon of flour, one pound of butter rubbed
well into it : pour in one teacupful of good ale yeast

(not bitter), and put it to rise; mix and knead it as you would bread, and add in six well-beaten eggs, three-quarters of a pound of sifted sugar, one grated nutmeg, and a little warm milk. The dough must not be mixed too soft at first, or it will be too soft to roll up subsequently. Leave it again by the fire to rise for an hour or two. Then take out small lumps of dough, the size of a smallish orange, insert into the centre of each a piece of candied peel and some currants (some grated lemon-rind also is a great improvement); roll it up securely. Have ready a deep pan of quite boiling lard, and be sure that it is quite boiling when the doughnuts are put in: let them be completely covered with the lard, and boil fifteen minutes over a slow fire. Take out, set to drain on paper, and let them get cool gradually and not stand in a draught. Dust over with sifted sugar. These are first-rate.

764. AMERICAN DOUGHNUTS

One cupful of self-raising flour, half a cupful of sugar, half a nutmeg. Mix together with milk, roll out on a board, cut with a sharp, round cutter. Make a hole in the centre about the size of a shilling, and fry in boiling lard. When a nice golden brown one side, turn and fry the other. Serve immediately.

765. DURHAM YULE CAKE

Take one and a quarter pounds of dough, work into it a quarter of a pound each of butter, sugar, sultanas, and currants, one small teaspoonful of allspice, a quarter of a pound of candied citron, a quarter of a pound of lemon peel (cut into thin slices). Melt the butter and beat it up with a knife before putting it in. The cake should be rolled out about one and a half inches thick, marked with a knife at the top into small squares, and brushed over with white of egg.

766. ECCLES CAKES (Cumberland)

A quarter of a pound of currants, which should be well washed, a quarter of a pound of moist sugar, a little nutmeg, and a little rum, well mixed. Rub a pound of butter into a pound of flour, roll out about half an inch thick, cut into squares about three inches across, then put some of the currant mixture in the centre of each square. Wet the edges and join the four corners of each square in the centre; turn over and roll lightly with the rolling pin, to make a round cake. Bake in a hot oven, not too hot.

767. ETHEL'S CAKES (Sussex)

Two eggs, their weight in flour and sugar, one teaspoonful baking powder. Beat the sugar and eggs till creamy and frothy ; when bubbling all over, add flour and baking powder and turn into greased tins, and bake in a very hot oven ; when firm on top, they are ready. Scoop out the inside and put in whipped cream, and place one on another with chocolate icing.

768. DELICIOUS FINGER CAKES (Hertfordshire)

Mix two tablespoonfuls of cornflour into one pound of powdered sugar, and stir them gradually into

the stiffly whipped whites of two eggs. Bake on
buttered tins in a moderate oven until very delicately
brown. For chocolate fingers, add two tablespoonfuls of finely grated chocolate to two tablespoonfuls
of corn starch, and one pound of powdered sugar,
and stir gradually into two beaten eggs. For coconut fingers add four tablespoonfuls of grated coconut.

769. FLEED CAKES (Kent)

One pound of flour, half a pound of fleed, quarter
of a pound of good butter. Rub the fleed and
butter into the flour and roll well.

Fleed cakes (says the sender of this recipe) were
usually seen on every tea-table in Kent when I was
a girl. Very rich these homemade cakes were. I
never see or taste such fleed cakes nowadays, puffed
up in delicate flakes! In winter we had another tea-
cake, made simply of flour and suet cut into the
shape of a diamond. They were served hot from
a Dutch oven placed in front of the fire. We know
an old " woman of Kent " who has her own recipe
for fleed cakes. Instead of pig's fleed, she uses
rabbit's fleed. Her hobby is to keep pet rabbits,
feed them well and keep them happy, when they
will grow fat. Then kill them, skin them, cut
them open and take out all the inside fat, or *fleed*,
cook the rabbit as you like it for your dinner, but
make delicious cakes for your tea with the fleed.
Bake the cakes in an old-fashioned Dutch oven
in front of the fire.

770. GALETTE (French)

Take equal quantities of butter and flour, a little salt, and two eggs (in the commoner sorts of galette, however, no eggs are used, the ingredients are merely flour, butter, and salt), knead the whole together into a paste, roll it as thin as a crown-piece (here we must beg to observe that the Paris galette is usually rolled to twice the thickness of a crown-piece), and make it the size of a dessert plate (or much larger) ; mark it with a knife so as to form diamonds ; put it into the oven for a quarter of an hour, take it out, beat up two eggs with a little cream and some salt, pour it over the cake, and return it to the oven to bake for another quarter of an hour.

771. GÂTEAU À LA MOCHA (Hertfordshire)

Beat up the yolks of four eggs, with a quarter of a pound of powdered loaf sugar, add gradually two ounces of flour, two ounces of potato flour, lastly the whites of four eggs, whipped to a stiff froth. When the whole is well mixed, put it in a buttered plain mould and bake ; turn out the cake when done, and when it is quite cold, cover it all over with the following icing, ornamenting it with piping of the icing squeezed through a small rose pipe. When the cake is finished it should be put in a cold place on ice till wanted. For the icing, take half a pound of fresh butter, and beat it into a cream in a bowl, adding drop by drop during the process half a teacupful of the strongest coffee that can be made.

772. GERMAN GAUFRES

Blanch a pound of sweet almonds, and cut them into small thin chips, put them in a vessel with three-quarters of a pound of powdered sugar, and a small quantity of candied orange-flowers : mix these ingredients well up with whites of eggs, beaten with a little good cream, and bake them in shapes. Serve hot, with sugar strewed over them.

773. ITALIAN GAUFRES

Beat well together eight eggs, a pound of loaf sugar finely pounded, six ounces of cream, as much milk, a little orange-flowers, and the rind of a lemon grated ; mix the whole well together, taking care that the batter is not lumpy ; bake in gaufre irons, as for ordinary gaufres.

774. HARD GINGERBREADS (Hertfordshire)

A cupful of treacle, a tablespoonful of butter, a tablespoonful of cold water, a teaspoonful of ginger, a teaspoonful of bi-carbonate of soda, and enough flour to make a dough ; bake in a brisk oven.

775. GINGERBREAD (Kent)

I

One pound of flour, one pound of moist sugar, a few cloves pounded, one pound of treacle, one ounce of butter, a little ginger.

II

One pound of treacle, two pounds of flour, one and a half ounces of ginger, one pound of sugar,

three and a quarter pounds of butter. The treacle
and sugar to be dissolved and poured over the other
ingredients.

III

One pound of flour, three-quarters of a pound of
treacle, four ounces of butter, six ounces of brown
sugar, one ounce prepared ginger, the peel of one
lemon chopped fine. Mix them well together, and
bake them in a slow oven. One egg is an improvement.

776. GINGERBREAD CAKE (Lancashire)

One and a half pounds of flour, one and a quarter
pounds of treacle, one ounce of ginger (ground
freshly), six ounces of butter, a quarter of a pound of
brown sugar, a lemon or Seville orange (both peel
and juice), three teaspoonfuls of baking powder.
Melt the butter in the treacle, add a little warm
milk, and pour into the dry ingredients. Mixture
must be rather soft. Bake four hours in a slow oven.
This is an old and excellent recipe.

777. GINGERBREAD (Middlesex)

Three pounds of treacle are to be mixed with
three pounds and a half of good flour, a pound of
fresh butter, and a pound of brown sugar, five
ounces of caraway seeds, six ounces of candied
orange and lemon peel, cut very small, a quarter
of a pound of powdered ginger, five eggs, and
rather more than half an ounce of pearl-ashes : the
butter is mixed with the other ingredients by being
beaten to a cream. The mixture must stand for

20

twenty-four hours, and on the following day is to
be worked up like bread, and baked into a cake,
of about an inch thick, in a slow oven. The same
mixture, made more liquid, and without the pearl-
ashes, the butter being melted instead of beaten,
dropped with a spoon upon a buttered tin, makes
gingerbread nuts ; but it is usual to put a larger
quantity of ginger. Gingerbread nuts are also made
by rubbing up a pound of butter with two pounds of
flour, a pound of brown sugar, and rather more
than an ounce of powdered ginger. These are
mixed together with as much treacle as will form
them into the consistency of dough : it is then made
into the form of nuts, and baked upon tins. In order
to make them richer, a little powdered allspice
and powdered cinnamon may be added. Nutmeg
and crushed or powdered almonds may be added
either to gingerbread or gingerbread nuts.

778. GINGERBREAD (Yorkshire)

Two pounds of flour, one pound of treacle, one
pound of sugar, twelve ounces of butter, with a little
lemon-peel and ginger to taste. For rolled gingerbread, it must be made the night before.

779. TRANSPARENT GINGERBREAD (Lancashire)

To ten ounces of flour take twelve ounces of
butter, one pound of treacle, and one pound of sugar.
Melt the butter and mix well with the treacle and
sugar ; put in the flour, and about a quarter of an
ounce of cinnamon and mace, with a little lemon
peel grated or shredded very fine. Beat all well together, drop it very thin and bake in a moderate

oven. Cut it out in squares and just turn it round
the finger, and put it in a canister. Take it out
only as it is wanted for use, or it will turn soft.
(This is equivalent to Ormskirk gingerbread, a well-
known Lancashire dainty. But the ginger has been
omitted. It would be as well to add about half
an ounce of ground ginger. Ed.)

780. GINGER-CAKE (Isle of Wight)

Mix into one pound of flour, a quarter of a pound
of butter, one tablespoonful of powdered sugar, one
penny packet of baking powder, two teaspoonfuls of
powdered ginger. Beat up and add two eggs, and
a full half-pound of thick treacle—*not* golden syrup,
but the old-fashioned treacle sold at oil-shops.
You may need to thin the treacle with a little milk,
before you can work it in. Beat all well together,
and bake for two hours in a slow oven.

781. GINGER CAKES (Kent)

One pound of flour, six ounces of sugar, one egg,
six ounces of butter, half an ounce of best ground
ginger, one glass of brandy, four drops of oil of
cassia.

782. GINGER CAKE (Lancashire)

Half a pound of butter, half a pound of sugar,
two ounces of ground ginger, one dessertspoonful of
baking powder, one pound of syrup, a little salt, a
gill of milk, four eggs, the rind of two lemons. Stir
into this mixture as much flour as will give it the consistency of very thick batter. Put it into a buttered
tin and bake for an hour in a moderate oven.

783. SHEET GINGER CAKE (Hertfordshire)

One pound of flour, half a pound of treacle or
golden syrup, half a pound of butter, half a pound
of brown sugar, half an ounce of ginger, one teaspoonful of carbonate of soda, three eggs ; warm
the butter, sugar, and treacle in a stewpan, then
add the eggs beaten, ginger, and soda; stir in the
flour. Not to be baked hard.

784. WHOLEMEAL GINGERBREAD CAKE (Surrey)

One pound of wholemeal or entire wheat flour,
one pound of coarse oatmeal, one pound of golden
syrup, quarter of a pound of butter, six ounces of
moist sugar, half a pint of milk, three large teaspoonfuls of baking powder or yeast powder. Put
the milk and golden syrup together into the oven
to warm, rub the butter into the meal in a dry
state, and all the other dry ingredients, then pour
in the warmed syrup and milk, mixing lightly with
a wooden spoon. Turn into two well-buttered
baking-tins, place immediately in a very slow oven.
Bake very slowly for two hours, or longer if
necessary.

785. MRS. GURNEY'S GINGER SNAPS (Gloucestershire)

Take a cupful of sugar, one of golden syrup, one
of melted butter (or butter and a little lard), two
teaspoonfuls of ground ginger, one of carbonate of
soda dissolved in two tablespoonfuls of hot water.
Just work in as much flour as will make a very stiff
dough. Roll on a floured board as thin as possible,
and cut into small rounds. Bake on a flat oven
plate in a moderate oven.

786. GINGERBREAD NUTS (Kent)

One and three-quarter pounds of flour, one and a half pounds of treacle, one pound of sugar, one ounce of ginger, half an ounce of allspice, quarter of a pound of butter, quarter of a pound of lard. The sugar to be rubbed in first, every lump broken, then the lard and butter, then the spice, which must be *very* fine.

787. FINE SWEET GINGERBREAD NUTS (1815)

Take two pounds of the best treacle, and put it in a large basin ; then take half a pound of the best fresh butter, and carefully melt it, not to oil ; pour the butter to the treacle, and stir it well as you pour it in ; add three-quarters of an ounce of the best pounded ginger, and put it with two ounces of preserved lemon and orange peel cut very small, two ounces of preserved angelica cut very small, one ounce of coriander seed pounded, one ounce and a half of caraway seeds whole ; mix them well together ; then break two eggs, yolks and whites together, and mix as much flour as will bring it to a fine paste ; make them the size you choose, put them on a tin plate, and let your oven be rather brisk.

788. GIRDLE CAKE (Lancashire)

Rub six ounces of sugar into two pounds of flour : add a little salt, make it into a paste with some good milk or buttermilk : roll it out, cut into shapes, and bake on a girdle (sometimes known as griddle. Ed.).

789. GIRDLE CAKE (Kent)

Sift together one pound of flour and two full teaspoonfuls of baking powder, then crumble into this three ounces of butter with the tips of the fingers as lightly as possible till it is all fine like bread crumbs. Next work in by degrees half a pint of milk till it forms a firm dough; halve this dough and knead each piece into a flat cake.

790. GOLD CAKE (American)

Half a cupful of butter, one cupful of sugar, two and a half cupfuls of flour, half a cupful of milk, half a teaspoonful of soda, one teaspoonful of cream of tartar, the yolks of six eggs, one teaspoonful of vanilla. Frost with yellow frost. The yellow frost is made with the yolk of one egg to nine lumps of sugar and flavoured with vanilla.

791. HONEY CAKES (Middlesex)

To two pounds and a half of dried flour, add a pound of honey, three-quarters of a pound of pounded loaf sugar, half a pound of citron, and the same quantity of orange peel; cut into thin strips, add half an ounce each of ginger and cinnamon, pounded; melt the sugar with the honey, and mix in the other ingredients; roll out the paste, cut into forms, and bake on floured tins.

792. COMMON JOHNNY CAKE (Ireland)

Into one quart of meal stir one pint of boiling water, with salt; spread it on a board an inch thick, and bake it before the fire, or on an iron over the fire.

793. JOHNNY CAKE (Lancashire)

One teacupful of fine sugar, two teacupfuls of flour, one teacupful of semolina, two ounces of butter or lard, two teaspoonfuls of baking powder. Mix with milk rather dry. Bake in moderate oven for about twenty minutes.

794. JOHNNY CAKE (Surrey)

To one quart of milk add three eggs, one teaspoonful of carbonate of soda, one teacupful of wheaten flour, mixed with enough Indian meal to form a thickish batter. Bake very quickly and eat hot, with golden syrup or butter.

795. JUDGES' BISCUITS (1815)

Take six eggs and break them into a copper pan, yolks and whites together; whisk them well for about five minutes; mix half a pound of powdered sugar with the eggs, and whisk them for ten minutes; put as many caraway seeds as you think proper, and half a pound of sifted flour; mix it well with a wooden spoon, and put three papers on your plates; then take a spoon and drop them on papers about the size of a crown-piece, sift some powdered sugar over them; let them be rather thick in the middle, and the oven rather sharp, and when they come out, cut them off the paper while hot. (Rice paper is advisable here. Ed.)

796. JUMBLES (Middlesex)

Well beat the whites of three eggs and remove the froth. Then take about one tablespoonful each of flour, sifted sugar, and milk. Add a very few caraway seeds ; a little ginger may be added at pleasure. Mix all together into a very stiff paste, and roll it flat. Cut it out into various shapes, and bake on a sheet of white paper.

797. KENTISH CAKES

Rub four ounces of butter into three-quarters of a pound of flour ; add some caraway seeds, and half a pound of loaf sugar finely pounded ; mix these into a stiff paste with a little water, roll out to the thickness of a crown piece, cut them out with a glass, or into squares, prick them, and bake on floured tins.

798. KING CAKES (Yorkshire, 1769)

Take one pound of flour, three-quarters of a pound of butter, half a pound of sugar, and half a pound of currants, well cleaned. Rub your butter well into your flour, and put in as many yolks of eggs as will make it supple ; then put in your sugar, currants, and some mace, as much as will give them a taste. So make them up in little round cakes, and butter the papers you lay them on.

799. KRINGLES (Kent)

Beat well the yolks of eight and the whites of two eggs, and mix with four ounces of butter just warmed, and with this knead a pound of flour and four ounces of sugar to a paste. Roll into thick or thin biscuits, prick them, and bake on tin plates.

800. LANCASHIRE CAKE

Beat well the yolks of twelve and the whites of seven eggs for half an hour, add a pound of pounded loaf sugar, half a pound of flour, and the peel of a lemon grated ; beat all well together and bake in a floured tin.

801. LEMON CAKES (Hertfordshire)

Sift four ounces of castor sugar and beat it into the grated rind of two lemons ; whip the whites of three eggs to a firm froth, and add it gradually to the sugar and lemon ; beat all together for half an hour. Make this mixture up in pyramid shapes, and place on rounds of short crust. Set in a moderate oven, and bake for six or eight minutes.

802. LIGHT CAKE (Welsh)

Put one pint of buttermilk (two days old) into a basin. Drop into it one egg *un*beaten ; add seven or eight tablespoonfuls of flour to make it into the consistency of *thick* batter, and one teaspoonful of salt. Beat together very well until light. Then put one teaspoonful of carbonate of soda, and the same of granulated sugar, into a cup with half a teacupful of buttermilk. Mix well, and add to the other batter. Beat all together *thoroughly well.* Take a small frying-pan, and rub it with a piece of bacon-rind when it has been made *very hot.* Pour in two tablespoonfuls of the batter, and fry. Turn the cake over with an egg-slice to brown the other side. Serve very hot, with butter.

803. LUNCH CAKE (Kent)

Half a pound of flour, three ounces of sugar, two ounces of butter, one egg, one teaspoonful of baking powder, one teacupful of warm milk ; caraway seeds, currants, or raisins to taste.

804. LUNCHEON CAKE (Westmorland)

One pound of flour, half a pound of butter, six ounces stoned and chopped raisins, and candied peel, caraway seeds to taste, half a pound of moist sugar, three eggs, teacupful of milk (boiling), one teaspoonful of carbonate of soda. Pour the boiling milk on to soda in a small basin, stir occasionally till cold. Put dry ingredients into large basin, then mix and add milk and eggs. Beat all with a wooden spoon for twenty minutes. Bake one and a half hours in a moderate oven. (Excellent cake.)

805. MACAROONS (Middlesex)

Take half a pound of blanched sweet almonds, and a quarter of a pound of shelled bitter almonds ; beat them each very smooth, and mix them together ; if prepared the day before, it will be the better. Next take a large teaspoonful of mixed spice, nutmeg, mace, and cinnamon, which must be well pounded and sifted ; beat the whites of three eggs till they stand alone ; add to them gradually, twenty-four large teaspoonfuls of powdered loaf sugar, a tea-spoonful at a time ; beat it very hard, and put in by degrees the spice and a tablespoonful of rose-water, after which stir in gradually the almonds. Should the almonds not prove sufficient to make the

paste as thick as a good soft dough, prepare a few
more, and stir them in.   When all is well mixed,
put some flour in the palm of your hand, and taking
up a lump of the paste with the point of a knife, roll
it with the flour into a small ball : have ready an
iron or a tin pan, and lay the balls in it as they are
made up, placing them about two inches apart, and
then bake them for about eight or ten minutes in a
moderately heated oven, until they become of a
pale brown colour.   The top of the oven should be
hotter than the bottom, so that they may crack on
the surface.

806. MADELEINE CAKE (Staffordshire)

One ounce of butter, one ounce of castor sugar, one
egg, quarter of a pound of self-raising flour, and
about two tablespoonfuls of milk.   Well beat the
egg, then add the sugar, the butter (which must be
creamed), and beat all well again.   Then add the
flour and milk, making the mixture moderately stiff.
Butter a medium-sized Yorkshire pudding-tin, put
in the cake and bake a nice brown.   Turn it out of
the tin, and when it is cooled a little, cut it in two,
spread jam on the one half and put the other over it.
Cut into finger-pieces and pile in a glass dish.

807. MADEIRA CAKE (Gloucestershire)

A quarter of a pound each of butter and castor
sugar, half a pound of flour (sifted), three eggs.
Work in one at a time.   One teaspoonful of baking
powder, one tablespoonful of milk.   Place a slice of
citron on top when mixture has been put in cake

tin lined with greased paper. Bake in moderate oven about three-quarters of an hour.

808. MADEIRA CAKE (Hertfordshire)

Six ounces of butter, six ounces of castor sugar, six eggs, twelve ounces of flour, a little grated nutmeg, citron. Slightly warm butter and beat it to a cream ; add the sugar and beat five minutes ; add the eggs one at a time and then the flour ; mix gently and then pour into a lined cake tin ; put citron on top. Bake for hour and half.

809. MAIDS OF HONOUR (Surrey)

Eight teaspoonfuls of sifted sugar, one egg, two ounces of ground almonds, a pinch of baking powder. The sugar and egg to be beaten well together, then the almonds stirred in. Put the baking powder last. Have some patty-pans lined with puff-paste, lay a little raspberry jam at the bottom of each, and cover with a teaspoonful of the mixture. Bake in a moderate oven.

810. MERINGUES (Middlesex)

Whisk to a froth the whites of twelve eggs, and when it is well raised, add some powdered sugar and grated lemon-peel. Continue whisking lightly to mix those ingredients, but without melting the sugar ; put the meringues in little portions about the size of half an egg upon a sheet of white paper, and place them under a cover that will contain hot ashes on the top ; when they are done on the outside, and of a good colour, remove them from the paper, take out the part of the inside which is not done, and supply its place with sweetmeat; join the two sides of them well together again, and serve as dry as possible.

811. RAG CAKE (Ireland)

Take three breakfastcupfuls of sugar, two of flour, and one of sour cream or milk. Take four eggs, and well beat the yolks and whites separately. Cream the butter and sugar, and beat them up again with the beaten yolks of eggs. Add one table-spoonful cream of tartar to the flour, one teaspoonful bi-carbonate of soda to the cream, and add these to the eggs and sugar. Put the whites of the eggs in last. Bake in a tin, and ice at pleasure.

812. RATAFIA PUFFS (Seventeenth Century)

Take half a pound of bitter almonds, beaten very stiff, and one and a half pounds of sifted sugar. Make it up to a stiff paste with white of egg whipped to a froth. Beat it well in a mortar, and make it up into little round loaves. Bake them in a very cool oven, on paper and tin plates.

813. GROUND RICE BISCUITS (Isle of Wight)

Three ounces of butter, three ounces of white sugar, six ounces ground rice, three ounces of flour, half a teaspoonful of baking powder, one egg (beaten), a little milk, grated lemon rind. Cream the butter and sugar, then add the egg and dry ingredients. The mixture should be like pastry ; turn on to a floured board, roll lightly (as it will stick), and cut into biscuits about a quarter of an inch thick. Place on a greased tin ; bake in a moderate oven to a golden brown.

814. RHODA'S RICE BUNS (Gloucestershire)

Three-quarters of a pound of flour, quarter of a pound of ground rice, six ounces of butter and lard, three-quarters of a pound of sugar, two teaspoonfuls of baking-powder, six eggs, and a little milk. Mix well. These take from ten to fifteen minutes to cook in moderate oven.

815. RICE CAKE (Yorkshire)

Two eggs beaten well for a quarter of an hour ; quarter of a pound of sugar, put to the eggs and beaten ten minutes ; quarter of a pound of rice, put to the eggs and sugar, and beaten five minutes. Butter a tin or mould and bake three-quarters of an hour.

816. RICE CAKES (Kent, 1809)

A quarter of a pound of ground rice, the same of flour, one pound of white sugar, sifted, a quarter of a pound of melted butter, four eggs, leaving out two whites. The rice, flour, and sugar to be mixed together, the eggs and butter to be added when the batter is nearly cold. If you choose currants, put a quarter of a pound.

817. RICE CAKE (Middlesex)

Whisk separately for an hour the yolks of eight and the whites of six eggs ; add to them half a pound of rice flour, three-quarters of a pound of finely powdered loaf sugar, and the peel of a lemon grated : beat one pound of butter into cream, and mix the above ingredients well with it ; bake in a buttered tin in moderate oven.

818. RICHMOND CAKE (Hertfordshire)

Six ounces of butter, a quarter of an ounce of mixed spice, the same of ground ginger ; mix till they are a cream ; add a quarter of a pound of brown sugar, a quarter of a pound of treacle ; mix all together with half a pound of flour, two ounces of ground rice, two tablespoonfuls of dried coconut, four eggs, half an ounce of baking powder.

819. RICH CAKE (Hampshire)

Nine ounces of currants, four and a half ounces of raisins chopped, four and a half ounces of butter, four and a half ounces of flour, four and a half ounces of sugar, half a nutmeg grated, quarter of a teaspoonful of mace pounded, two and a quarter ounces of citron, three eggs. Bake two and a half hours. This is very good. If the cake be iced, remember to beat the white of an egg to a solid froth *before* adding the pounded white icing sugar, and place it on the cake directly it is drawn from the oven.

820. RICH PLUM CAKE (Devonshire)

Eight ounces of fresh butter, eight ounces of castor sugar, eight ounces of mixed peel, eight ounces of dried cherries, three-quarters of a pound of flour, half a pound of sultanas, four ounces of

almonds, a quarter of a pint of brandy, five eggs,
half an ounce of allspice, half a teaspoonful of salt.
Cream the butter and sugar. Sift in flour and salt ;
gradually add eggs one at a time and beat in well.
Chop the cherries, the peel, and the almonds ; add
these with the sultanas and allspice ; mix all well
together. Add the brandy last, a little at a time.
Be sure all is thoroughly mixed. Line a cake tin,
putting three rounds of paper at the bottom. Bake
three hours in a moderate oven. Don't let the
heat rise after the cake has gone in.

821. ROUT CAKES (Middlesex)

Rub into two pounds of flour an ounce of fresh
butter, washed in orange-flower water ; then add
half a pound of well beaten loaf sugar, the same
weight of candied orange and lemon cut into strips,
and a quarter of a pound of well-dried currants ;
mix all these ingredients well together with five
eggs, well beaten, and half a glass of brandy or
ratafia, or a little of both ; drop this paste in small
rough knobs upon floured tins, and bake in a quick
oven ; they will require but a very short time to
bake, as they must not be high-coloured.

822. OAT-CAKES (Scotland)

Mix into one and three-quarter pounds of medium
Scotch oatmeal, one teaspoonful of carbonate of
soda and two teaspoonfuls of salt. Then rub in
three or four ounces of lard or dripping, and
add enough hot water to mix into a dough. It
must not be too dry, and must not cool off, but
should be done very quickly. Dust some fine

oatmeal over the board, roll the dough out as thin as it will stand, and cut it into round or triangular shapes, and bake it in a quick oven. If you try to get the rolled dough too thin, it will break.

823. OATMEAL CAKES (Lancashire)

Six ounces of oatmeal, five ounces of flour, three ounces of butter, two tablespoonfuls of milk, one ounce of sifted sugar, one egg, one tablespoonful of baking powder. Mix the dry ingredients, rub in the butter, mix up with the egg and milk. Roll it out like pastry, cut it with a round cutter. Bake these biscuits for about ten minutes.

824. ORANGE CAKE (Somerset)

Six ounces of flour, six ounces of castor sugar, two and a quarter ounces of butter, one small teaspoonful of baking powder, the rind of two oranges grated, and sufficient juice to make it soft, two eggs. Beat the butter and sugar to a cream, add the eggs one at a time, with a little flour ; beat well, then add the rind, flour, and baking powder, all mixed together by degrees. Bake one hour. Make an icing with six ounces of icing sugar, and the juice of half an orange; spread it over the cake when cool.

825. OSWEGO CAKES (Kent)

One pound of oswego or cornflour, quarter of a pound of butter, quarter of a pound of fine white sugar, two teaspoonfuls of baking powder, quarter of a pound of currants, two eggs (yolks and whites beaten separately for quarter of an hour). Mix all together, beat well for a quarter of an hour before pouring into a buttered shape. Bake a nice brown.

21

826. PAISLEY CIRCLES (Kent)

Three-quarters of an ounce of Paisley flour, six ounces of ordinary flour, one ounce of butter, one ounce of castor sugar, one egg, a little milk. Put the flour in a basin and rub the butter in lightly ; add sugar and Paisley flour. Mix well. Beat up egg and add, with enough milk to make a rather stiff dough. Roll out rather less than a quarter of an inch thick. Cut into rounds with cutter two and a half inches in diameter, then cut out centre with a small cutter. Fry the circles in smoking hot fat (a few at a time). They will drop to the bottom of the pan. Do not try to lift them, they will rise of themselves. Directly they rise turn over if nicely browned and cook the other side. They will not take more than a few minutes. Drain on paper, let get cold. Split open circles carefully. Spread with preserve or lemon curd. Lay one half over the other and dust with castor sugar.

827. PARKINS (Derbyshire)

One pound of fine porridge oatmeal, half a pound of butter or beef dripping, six ounces of brown sugar, almonds (a few), half an ounce of ground ginger, nine ounces treacle, pinch of salt. Mix all dry ingredients well together, rub butter into meal, add treacle last and make stiff enough to roll out, half an inch thick, on a floured pasteboard. Cut out in rounds, place half almond in centre of each. Place immediately in slow oven, to cook half to three-quarters of an hour.

828. PARKIN (Lancashire)

Four pounds of oatmeal, four pounds of treacle, half a pound of butter, ginger and candied lemon according to taste.

829. PARKIN (Shropshire)

Rub a quarter of a pound of butter and a quarter of a pound of fresh lard into two pounds of fine oatmeal. Add a quarter of a pound of moist sugar, half an ounce of ground ginger, and a little candied lemon peel. Stir half a breakfastcupful of hot milk into one and three-quarter pints of good treacle, and heat this a little, so that it may mix easily with the meal. Beat all together and bake in a slow oven. To be kept in a closely covered tin box.

830. YORKSHIRE PARKIN

Half a pound of flour, half a pound of fine oatmeal, two ounces of lard, two ounces of butter, half a pound of treacle, two ounces of sugar, one teaspoonful of ground ginger, one teaspoonful mixed spice, one teaspoonful baking powder, pinch of salt, a little milk. Rub the lard and butter into the flour, add all dry ingredients, warm the treacle, and add with a little milk, mix well, pour into a flat tin, well greased. Bake in a very moderate oven about forty minutes.

831. ANOTHER WAY

One pound of flour, half a pound of oatmeal, half a pound of sugar, half a pound of butter, half an ounce of ground ginger, one pound of treacle

two eggs, pinch of carbonate of soda. Melt butter
and sugar together, add flour, oatmeal, etc. Bake
in a flat tin in a moderate oven.

832. PLAIN CAKE (Cape Colony)

Take the weight of four eggs in sugar and butter
and the weight of six in flour, two teaspoonfuls of
baking powder, two or three eggs. Flavour as required. Stir the sugar, butter, and eggs together
with a spoon, then gradually add the dry ingredients
previously mixed. If less eggs are used they can be
substituted by a little milk.

833. PLAIN CAKE (Surrey)

Three-quarters of a pound of flour, a quarter of a
pound of ground rice, three eggs, some candied peel,
one tablespoonful of baking powder, six ounces of
sugar. When mixed it should be rather moist, and
if the eggs do not make it sufficiently so, add a
little milk or water.

834. PLAIN CAKE (Yorkshire)

Half a pound of flour, six ounces of currants, six
ounces of sugar, two ounces of butter, three eggs,
two ounces of candied lemon, two teaspoonfuls of
baking-powder ; bake one hour.

835. PRIMBLES (Hertfordshire)

A quarter of a pound of flour, three ounces of
sugar, two ounces of butter, rind of a lemon, two
eggs. Mix perfectly smooth, force through a rose-
pipe, bake in brisk oven. Should be a pale gold
colour.

836. POTATO-CAKES, SALT (Ireland)

I

This recipe is most excellent. Take an equal weight of cold cooked potatoes pressed through a sieve, and of flour. Rub in beef dripping in the proportion of four ounces to the pound, and salt to taste. Moisten with a little milk, roll out about half an inch thick, cut the paste into little cakes with the top of the flour dredger. Bake in good hot oven till the cakes are a golden brown. Split, butter, and serve piping hot. Suitable either for breakfast, tea, or for dinner as a substitute for potatoes ; in the latter case, very good with cold meat.

II

About one pound of boiled potatoes. Mash well, with some milk and water, salt, and a little butter, into a thick batter. Then work in about double the quantity of flour, with which you have previously mixed a dessert-spoonful of yeast powder. The mixture becomes softer the more you work it. Make it into little cakes and bake in good oven.

837. POTATO-CAKE, SWEET (Devonshire)

I

Take three or four warm potatoes, mash these ; half a pound of flour, quarter of a pound of fat (two ounces of butter, two ounces of lard), a few currants or sultanas, a little Demerara sugar, salt ; well mix together with milk ; roll out to about one inch or one and half inches thick, and put on flat greased tin.

II

Two pounds of boiled potatoes mashed, add quarter of a pound of flour, quarter of a pound of butter, quarter of a pound of currants, two table-spoonfuls of sugar. Work all well together, roll out nearly an inch thick, cut into round cakes and bake. To be eaten whole, or split and buttered.

838. QUEEN CAKES (Gloucestershire)

Cream a quarter of a pound of butter and then add quarter of a pound of castor sugar, two eggs— work in one at a time—five ounces of flour (sifted), a little grated nutmeg, one ounce of currants, one teaspoonful of baking powder. This is a rather stiff mixture. Well grease queen-cake tins, and bake from ten to fifteen minutes in moderate oven.

839. QUEEN CAKES (Surrey)

Put into a bowl a quarter of a pound of fresh butter with a quarter of a pound of castor sugar and cream it. Add, to six ounces of flour, one teaspoonful of baking-powder, the grated rind of a lemon, a pinch of salt. Beat up two eggs, and add these, *alternately with the flour mixture*, to the bowl of creamed butter and sugar, until all is in, beating well. Lastly, add three ounces of glacé cherries or of sultanas, and two ounces of candied peel thinly cut : pour into patty-pans, or very small " castle pudding " tins, and bake in a good oven. These cakes may be decorated on top with glacé cherries or candied peel. They are most delicious.

840. SAND CAKE (Gloucestershire)

Weight of two eggs in butter, sugar and cornflour (Colman's is the best for this recipe), one teaspoonful of baking-powder. Bake in a moderate oven. Pour over a little water or lemon icing. Just warm two or three tablespoonfuls of icing or castor sugar, wetted with about a tablespoonful of lemon juice, and pour over cake.

841. SANDWICH CAKE (Devonshire)

Three eggs, the weight of two eggs in flour and sugar, beat the sugar and eggs together for twenty minutes, gradually sift in the flour. Bake in a quick oven for ten minutes.

842. SANDWICH CAKE (Gloucestershire)

Take the weight of two eggs in butter, castor sugar, ground rice, and flour—add one teaspoonful of baking-powder. Bake in large flat cake tin. When cold, split and insert raspberry jam. Takes about twenty to thirty minutes to cook in a moderate oven.

843. SCOTCH CAKE

Four pounds of well-dried flour, two pounds of good butter, half a pound of candied citron and lemon peel, the same quantity of pounded loaf sugar, quarter of a pound of sweet and half the quantity of bitter almonds blanched, and half a pound of caraway comfits; cut the citron and lemon peel into thin strips, the almonds into small chips, and mix them with little more than half of the flour, part of the comfits, and the sugar; melt the butter, and when nearly cool pour it into the flour mixing it briskly all the time; then form it with the hands into a large round, about an inch thick, using the remainder of the flour to make it up with; cut it into four, pinching each part round the edge with the finger and thumb; prick and strew the remainder of the comfits over them; bake on paper on floured tins in a moderate oven.

844. SEED CAKE (Cheshire)

Take one pound of flour, one pound of sugar, one dozen eggs, quarter of a pound of caraway seeds. Put one pound of butter before the fire till it gets soft enough to beat it up; when well beaten with the hand, put in the sugar and beat it well, then the eggs, and afterwards the flour. They must all be beaten as they are put in. Line your pan with buttered paper and put in the batter.

845. SEED BISCUITS (Kent)

Take three and a half pounds of flour, one pound of moist sugar, one and a half ounces of caraway seeds, one and a half pints of milk, and a little volatile salts. Wash them over with egg and sugar, and bake in a quick oven.

N.B.—The sugar should be dissolved in the milk and strained, for all biscuits.

846. SEED CAKE (Gloucestershire)

(Rich)

Take one pound of flour and a pinch of salt, six
ounces of butter, three-quarters of a pound of castor
sugar, four eggs, one teaspoonful of caraway seeds,
one ounce of baking powder, one gill of milk or
cream. Add the eggs well beaten, and work well
together; thin down with milk. Add baking-
powder and seeds last. Let it stand on plate rack
over oven (coolest part) for about one hour. Then
bake in moderate oven about one hour. Sufficient
for two medium-sized cakes.

847. SEED CAKE (Ireland)

Take one pound of butter beaten to a cream.
Beat in one pound of powdered sugar (white);
then beat in, one by one, a pound of eggs, each
whole. Keep beating all together with a wooden
spoon. Then add one pound of flour, well dried
at the fire, and lemon or hawthorn whisky to
flavour—a wineglassful. Beat at least one hour
from the commencement. Bake in tin shapes
lined with buttered paper. Bake about two hours.
(The seeds have been omitted. Two ounces of
caraways should suffice. Ed.)

848. COMMON SEED CAKE (Yorkshire)

Two and a half pounds of flour, half a pound of
loaf sugar, one tablespoonful of thick yeast, half a
pint of warm milk, half a pound of butter, one ounce
of caraway seeds. Line a tin with buttered paper,

put in the mixture, and set it before the fire to
rise. Bake it about one hour in a rather hot oven.
When done, brush the tops over with milk.

849. TIPPERARY SEED CAKE (Ireland)

Wash a pound of butter in a little orange-flower
water, and beat it to a cream ; then mix into it by
degrees a pound and a half of pounded loaf sugar
and sixteen eggs well beaten ; add one pound of well-
dried flour, half a pound of sweet almonds, blanched
and pounded in a little rose-water, two ounces of
caraway seeds ; beat the whole well together for
half an hour, pour it into a buttered tin lined with
buttered paper, and bake in a quick oven for two
hours.

850. AYRSHIRE SHORTCAKE (Scotland)

Mix together in a basin a quarter of a pound of
flour, two ounces of castor sugar, and a pinch of salt ;
rub in gently but thoroughly a quarter of a pound of
butter. Slightly beat up one egg, mix with it one
tablespoonful of milk or cream. Make a hole in
the middle of the flour, pour in the egg and milk ;
mix into the flour with a knife, and then knead it
well with the hand till all the flour is well mixed.
It must be a soft paste. Flour a board and roll
out the paste half an inch thick and cut into any
shape desired. Ornament the edges, decorate the
top with caraway seeds, place on a greased paper
on a tin, and bake.

851. SAFFRON CAKE (Cornwall)

One and a half pounds of flour (if self-raising flour is not used, add four teaspoonfuls of baking powder), half a pint of milk, one pound of fruit (raisins, currants, or both), three ounces of candied peel, six ounces of brown sugar, six ounces of butter (to be creamed along with the sugar), two eggs, a pinch of salt, and three pennyworth of saffron. Put the saffron in the oven over-night, or for an hour when the oven is quick, to "draw" it well, in a cup with a little hot water. Then strain it, well squeezing out the essence. Add it to the milk and eggs, which have been well beaten (yolks and whites separately), and mix this to the dry ingredients. The above amount will make two good-sized cakes. Bake two hours or more. (Some people dry their saffron, then crush it to powder and mix it with the flour.)

852. SHORTBREAD (Kent, 1809)

Take one pound of fresh butter, beaten to the consistency of cream; add to it, by degrees, three pounds of flour, half a pound of loaf sugar, sifted quite fine, which must be mixed with the flour previous to its being crumbled into the butter, two ounces of sugar plums, one ounce of lemon peel, one ounce of orange peel sliced. After the ingredients are mixed together, form them into cakes, eight in number. The orange peel and sugar plums are to be placed on the top.

853.　SHORTBREAD (Leicestershire)

A quarter of a pound of butter, a quarter of a
pound of flour, two ounces of ground rice, two
ounces of castor sugar, strip of citron peel. Put all
the ingredients in a bowl together ; work well with
the hand until all is mixed into a stiff paste (without
any liquid added). Turn on to a floured board,
press well with the hand until the cracks are out ;
cut into squares and place on each a piece of peel.
Bake on a greased tin until a nice brown colour.

854.　SHORTBREAD BISCUITS (Hertfordshire)

Mix together in a basin a quarter of a pound of
flour, a quarter of a pound of rice flour, two or three
ounces of castor sugar, a pinch of salt. Rub gently
into this a quarter of a pound of fresh butter.
Slightly beat an egg, mix with a tablespoonful of
cream, pour this into the shortbread mixture ; stir
it with a knife.

855.　GINGER SHORTBREAD (Hertfordshire)

Rub a quarter of a pound of butter into half a
pound of flour, to which a pinch of salt, a quarter
of a pound of castor sugar, an eggspoonful of baking
powder, and one and a half teaspoonfuls of ground
ginger has been added. Mix into a paste with an
egg.

856.　SHREWSBURY CAKES (Shropshire)

Beat to a cream one pound of fresh butter ; add
the same quantity of well-dried flour, a pound of
sugar pounded and rolled with a bottle, an ounce

and a half of caraway seeds and six eggs well beaten
in a little orange-flower water ; add, last of all, half
a glass of ratafia, and mix the whole well together ;
make it into a paste, roll to the thickness of a crown-
piece, cut into shapes, and bake on floured tins.

857. SHREWSBURY CAKES (Kent)

Take one pound of butter beaten to a cream, one
and a half pounds of flour sifted and dried, one pound
of loaf sugar, four eggs, a little mace and cinnamon
pounded. Work all together; roll it out thin and
cut it into shapes. To be baked in a slow oven.

858. SHREWSBURY CAKES (Staffordshire)

Take one pound of flour, six ounces of butter,
rubbed into the flour, three-quarters of a pound of
castor sugar, two eggs, leaving out one white. Mix
all well together, first butter, sugar, and flour, then
eggs. Roll out very thin and cut in rounds with a
wineglass or small tumbler, and bake in a slow oven.

859. SILVER CAKE (American)

Take one cupful of butter, half a teaspoonful of
soda, two cupfuls of sugar, one teaspoonful of cream
of tartar, three cupfuls of flour, the whites of six
eggs, half a cupful of milk, one teaspoonful of lemon
juice. Frost with white frost.

860. SIMNEL CAKE (Gloucestershire)

Take a quarter of a pound of flour, three ounces of
mixed peel, quarter of a pound of butter, three good-

sized eggs, quarter of a pound of castor sugar, two
ounces of ground almonds, three-quarters of a pound
of currants. Beat butter to a cream, add sugar and
beaten eggs gradually, and work well together.
Add flour sifted; beat thoroughly, then add remaining ingredients. Line a tin with greased paper,
pour in mixture, and bake in gentle oven from
two to three hours. When cold, make some almond
paste. Put a layer on top of cake. Form remainder
into round balls. Brush the cake over with white of
egg and dust with castor sugar. Set in a cool oven
till balls are lightly browned, and decorate with
crystallised fruits.

861. MRS. STOCKDEL'S SMALL CAKES

(Seventeenth Century)

Take three pounds of very fine flour; add one and
a half pounds of butter, and as much each of currants and of sugar. Add the yolks and half the
whites of seven eggs, well beaten, knead all well
together into a paste, adding one grated nutmeg
and a little rose-water. Make them up about the
bigness of your hand, and bake them upon a tin
plate.

862. SLIM CAKES (Kent)

Take one and a half pints of flour—put one egg
in it, as much milk as will wet it, put one ounce of
butter in the milk, beat it over the fire till the butter
melts—add it to the flour; roll out and bake on a
griddle (or girdle).

863. SODA CAKE (Kent)

Take five ounces of flour, six ounces of raisins, three ounces of brown sugar, two ounces of butter, one egg, a little essence of lemon, and a small teaspoonful of carbonate of soda dissolved in a teacupful of cold milk. Rub the butter into the flour, then add the raisins and sugar, then all the rest by degrees, the soda and milk last, and *bake directly.*

864. ANOTHER WAY

Take two pounds of flour, half a pound of butter, half a pound of currants, one ounce of caraway seeds, two drachms of carbonate of soda, two drachms of ginger, half a pound of sugar, and four eggs. Mix with one pint of new milk. To be baked in a moderate oven for two hours.

865. SODA CAKE (Yorkshire)

One pound of flour, half a pound of lump sugar, half a pound of currants, one gill of milk, four ounces of butter, one teaspoonful of carbonate of soda, one egg. Rub the butter in the flour, and put the milk, sugar, and egg together. Put the currants into the flour, and mix them together before you add the milk, sugar, and egg. Dissolve the carbonate of soda in the milk. Directly you have mixed all together, put in the oven.

866. SPONGE CAKE (Surrey)

Three eggs, their weight in castor sugar, the weight of two eggs in flour, three drops essence of lemon. Beat the eggs and sugar together, till light (quite twenty minutes' good beating), stir in the flour, but do not beat it, add the flavouring, put into a greased and sugared tin, and bake at once in a moderate oven, about thirty minutes.

867. CHEAP SPONGE CAKE (Surrey)

Three eggs, three cupfuls of flour, two cupfuls of sugar, half-cupful of milk, one teaspoonful of cream of tartar, half teaspoonful of soda, lemon. Bake quick. (Breakfast-cups are apparently intended. Ed.)

868. RICH SPONGE CAKE (Hampshire)

Break twelve large eggs into a deep basin, beat for ten minutes, sift in by degrees one pound of castor sugar ; when this has been beaten all together twenty minutes, sift half a pound of pastry flour and half a pound of self-raising flour, previously well mixed together and warmed. Continue to beat, till the time in all is half an hour. Put into tins well buttered and sugared, and bake for one hour.

869. SULTANA CAKE (Devonshire)

Three-quarters of a pound of flour, six ounces of sugar, a quarter of a pound of butter, six ounces of sultanas, one egg, two teaspoonfuls of baking powder, one and a half ounces of citron. Beat butter and sugar to a cream, and add the egg well beaten, mix in the other ingredients, and add to the mixture, if necessary, a little warm milk. Bake one and a half hours.

870. SUSSEX CAKES

To two pounds of well-dried flour, mix three-quarters of a pound of pounded loaf sugar, four ounces of sweet and one ounce of bitter almonds pounded in a little orange-flower water, and one pound of fresh butter beaten to a cream ; mix these well together, bake in small tins, well floured, or drop on small tins.

871. SWEET BISCUITS (Yorkshire)

Take five eggs well beaten, one pound of sugar, one pound of flour ; beat all together half an hour and bake in tins.

872. SWISS ROLLS (Kent)

Take a cupful of sugar, another of flour, three eggs, a little milk ; well beat the eggs, then add together with one teaspoonful of baking-powder, mix well ; grease a baking tray ; pour in ; bake in moderate oven for fifteen minutes. Spread raspberry jam on, and roll up, or fold over.

873. TEA BISCUIT (Surrey)

Four teacupfuls of flour, one heaped teaspoonful of cream of tartar, one *small* teaspoonful of carbonate of soda, butter to taste rubbed into flour. Mix into a dough with milk, not at all stiff, and bake directly in a quick oven. Buttermilk will do instead of cream of tartar.

22

874. LITTLE TEA-BISCUITS (MACAROON AND COCONUT) (Surrey)

Beat up the white of an egg to a stiff froth in a basin. Gradually add half a pound of castor sugar and a few drops of essence of almonds. Mix into a thick white paste, and drop pieces of it, with a spoon, upon a sheet of rice paper or tissue paper, keeping them about half an inch apart. This paper, of course, must be first laid upon the oven sheet. Put the biscuits in a slow oven till they colour to a pale drab, then take them out, and when cold remove them from the paper with a sharp silver knife. A somewhat similar style of biscuits may be made, by substituting a quarter of a pound of grated coconut for the castor sugar and almond essence. About a teaspoonful of sugar will be required only ; and a little cochineal will colour some of these as a pretty variety.

875. TEA CAKES (Middlesex)

Take one pound of flour, half a pound of butter, nine ounces of pounded loaf sugar, the peel of a lemon grated, a few caraway seeds, the yolks and whites of three eggs beaten separately; mix these together into a stiff paste, roll it out, and cut it with a glass; bake upon tins.

876. BUTTERMILK TEA CAKES (Somerset)

Half a pound of flour, three ounces of dripping or butter, a quarter of a pound of sultanas, a teaspoonful of baking powder, a little candied peel and sugar, one small egg, salt. Mix in the flour first, sugar, powder, and salt ; then rub in the dripping, and lastly put in the sultanas and peel ; mix with egg and buttermilk (not too moist). Bake in moderate oven.

877. FRIED TEA CAKES (Somerset)
Very old recipe

One pound of flour, two ounces of currants, two ounces of dripping or lard, one teaspoonful of baking powder. Mix these with milk in the morning, stiff to the consistency of pastry : roll out in the afternoon, a quarter of an inch thick. Cut with a round cutter and fry in boiling lard in a saucepan or deep frying-pan. Serve hot, with castor sugar sprinkled over.

878. POTATO TEA CAKES (Isle of Wight)

Boil some nice potatoes dry, and when cold pass them through a sieve, or mash well. Take three ounces of mashed potatoes, three ounces of flour, one teaspoonful of baking powder and a pinch of salt. Mix all well, and then rub in lightly three ounces of lard or dripping. Add sufficient water to make all into a stiff paste. Roll out thin, cut with round cutters and bake at once. Serve hot with butter. Sultanas or currants and a little sugar added are also liked.

879. TREACLE CAKE (Yorkshire)

Three-quarters of a pound of golden syrup, one and a half pounds of flour, quarter of a pound of sugar (Demerara), two ounces of butter, two ounces of lard, one egg, and one teaspoonful of ground ginger, one teaspoonful of carbonate of soda dissolved in half a teacupful of cold milk. Have the golden syrup hot. Rub in butter and lard to the flour, then add syrup, lastly the egg and milk (with carbonate of soda in). Bake in moderate oven about half an hour in ordinary square or oblong "dripping" tins. Cut in squares when cold.

880. ICED TRIFFIES (Hertfordshire)

Whisk three eggs with five ounces of castor sugar to a stiff batter, and flavour with a few drops of vanilla essence, then sift in five ounces of pastry flour. With the batter, half fill some fancy-shaped bun-tins which are well greased with butter, and bake in a sharp oven from ten to twenty minutes. During this time prepare the icing as follows : Mix in a basin six ounces of pounded sweet almonds, a dessertspoonful of pounded bitter almonds, four ounces of grated chocolate, and four ounces of fine icing sugar. Meanwhile dissolve in a double boiler one ounce of butter and a beaten egg. This dissolved butter and egg should be gradually added to the dry ingredients till the icing is of the right consistency. Spread this over the top and sides of the little cakes, smooth with a knife dipped into boiling water, and set in a cool oven to harden a little. Afterwards place each little cake in a small fancy d'oyley or paper.

881. WAFFLES (Hertfordshire)

Two cupfuls of flour, two eggs, one teaspoonful of baking powder, one and a quarter cupfuls of milk, one tablespoonful of creamed butter, a pinch of salt.

Mix flour, baking powder, and salt together. Mix
yolks with milk, then mix with the dry ingredients,
adding last the whites and creamed butter. Have
the waffle iron very hot and well greased with
lard, bake on both sides until a nice deep brown.
(Breakfast-cups are indicated. Ed.)

882. WALNUT CAKE (Hertfordshire)

Six whites, six yolks of eggs, six ounces of flour,
half a pound of sugar, half a pound of butter, half a
teaspoonful of baking powder, one pound of walnuts,
three drops of vanilla. Chop walnuts very finely
(there should be six ounces when shelled), beat
butter and sugar to a cream, add yolks one by one,
whisk whites very firmly, add walnuts to the
whites, add flour and whites alternately.

883. WENNINGTON CAKES (Yorkshire)

Take half a pound of flour, half a pound of lump
sugar, six ounces of butter rubbed into the flour, a
few currants or almonds, which you please ; three
eggs, the rind of a lemon grated ; mix all well
together, lay them in lumps upon the tins—a few
minutes will bake them.

884. THE MOST WHOLESOME OF CAKES (Surrey)

Two pounds of wholemeal flour, half a pound
of raisins, half a pound of sultanas, half a pound
of butter, half a pound of moist sugar (more if
liked), one teaspoonful of mixed spice, two large
teaspoonfuls of yeast powder ; mix with about
a pint of new milk. Rub the butter into the

dry meal. Add all the other dry ingredients, then stir in the milk as quickly and lightly as possible with a wooden spoon; no kneading required. Turn out at once into two well-buttered baking-tins, place immediately in a good but not over-heated oven. Bake about two hours, taking care not to burn.

885. WIGGS (Yorkshire, 1769)

Take two pounds of flour, one pound of butter, one pint of cream, four eggs (leaving out two of the whites), and two tablespoonfuls of yeast. Mix well and let it rise a little. Then add half a pound of sugar, and half a pound of caraway comfits, make up the dough with these, and bake in a dripping pan.

CHAPTER XIX

BREAD, ROLLS, BUNS, MUFFINS, TEA-CAKES, SCONES, ETC.

NOTE.—That the art and practice of making our own bread has, in large measure, died out from among us, is one of the most lamentable signs of modern so-called civilisation. We allow the baker, with his alum, bone-flour, and other unnecessary ingredients, to supply us with that " staff of life," which should surely be a sound and trustworthy staff if it is to be any good at all. We speak of home-made bread as though it were some treasure beyond our attainment. Now, in remote country villages, where brewer's yeast is almost unprocurable, one can understand the art of bread-making dwindling down to nothing ; although, even there, yeast can be made quite easily—witness the recipes at the end of this section. But in towns, where the breweries are only too glad to get rid of their yeast for the asking, there need be no such difficulty. (I do not allude to German or composition yeast ; it really is not a patch upon the genuine article.) Then, the absence of the old-fashioned brick oven is a great drawback in towns ; but here, again, some of the best bread I have ever eaten was baked by a Hammersmith woman in an

343

oil-stove. The *Daily Mail* bread-making competition
proved, to the satisfaction of all well-wishers to
humanity, that there are still many wives and
mothers who have solved one of the secrets of good
health ; for that home-made bread and good health
are frequently synonymous, is a fact to be verified
by experience.

The few and uninteresting breads, buns, scones,
etc., obtainable at a shop, can be supplemented
—or, I hope, replaced—from the following list, with
the most varied and toothsome productions. I
desire to commend this section to everybody who
can appreciate the difference between bread made
for eating, and bread made for selling. It is a difference not to be stated in mere words.

Amongst minor items, the reader should particularly note the delicious Cornish Saffron Buns.

886. TO MAKE HOUSEHOLD BREAD OR ROLLS
(Middlesex)

Take ten pounds of flour, and three quarts of water
which is about lukewarm, if in summer, and rather
warmer in winter. Put the water in a large pan,
and add a tablespoonful of salt. Add a portion of
the flour, stirring it up well, until it is of the consistency of butter, adding rather more than a pint
of good yeast; then add more flour, mixing the
whole well, and put the pan, covered with a cloth,
and throwing flour over the dough, before the fire
for a few minutes. About a third of the flour is to
be kept back in the first operation, and this is to be
well kneaded in when the mixture which has been

placed before the fire has risen properly. Put the
dough again before the fire, and let it rise for a few
minutes, then knead again, and bake in a quick oven,
having previously put the dough into pans, and
pricked the surface of the dough with a fork, and
placed it again before the fire in the pans. The
baking, in an ordinary oven, will require about an
hour for a four-pound loaf and fifty minutes for a
loaf of three pounds. If a heated oven is used,
it must be well-heated before the dough is put
into it. If potatoes be mixed with the bread in
the proportion of an ounce to two ounces to the
one pound, the flavour, (to some people's thinking)
will be improved. The potatoes must be first
boiled in their skins, then skinned, and when
dry, rubbed well up in milk or water boiled and allowed to stand for a few minutes before it is used.
Then add the mixture to the dish in which the dough
is mixed. Rice may also be used. Take a pound
of rice to ten pounds of wheat flour, boil it in one
quart of water till the rice has become a complete
pulp. Strain off the water, and beat the rice well in
a mortar until it is completely crushed, and is
entirely dissolved, then add the water in which it
was boiled, and a pint of milk, and boil the whole together for an hour. Strain off the liquid and add it
to the dish in which the dough is made, suppressing
as much water from the process as the quantity of
liquid obtained from the boiling of the rice will
supply. The dough must in all cases be thoroughly
kneaded. Filtered rain water is the best to use
for bread-making ; if the water be hard, a drachm
of carbonate of soda may be added to three quarts
of water, but this is unnecessary when the water

is of a soft nature. If rolls are to be made, take a portion of the dough and mix it up with a few tablespoonfuls of cream, in which the whipped whites of two or three eggs have been put ; knead them carefully, and add a little flour if they be too moist. The dough for rolls should be taken off when it has risen the second time, as above stated, before the fire. After taking the dough from the fire the second time, it must be kneaded for half an hour on a board strewed with flour, if intended for loaves, but the rolls will not require more than five or six minutes kneading. They are then to be baked in a quick oven until they are nicely browned. A minute or two before they are done, they should be taken out of the oven, and a brush dipped in the white of egg passed over the top ; then they are to be put into the oven again for one or two minutes. When there is reason to suspect, either from the appearance or smell of the flour, that it is not good, and there is still a necessity for using it, let it be baked for an hour in a very slack oven, and add to it, when making into dough, about ten grains of fresh carbonate of ammonia, carefully powdered, for every pound of flour. This will frequently correct any bad qualities of the flour, and render the bread palatable. Milk may be substituted for water in the manufacture of bread, but it does not improve the flavour if the flour be good.

887. HOME-MADE BREAD (Middlesex)

One quartern of best flour, half an ounce of German yeast, one teaspoonful of salt, one and three-quarter

pints of warm water. Mix all into a dough, put
into a wooden or earthen basin, cover with a thick
cloth, stand it in a warm corner of the kitchen, let
it rise for two or three hours. Knead it up well,
put it in two baking tins, bake in a brisk oven.

888. HOME-MADE BREAD (Essex)

Take one and a quarter pounds of flour, two
ounces of yeast, one saltspoonful of salt, and about
one pint of milk or more, with a little warm water to
make the temperature of blood heat. Have a deep
basin, or better still a small bread-pan, put the flour
in and pile it all round the sides of the basin to
make a deep hole in the centre, mix the yeast in a
cup with a little milk and water till it is nice and
smooth but not thick. Now pour it into the centre
of the flour and sprinkle a little flour on the top of
the yeast, cover the basin with a cloth and put it in
front of the fire, to rise for about an hour, continually turning the basin round. Then mix lightly
with a wooden spoon so that the yeast is well mixed
in the flour; then, with the hand, mix in gradually
the milk and water, till the dough is nice and light
but not too moist. Put the basin on a chair and
knead well with the knuckles till the dough looks
nice and smooth. Butter a tin or tins, put the
dough in, cover with a cloth and place in front of the
fire to rise nicely but not too much. Now have a
nice hot oven ready, put the bread on the lower
shelf for three-quarters of an hour, and then on
upper shelf with a greased paper on top of the tins
for another three-quarters of an hour. Watch it

about every twenty minutes, for to open the oven too often spoils the bread.

For making brown bread use wholemeal flour instead of the ordinary flour.

889. CORN BREAD (Ireland)

To one quart of sifted meal add one teacupful of cream, three eggs, a teaspoonful of carbonate of soda dissolved in water, enough buttermilk to make it quite soft ; stir well, and bake in a baking kettle or oven.

890. ITALIAN BREAD

Make a stiff dough, with twelve tablespoonfuls of fine flour, six of white powdered sugar, three eggs, the raspings of a lemon, and two ounces of fresh butter ; mix them in a pan with a wooden spoon, and if the dough is not sufficiently firm, add more flour and sugar. Then turn it out and work it well with the hand, cut it into the shape of round long biscuits, and glaze them with white of egg. They are then to be baked in a hot oven.

891. MANNHEIM BREAD (German)

Take two eggs, six tablespoonfuls of flour, three of sugar, some salt, and a little essence of aniseed to give it a flavour ; when worked well together, cut into pieces as above, and bake in a quick oven.

892. POTATO BREAD (French)

Take the quantity of potatoes required ; boil them in their skins. When done, peel them, and bruise them with a rolling-pin to the consistence of a paste. To this add as much flour as there is potato pulp, and some yeast. Knead them well, putting as much water as may be necessary. When properly kneaded, form into loaves, and place in the oven, taking care that it be not quite so hot as for common bread, or it will become hard on the outside before the inside is properly baked. The door of the oven should not be closed so soon as on ordinary occasions. This bread must be allowed longer time to bake than any other.

893. YANKEE BROWN BREAD (Ireland)

To two quarts of corn meal, pour one quart of boiling water ; stir yeast into two quarts of rye meal, and knead all together with two quarts of water lukewarm. Add, if you choose, one gill of molasses.

894. LITTLE LOAVES (Kent)

One quart of flour, one small teaspoonful of soda, as much tartaric acid as would fit on a sixpence, mixed with either milk or water, a pinch of salt. Mix the salt and soda with the flour, then dissolve the tartaric acid in the milk, and make your dough.

895. FRENCH ROLLS

Two pounds of fine flour, two tablespoonfuls of fresh table-beer yeast, a full pint of warm water or milk, a little salt. Mix all together, and make the dough quite tender ; cover it over with a napkin and let it rise before the fire about half an hour, then mould it into rolls, and let them rise about half an hour more ; bake them half an hour in a quick oven.

896.   MILK ROLLS (Devonshire)

Half a pound of flour, one teaspoonful of baking
powder, a pinch of salt, one ounce of butter, a teacupful of cold milk. Sift the flour, baking powder,
and salt, and mix well ; rub in butter, mix with the
milk, make quickly into rolls, and bake at once;
brush over with milk when half baked.

897.   SUFFOLK RUSKS

Half a pound of flour, one egg, and a little milk.
Three ounces of butter, salt, and baking powder.
Work all together as for pastry, and cut into rounds
with a cutter, and bake. When nearly done, take
out and cut in half ; bake again for a few minutes.
To be eaten with butter or cheese.

898.   RUSKS (Kent)

Three pounds of fine flour, three ounces of fresh
butter, three ounces of sugar. Rub all together. Lay
a leaven with a few tablespoonfuls of yeast and three
eggs beaten together. Let it stand for half an hour,
then mix it up with a pint of warm milk. After it
has stood half an hour longer, make it into small
loaves ; when baked as much as cakes of the same
size should be, put them back into the oven to dry.

899.   TOPS AND BOTTOMS (Kent)

Two eggs, one pound of flour, three ounces of
butter. The butter to be dissolved in a sufficient
quantity of milk to make it into a stiff paste, with
as much yeast as will make it light. Afterwards
roll it out, and cut them into whatever shapes you

please. Put them on tins in a warm place for twenty minutes, then in rather a cool oven ; when cooked through, divide them and put them again in the oven till quite crisp.

BUNS

900. BUNS AND FRENCH BREAD (Hertfordshire)

Two pounds of flour, two ounces of sugar, two ounces of butter, two ounces of German yeast, two eggs, one pint of milk. Dissolve yeast in a little warm water, make a well in centre of flour, pour it in ; well whisk eggs, add the milk made hot, and mix all into a light dough ; heat it for about ten minutes, then leave it to rise and make into any shapes preferred. For the buns, add a little more sugar and sultanas ; if for dough cakes, raisins ; always leave to rise for about half an hour, when made into shapes ; then bake in a quick oven ; half an hour for dough cake ; ten minutes each for buns and rolls.

901. BROWN MEAL BUNS (Hertfordshire)

One pound of fine meal, six ounces of butter, three ounces of sugar, one teaspoonful of baking powder, two eggs.

902. BATH BUNS (Kent, 1809)

Four eggs, yolks and whites, beaten up and mixed in two spoonfuls of table-beer yeast, and strained through a sieve ; eight ounces of butter, melted in half a pint of milk, and mixed with the eggs and yeast into two pounds of flour ; make it up into

dough, and let it rise an hour and a half. Mix
seven ounces of sifted sugar in the dough, and
make it up into twelve cakes, then let them rise
three hours and a half, taking care not to place
them too near the fire. Strew a little sifted sugar
over them before baking.

903. BUTTERMILK BUNS (Kent)

Three pounds of flour, half an ounce of carbonate
of soda, well-pounded and mixed with one teaspoonful of ground spice and two teaspoonfuls of
salt which must then be well mixed with the flour ;
three and a quarter pounds of moist sugar and a
tablespoonful of caraway seeds. The oven should
be rather hotter than for bread. When the oven
is quite ready, add to the ingredients sufficient
buttermilk to make it into a thin batter, which
must be dropped with a spoon on a floured tin.

904. COBURG BUNS (Northumberland)

Three ounces of castor sugar, four ounces of
butter, six ounces of flour, two eggs, half a teaspoonful of carbonate of soda, half a teaspoonful
of cinnamon, one teaspoonful of ground ginger, half
a teaspoonful of nutmeg, two teaspoonfuls of golden
syrup. Beat the butter and sugar to a cream, add
the eggs well beaten, mix in the dry ingredients
(which have been previously well mixed in a basin)
without beating, add the syrup last. This mixture
fills one dozen small tins. If liked, put split almonds
in the bottom of each tin. Be sure to butter or
lard the tins very thoroughly. Bake in a sharp
oven until nicely browned.

905. COFFEE BUNS (Somerset)

Six ounces of butter, six ounces of Demerara sugar, six ounces of sultanas, a quarter of a pound of flour, one and a half teaspoonfuls baking powder, two eggs. Cream the butter and sugar, add the well-beaten eggs gradually with a little flour, lastly add all the dry ingredients, mix to a stiff paste, form into round balls with the hands pressed slightly. Place on a greased baking sheet; brush over with egg, and bake in a fairly quick oven twenty to thirty minutes. Sufficient for two dozen buns.

906. EASTER BUNS (Surrey)

Take one cupful of yeast, three of milk, and enough flour to make a thick batter : mix lightly, and set it over-night. Next morning, add one cupful of sugar, half a cupful of butter, melted (but not creamed), half a nutmeg, one saltspoonful salt, and sufficient flour to make the mixture roll out like biscuit. Mix and knead all well, and leave it for five hours to rise. Then roll it out half an inch thick, cut it into round cakes, lay them on a buttered baking-sheet for half an hour ; then mark a cross on each with a knife, and bake immediately till they are a good light brown. They can be brushed with white of egg and sugar. (Tea-cups indicated. Ed.)

907. LEMON BUNS (Kent)

One pound of flour, quarter of a pound of butter, two ounces of sugar, two ounces of lump sugar, rubbed on the rind of one lemon ; squeeze the lemon-

23

juice into the ingredients. Dissolve your butter in half a teacupful of warm milk. Mix well with a wooden spoon, drop them on your baking-sheet, and bake in a quiet oven twenty minutes. When half done, sprinkle some powdered sugar on them.

908. PLAIN BUNS (Kent)

Rub four ounces of butter into two pounds of flour, mix in four ounces of sugar, one nutmeg, a few Jamaica peppers, a dessertspoonful of caraways. Put one or two spoonfuls of cream into a tea-cup of yeast, and as much milk as will make it into a light paste. Set it to rise by the fire till the oven is ready. Bake on tins.

909. PLAIN BUNS (Cape Colony)

Two full breakfastcupfuls of flour, three-quarters of a breakfast-cupful of sugar, two to four ounces of butter or beef dripping, one nutmeg grated, two eggs, two teaspoonfuls of baking powder, a pinch of salt, and enough milk to mix the whole into a fairly moist dough. Stir the butter (which should be soft), sugar, and eggs together with a spoon, add a little milk. Mix all the dry ingredients and add gradually to the rest ; if the dough is too stiff, put a little more milk. Place large spoonfuls on baking tin, sprinkle white sugar on each bun. Bake from ten to twenty minutes according to heat of the stove.

910. SAFFRON BUNS (Cornwall)

To half a quartern of dough add a quarter of a pound of currants, two ounces of grated lemon-peel, Demerara sugar to taste (say about quarter of a pound), half a teaspoonful of mixed spice, six ounces of lard or dripping, two-pennyworth of saffron (pour boiling water on this and leave it overnight); warm the dough and melt the lard before mixing, and add (while the mixture is not too hot) two well-beaten eggs. Do not let the lard be too hot. Knead all together with the hands, then leave in a warm place covered with a cloth, until the whole has " plimmed up " or risen ; then divide into small lumps, place on a greased tin, and bake in a slow oven until slightly coloured.

(For other buns, see Chap. XVIII.)

911. CURRANT LOAF (Hertfordshire)

Two pounds of flour, a quarter of a pound of butter, five ounces of sugar, five ounces of currants, five ounces of sultanas, three ounces of candied peel, three eggs, three-quarters of a pint of warm milk, a pinch of salt, one pennyworth of German yeast. Rub butter into flour, add fruit and sugar, beat up eggs, milk, and yeast, set aside for a little time, then knead and stand aside to rise. Bake in good oven.

SCONES

912. SCONE FLOUR (Hertfordshire)

Eight pounds of flour, one ounce of soda, two ounces of cream of tartar.

913. SCONES (Devonshire)

One pound of flour, three and a half ounces of lard, three ounces of white sugar, half an ounce of cream of tartar, a quarter of an ounce of carbonate of soda, one ounce of sultanas, one egg, one pinch of salt, little milk. Mix all the dry ingredients together, then add the eggs and milk, and mix to a nice dough, not too stiff; roll out on floured board half an inch thick, cut into diamond shapes, allow them to rise before the fire for ten minutes. Bake for twenty minutes in moderate oven.

914. SCONES (Hertfordshire)

One pound of flour, two ounces of butter, two ounces of sugar, a quarter of an ounce of carbonate of soda, a quarter of an ounce of cream of tartar, one egg. Bake twenty minutes.

915. SCONES (Kent)

I

One pound of flour or brown meal; rub into it two ounces of butter, one teaspoonful of baking powder, one teaspoonful of pounded white sugar, and a little salt. Mix with lukewarm milk to a stiff paste; roll out, cut with a tumbler or tin circle into rounds, and bake them on a tin. To be eaten hot, cut in halves and buttered—or toasted next day.

916. ANOTHER WAY

Half a pound of finest flour, two ounces of butter, a pinch of salt and of sugar, a teaspoonful of baking powder, and three-quarters of a gill of milk. Rub the butter into the flour with the sugar, salt, and baking powder, and mix in the milk with an iron spoon as lightly as possible. Roll out with a little flour to the thickness of an inch, and cut into three-cornered shapes. Bake in a quick oven twenty minutes, and serve up on a napkin. For these scones wholemeal flour can be used if preferred to white.

917. ANOTHER WAY

One pound of flour, one ounce of butter, two teaspoonfuls of baking powder, two teaspoonfuls of castor sugar, half a pint of milk, a little salt. Rub the butter in the flour, then add the baking powder, sugar, and salt. To be sent to the table hot.

918. IRISH SCONES

Six tablespoonfuls of plain flour, one tablespoonful of Paisley flour, one tablespoonful of lard, half a saltspoonful of salt. Mix with milk and roll out on a board. Cut with sharp round cutter, and bake in a quick oven. May be served either hot or cold, with butter.

919. SCOTCH SCONES (Lancashire)

One pound of flour, three tablespoonfuls of sugar, three ounces of dripping or butter, one tablespoonful of bicarbonate of soda, two teaspoonfuls of cream of tartar, one teacupful of milk. Mix flour and sugar, soda and tartar, rub in butter, mix up with milk, roll out and cut into scone shapes, and bake twenty or thirty minutes.

920. SODA SCONES (Scottish)

Eight tablespoonfuls of flour, two teaspoonfuls of cream of tartar, one teaspoonful of carbonate of soda, a little salt. Mix well together, dry; then rub in a little butter, about the size of a nut, and make all into a soft dough, with a little milk or milk-and-water. Put it on a well-floured board, roll it out about half an inch thick. Cut it into rounds with a cutter, or roll it out in one large round and divide it in four. Bake for about ten minutes in a moderate oven.

921. WHEATMEAL SCONES (Isle of Wight)

Half a pound of wheatmeal, one teaspoonful of sugar, a pinch of salt, one or two ounces of butter, one and a half teaspoonfuls of baking powder. Rub the butter into the meal, add the salt, sugar, and baking powder. Mix to a stiff paste with cream or milk; turn on to a floured board, roll out about half an inch thick. Cut with a round cutter, or in triangles. Bake about fifteen minutes. Serve hot or cold, with butter.

CRUMPETS, ETC.

922. CRUMPETS (Kent)

Set two pounds of flour with a little salt before the fire till quite warm; then mix it with warm milk and water till it is stiff as it can be stirred. Let the milk be as warm as it can be borne with the finger. Put a cupful of this with three eggs well beaten and mixed with three tablespoonfuls of very thick yeast; then put this to the batter and beat all well together in a large pan or bowl; add as much milk and water as will make it into a thick batter; cover it close, and put it before the fire to rise. Put a bit of butter in a piece of thin muslin, tie it up, and rub it lightly on the heated frying pan ; then pour over sufficient batter at a time to make one crumpet. Let it do slowly, and it will be very light. Cook them all the same way. They should not be brown but of a fine yellow.

923. MUFFINS (Middlesex)

Mix a quartern of fine flour, one and a half pints of warm milk and water, with a quarter of a pint of good yeast and a little salt. Stir them together for a quarter of an hour, then strain the liquor into a quarter of a peck of fine flour ; mix the dough well, and set it to rise for an hour. Then roll it up and pull into small pieces ; make them up in the hand like balls, and lay a flannel on them while rolling, to keep them warm. The dough should be closely covered the whole time. When the whole is rolled into balls, the first that is made will be ready for baking. When they are spread out in the right form for muffins, lay them on tins and bake them, and as the bottoms begin to change colour, turn them on the other side.

924. PIKELETS (Staffordshire)

Take one and a half pounds of flour, half an ounce of carbonate of soda, a pinch of salt, and mix them to a batter with one quart of buttermilk. Have ready a hot iron plate or a heated frying pan, either of which must be rubbed with a piece of fat bacon before putting in the batter. Allow one small tea-cupful of batter for each pikelet. When it is a light brown, raise and turn it over gently with a sharp knife.

925. SALLY LUNN (Lancashire)

Make a light dough, using a little more yeast than in making a loaf. Mix with warm milk, with a little butter dissolved in it and a pinch of salt. Leave it to rise in the tin in which it is to be baked.

926. SALLY LUNN (Kent)

Beat up two eggs, melt a quarter of a pound of butter, one tablespoonful of thick barm, put all into a quart of flour with as much rich warm milk as you will want to wet it. Beat all with a spoon; let it stand for an hour, and bake in a pan.

927. SPLITS (Kent)

One pound of flour, one ounce of butter to be rubbed into it, two teaspoonfuls of baking powder, half a pint of milk; to be rolled out about an inch thick, and cut out with a small tin shape.

928. TEA-CAKES (Lancashire)

Put a halfpennyworth of barm into a little warm milk, then rub three ounces of butter into one and a half pounds of flour, and set it to rise. Beat up one egg, and put it in when you knead it, then let it rise again when you put it in your tins, before you bake the cakes.

929. TEA-CAKES (Yorkshire)

I

Take one quart of sifted flour and three spoonfuls of baking powder, mix them well together, and then rub one tablespoonful of lard into the flour, and moisten with water, kneading till you get a dough. Roll it on a pie board until thin, and cut in round cakes and bake immediately.

II

Take half a peck of flour, half a pint of yeast, one pound of currants, one pound of butter, half a pound of sugar, one ounce of caraway seeds ; to be made into large cakes. Set to rise a short time before being put into the oven.

930. TO MAKE BARM OR YEAST (Cheshire)

I

Boil one ounce of hops in six quarts of water till the hops fall to the bottom, then strain, and when blood-warm, add two tablespoonfuls of sugar and three pints of flour. Leave it at the fire two days, stirring it frequently—then add one pound of boiled potatoes, bruised, and well mixed through the barm. Strain all through a colander and set it by the fire till it rises in the vessel. Keep it in a cool place covered. One pint will answer for eight quarts of flour.

931. ANOTHER WAY.

A handful of hops to a breakfastcupful of malt. Pour four to five quarts of boiling water on it, and let it simmer down to about three quarts. Then strain, and when milkwarm, add half a pint of flour, and some old barm. Leave it a day to rise, and bottle it that day or the next.

932. TO MAKE BARM OR YEAST (Lancashire)

Half a pound of bruised malt, half an ounce of
hops, four ounces of sugar, four ounces of salt, two
gallons of water. Boil for an hour in a very clean
pan. Have ready two pounds of fine flour rubbed
very smooth with cold water in a deep mug (pan).
Strain the boiling liquid on the flour while some one
stirs it with a wooden spoon. About one quart of
old barm should be put to the new while it is warm.
Let it stand to work for two days and then cork it up
very tightly. Shake the bottle *well* before using it ;
it is better two or three days old. Fourteen pounds
of flour will require two teacupfuls of barm.

CHAPTER XX

BEVERAGES

NOTE.—In the olden days of home-brewed ale, a great many wines and beers were also made. Some of these, " tasting of Flora and the country green," in rural districts still survive.

The Surrey cottager regards the elder-bloom in the hedges as significant of the coming elderberry wine that shall " hearten a man up," as he puts it, in a drear-nighted December : elderberry wine and Christmas are for him synonymous. Cowslip wine, sweet, sticky, and innocuous—rhubarb, and turnip, and blackberry wine, are yet immensely popular in provincial places : and " currant wine is very good," as Jenny Wren said in the nursery rhyme.

But aerated drinks have largely superseded these pleasant beverages ; and the old-time recipes are rapidly becoming obsolete. Amongst those ensuing I would call attention to the various formulas for ginger beer—which is cheap, wholesome, and refreshing—to the home-made cordials and liqueurs, and to the notes on coffee and tea-making. It should be noted that many cottage wines are spoiled by the use of brown sugar, which renders them somewhat coarse and crude in flavour. White preserving sugar is nowadays just as cheap, and much more refined to the taste.

HOME-MADE WINES (ALCOHOLIC)

933. APPLE WINE (1822)

To make a wine nearly equal to the Rhenish, you must, to every gallon of the juice of apples, immediately after it comes from the press, add two pounds of common loaf sugar. Boil it as long as any scum rises ; strain it through a sieve, and let it cool ; add some good yeast, and stir it well. Let it work in the tub for two or three weeks, or till the head begins to flatten, then skim off the head, draw it clear off, and turn it. When it has been made a year, rack it off, and fine it with isinglass ; then add to every three gallons half a pint of the best rectified spirits of wine, or one pint of brandy (see note to No. 940). This wine will be found very superior.

934. BLACKBERRY WINE (Essex)

Put any quantity of blackberries in a pan, just cover them with boiling water, and allow them to stand in a cool oven or outside the cooking-stove all night to draw the juice; or the berries may be mashed with a mallet.

Measure and strain into a cask or stone bottle, and allow the juice to ferment for a fortnight. No yeast is required. Then add one pound of loaf sugar to every gallon of the wine, with a quarter of a pint of best brandy (see note, No. 940). It may be bottled in six months, but will improve by keeping.

935. BALM WINE (Yorkshire, 1769)

Put a peck of balm leaves in a tub or large jar, heat four gallons of water scalding hot, ready to

boil, then pour it upon the leaves. Let it stand all
night, then strain it off through a hair sieve. To
every gallon of liquid put two pounds of fine sugar,
and stir up very well. Take the whites of four or
five eggs, beat them very well, put them into a pan
with the liquor. Whisk it well before it be over
hot ; when the scum begins to rise take it off, and
keep it skimmed all the time it is boiling. Let it
boil three-quarters of an hour; then put it into the
tub. When it is cold, put a little new yeast upon it,
and beat it in, every two hours, that it may head
the better. So work it for two days, then put it into
a sweet keg, bung it up close, and when it is clear,
bottle.

936. COWSLIP WINE (1815)

To one gallon of water put four pounds of loaf
sugar, boil and skim it as long as any scum rises ;
to each gallon of water put the rind of a lemon or
orange, and boil with the sugar and water three
gallons of the flowers of cowslips. Let them boil
three minutes, then put it into a tub, and when
almost cold, toast a bit of bread and spread it with
very thick yeast, put it in the liquor, and let it
stand two nights : when you put it into the cask,
add all the juice of the orange or lemon which you
pared ; and if you make ten gallons of wine, you
must put two quarts of brandy, and so on in proportion for any quantity you wish to make. (See
note, No. 940.)

937. COWSLIP WINE (Surrey)

Boil twelve pounds of loaf sugar, with the juice of six Seville oranges, and the whites of three or four eggs well beaten, in six gallons of water, for half an hour, carefully skimming it all the time. In the meanwhile, put a peck of the finest and freshest picked cowslip flowers into a tub, with the rinds of two or three of the oranges, and, pouring on them the boiling syrup, stir the whole up, and leave it, well covered, to infuse. On its getting nearly cold, spread a thin toast of bread all over with good yeast, and put it into the tub to excite a fermentation. After it has worked two or three days, strain it off, having first pressed the cowslips in a coarse cloth to strain out all the juice. Having turned it up, keep the bung loose for a few days, and on finding the wine has ceased to work, which is always known by its ceasing to hiss, drive the bung tight. Let the liquor remain undisturbed for about three months and then bottle it off, either for present or future use. If, on running the wine, about a quarter of a pint of brandy be put in for every gallon (see note, No. 940), with a quarter of a gill of syrup of citrons, lemons, or clove gilly-flowers, it will make a very fine addition to its strength and flavour. (This is the best recipe of the three. Ed.)

938. ANOTHER WAY

To two gallons of water and half a peck of cowslip flowers, add two and a half pounds of powdered sugar. Boil them for half an hour, and take off the scum as it rises. Then pour it into a tub to cool, with the rinds of two lemons. Let it stand in the tub for two days, stirring it every two or three hours, and then put it into a barrel. Let it stand a month; bottle it, and put a lump of loaf sugar in each bottle.

939. CURRANT WINE (1815)

To three quarts of water add two quarts of currant juice and four pounds of good powdered sugar; let it stand two or three days before you put it into the cask; and if you make ten gallons, add three quarts of brandy (see note, No. 940), and one gallon of raspberry juice mixed with four pounds of sugar. Put the bung in, but do not stop it close till it has done hissing, which perhaps will not cease in less than a fortnight; then stop it close, and let it stand twelve months, if you make a large quantity. *N.B.* —As currant wine is seldom two years alike, on account of the different seasons for ripening the currants, it will be proper to try the wine in four or five months after it is made, as the sweetness goes off much sooner some years than others, but it will generally require to stand twelve months or more. If it is made with loaf sugar, it is fit to drain off much sooner; but the wine is not so strong as that made of powdered sugar. The raspberry juice and brandy should not be mixed with the wine till it is put into the cask.

940. CURRANT WINE (1822)

For a fine currant wine, take black currants, red currants, white currants, ripe cherries, raspberries, and strawberries, of each an equal quantity. To every four pounds, well bruised, add one gallon of

clear soft water. Steep three days and nights in
open vessel, and stir the mass frequently. Then
strain through a sieve, and press the pulp to dryness.
To each gallon of liquor put three pounds of good,
rich moist sugar. Let the whole stand three days,
skim the top, and stir frequently. Put it into
casks, to purge at the bung, for about a fortnight;
then to every nine gallons you can add a quart
of good brandy, and close the cask. Isinglass
finings may be applied, if necessary.

NOTE: Some of the finest-flavoured and strongest-
bodied home-made wines I ever met with, were made
without any addition whatever of brandy; and the
excellence they had attained from age, was a proof
that brandy was not necessary merely to enable them
to keep.

941. CURRANT WINE (Kent)

To every quart of juice put two quarts of water,
and to every gallon three and a half pounds of sugar.
Let it ferment in the cask three days, and then
bung it down with a quarter of a pint of brandy to
each gallon (see note to above, No. 940).

All home-made wines are better if you first boil
the sugar and water together, and add the juice when
cold.

Grape wines are made in the same proportion.

The fruit should be gathered in a dry season and
when quite ripe.

942. ELDERBERRY WINE (Essex)

Remove the berries from the stems and if necessary wash them. Place in a pan, mash well, and

pour over boiling water in the proportion of three quarts to four quarts of berries. Let them remain for twenty-four hours, then strain and press out all the juice that can be forced through the strainer. For every two quarts of juice add one and three-quarters of a pound of loaf sugar, a dozen allspice, an inch of ginger root, and a teaspoonful each of caraway seeds and powdered cinnamon. Boil all together for five minutes, and when quite cold, put in half an ounce of compressed yeast, which has been stirred till liquid with a teaspoonful of sugar. The fermentation will commence in a short time, and when it is quite finished the wine may be bottled.

As this wine is rather heady, many people prefer to substitute elder syrup, which can be made like blackberry syrup, and will make a nice hot drink for winter evenings.

943. ELDERBERRY WINE (Surrey)

Take five gallons of ripe elderberries, and boil them in ten quarts of water for half an hour. Then strain through a sieve, but do not squeeze the berries. Pour back the liquor into the boiler, measuring it. To every gallon add three and a half pounds of sugar, with the peels and juice of five or six lemons. Boil twenty minutes, and when at boiling point, add the well-beaten whites of five or six eggs. Stir all well, and fill the cask. When the liquor has cooled enough, put in some yeast, or a bit of toast with yeast on. When it is ready to be bunged, half a pound of bruised race ginger, in a muslin bag, should be tied so as to hang in the middle of the cask. In two months it will be ready to bottle.

24

944. ELDERBERRY WINE (Sussex)

Take about twenty pounds of very ripe elderberries (picked from the stalks), and put them into a deep earthen pan or small tub, with just enough water to cover them. Crush them every now and then with some heavy utensil, till all the juice is out of the berries. Then strain the liquor into a pan for boiling, with three pounds of Demerara sugar to every gallon of juice. Add some cloves, a stick of mace, the same of cinnamon, and six or seven pieces good " race " ginger. Let this boil for about one and a quarter hours, then pour it back into the former vessel (cleaned ready to receive it), and when it is fairly cold, put in a little yeast on a bit of toast, cover it up and leave it to work. In about five days you can strain out the wine into a cask, and leave the bunghole half open till fermentation ceases, when it must be securely fastened and left so for three months.

945. GINGER WINE (1815)

To five gallons of water put seven pounds of powdered sugar ; boil it a quarter of an hour, take the scum off as it rises, put the liquor into a tub, and, when cold, add six pounds of sun raisins. Have ready five ounces of ginger boiled in two quarts of water till it is reduced to one quart, and the peels of two large lemons boiled with it ; when it is cold put this to the liquor, with two ounces of isinglass. Toast a bit of bread, and spread it thick with good yeast, and put it in ; let it stand in the tub one night, take out the bread and put it into the cask

with a pint of brandy (see note, No. 940); stop it close
and let it stand six weeks, and it will be fit to bottle.

946. GINGER WINE (Kent, 1809)

Seven gallons of water, seven pounds of lump
sugar, half a pound of ginger well bruised; boil it all
one hour, then add the whites of four eggs, well
beaten to clarify it, and skim it well when boiled;
strain it into a tub, and let it stand till it is quite
cold, then put into a vessel, with the peels and juice
of seven lemons cut very thin, and two spoonfuls of
yeast. Stop the cask close. In a fortnight it will
be fit for bottling, and in a fortnight more for drinking. *N.B.*—The juice of the lemons should be passed
through a colander, or strainer, and the egg-shells
be boiled in it.

947. GOOSEBERRY WINE (1822)

To every two gallons of full-ripe gooseberries,
mashed, add an equal quantity of soft water, milk-
warm, and one pound of refined sugar, in process of
dissolving. Stir up the whole in a tub, and cover
with a blanket, to preserve the heat of fermentation.
Stir frequently for three days, then strain—first
through a sieve, and secondly through a coarse
cloth. The liquor must then be put into a cask,
kept full, and allowed to ferment from ten days to
three weeks, when two or three bottles of brandy
(see note, No. 940), according to the size of the
cask, in the proportion of one to eight, may be
poured in, with the same quantity of sherry,
together with a small quantity of isinglass, perfectly
dissolved in water. Close the cask tightly, and if

at the end of a fortnight it is not sweet enough,
add more sugar. Close finally for six months, and
then bottle ; or sooner, if it is wished to imitate
sparkling champagne.

948. GREEN GOOSEBERRY WINE (Lancashire)

Gather gooseberries when quite hard and sour.
To every pound of fruit when picked and bruised
put one quart of cold spring water. Let it stand
three days, stirring it twice every day. To every
gallon of juice, when strained, add three pounds of
loaf sugar. Put it in a brandy cask and to every
twenty quarts of the liquor add one quart of French
brandy (see note, No. 940), and a little isinglass.
Try it in six months, and if the sweetness is gone off,
bottle it. The corks should be wired down.

949. ANOTHER WAY

To one pound of bruised gooseberries, add one
quart of spring water. Let it stand two days and
then strain it off. To every gallon of liquor add three
pounds of loaf sugar ; when that is dissolved, barrel
it When the fermentation has subsided, to every
five gallons add one pint of brandy (see note, No.
940), and a little isinglass. Let it stand six months,
then bottle it.

950. GRAPE WINE (Kent)

To every gallon of water put four quarts of grapes
well bruised. Let it stand twenty-four hours, then
strain it through a hair sieve. To every gallon of
liquor put three pounds of loaf sugar ; when the

sugar is dissolved, put it into a cask, which must be quite full, then add a quarter of an ounce of isinglass to every five gallons, stirring it well with a stick. Take off the scum, which rises for several days, and when the liquor is clear, stop up the cask very close, and bottle it in March (September in Australia).

951. LEMON WINE (Kent, 1809)

Take a sufficient number of the best lemons to produce five quarts of juice, and pass the liquid through a strainer to free it entirely from the seeds. Peel all the lemons before squeezing, throw the pulps into a large tub, and cover them with water. When they have been steeped for two days, strain off the liquid, and pour it on seventy-five pounds of lump sugar, to which, when formed into a syrup, add as much of lemon peel as you obtain by putting half of the rinds, cut very thin, into a jug, and pouring on them about two quarts of boiling water, which, after being covered over for two days and nights will have sufficiently imbibed the flavour. Get a cask of twenty-one gallons measure (if one that has held brandy, sherry, or Madeira, it will be better), pour into it the juice of the fruit and the syrup mixture, and fill the cask up with water; leave the bung out for about six weeks, or even two months, and by that time it will have sufficiently fermented, but should there be the *least* hissing or the smallest quantity rising out of the bung hole, you must not stop it down ; the vent peg, for security, had better be left out for a few days. The wine must remain *two years* in the cask before it is bottled. Rain water or Thames water is much to be preferred in making the wine. It is all to be used *cold*, excepting that put to the rinds, and nothing is to be used to produce fermentation. If you should wish to bottle the wine before the expiration of two years, it may be done at the end of twelve months, but not sooner, by fining it down with isinglass. *N.B.*—At the expiration of a fortnight add two bottles of brandy (see note, No. 940); should the fermentation not have ceased in four days after adding the above, put in one bottle more brandy.

952. LEMON WINE (1815)

Pare four dozen of lemons, put the peels into one gallon of brandy, and let them stand fourteen days ; make the juice of the lemons into a syrup, with two pounds of lump sugar ; when the peels are ready, boil ten gallons of water with forty pounds of good lump sugar, for half an hour ; put it into a tub, and, when cold, add the brandy, peel, and syrup, and put it into the cask ; stop it close, and let it stand six months. *N.B.*—Beat the whites of six eggs to a froth, and mix with the water while it is cold.

953. MADEIRA WINE (Kent, 1809)

Thirty pounds of coarse, moist sugar, to ten gallons of water ; boil it half an hour, and take off the scum as it rises ; when cold, put to every gallon one quart of ale out of the vat, let it work well a couple of days, then put it in a barrel with one pound of sugar-candy and four pounds of raisins, with some isinglass in a pint of brandy (see note, No. 940). When it has done working, stop it up close and let it stand twelve months. October is the best month for making it.

954. MARIGOLD WINE (Surrey)

Take a peck of marigold blossoms, stand them in an earthenware pan, with one and a half pounds of stoned raisins. To three gallons of water, add two pounds of honey and seven pounds of sugar. Boil this, clear it with the whites and shells of three eggs, strain it, and put it to the flowers. Cover the pan close and leave it for twenty-four hours; then, next day, stir it up with a wooden spoon, and let it stand another twenty-four hours. Then strain it off into a cask, adding the thinly pared rinds of five or six oranges, a pound of sugar-candy, and about a wineglassful of brewer's yeast. Stir well, and leave it to work until it foams out at the covered bunghole. When fermentation is over, add one pint of brandy and about half an ounce of isinglass (melted), and stop up the cask (see note, No. 940). In four or five months' time it should be ready.

955. MEAD (1815)

To one gallon of water put five pounds of honey; when the water is hot put the honey into it, and let it boil one hour and a half; as soon as the scum begins to rise take it off, and continue skimming it as long as any scum arises; then put two ounces of hops to every ten gallons of liquor, and two ounces of coriander seeds, each ounce sewn up in a separate bag; add the rind of three or four lemons and oranges, if you like: when it is cool, put it into the cask with a bottle of brandy (see note, No. 940), and stop it up quite close. Mead made of this strength will generally require to stand six or nine months in the barrel; if you wish to have the sweetness gone off, it must stand longer.

956. MEAD (Middlesex)

Put into a large earthenware pan three gallons of water, five pounds of honey, half an ounce each of cinnamon, mace, and ground ginger ; four cloves, and the whites of two eggs well beaten. Mix all thoroughly well. Pour it into a deep lined saucepan, or large preserving pan, and stir it gently till it comes to the boil, then let it simmer for at least an hour. Take it off and let it go cold. Then stir in one tablespoonful of brewer's yeast, and strain it off into a cask to ferment. Keep the bunghole covered till fermentation ceases, then close it up and leave it for nine months or so, after which the wine can be bottled.

957. MEAD (Surrey)

Boil fourteen pounds of honey in six gallons of water for half an hour, breaking into it four eggs. Add some small bunches of marjoram, balm, and sweet briar, half an ounce each of cinnamon, cloves, mace, and bruised ginger, and boil for quarter of an hour longer. Pour it out to cool, toast a large slice of brown bread, spread it over with fresh yeast, and put it into the liquor. Let it ferment for one day, and then put it into a cask, which keep open till fermentation has ceased, then bung close. It may be bottled in a month, but the corks must be well wired.

958. METHEGLIN (Cornwall)

Take three and a half pounds of honey, one quart of white-currant juice, two gallons of boiling water, quarter of an ounce of cream of tartar, and stir all well together till the honey is quite dissolved. Then let it stand to ferment. When fermentation ceases, strain it off, add one pint of brandy (see note, No. 940), and bottle it. If it be properly corked and kept in a dry place, it will keep good for years.

959. ORANGE WINE (1815)

To thirty quarts of water, add forty pounds of lump sugar, and the whites of six eggs ; beat them to a froth, and mix it with the water while it is cold ; boil it half an hour, and take off the scum as it rises. Have ready ten quarts of the juice of Seville oranges, and put half the rinds into a tub, and pour the liqour boiling hot upon them ; let it stand till quite cold, and add the juice and a quart of brandy (see note, No. 940) ; put it in the cask and stop it close, and let it stand for six months, and if it is too sweet let it stand longer. If you wish to have it very rich, you may add what quantity you please of citron syrup. Wine made by this recipe is very rich without the syrup.

960. RAISIN WINE (1815)

To one gallon of water put six pounds of sun raisins ; let it stand in a tub twelve days, stir it frequently, press the raisins as dry as possible, and put the liquor into a cask the proper size ; if you have ten gallons, put a quart of brandy in it (see note, No. 940). If you wish to make it very rich, you may put seven pounds of raisins to the gallon, and dissolve five pounds of sugar-candy in the liquor before you put it into the barrel: when made thus, it requires to stand longer, and is equal to any foreign wine.

961. RHUBARB WINE (Suffolk)

Measure one pint of rhubarb, cut into small pieces, to one pint of water, to the quantity you require. Put all together into an earthen vessel and let it stand for a fortnight. Stir and squeeze it (with a wooden spoon) every morning. Then strain off, and measure half a pound of white sugar to every pint of liquid. Let this stand for a week; skim every morning, and bottle at the end of the week.

962. ENGLISH SHERRY (Kent, 1809)

Thirty pounds of moist Lisbon sugar to ten gallons of water. Boil it half an hour, then skim it clean. When quite cold, put to every gallon of the liquor one quart of new ale out of the butt. Let it work in the tub a day or two; then put it in the barrel with one pound of brown sugar-candy, six pounds of common raisins, one pint of French brandy, and two ounces of isinglass. When it has done working, stop it up. It should remain in the vessel two years, if not particularly wanted.

963. VALENTIA WINE (Kent, 1809)

One gallon of good spirits, one gallon of water, eighteen lemons, juice and rind, one ounce of cinnamon, two ounces of ginger, one ounce of nutmeg, three and a half pounds of loaf sugar, or brown, one ounce of bitter almonds. The spices to be powdered together, the lemons grated, put together with the spices, and infused for three days in a quart of the spirits, afterwards to be strained. The sugar to be dissolved in water and added to the other ingredients. The whole to be mixed well in a cask, and three quarts of boiling milk poured into it, keeping the mixture stirring all the while the milk is pouring in. The cask to be covered close and let stand twenty-four hours. The liquid then to be strained through a thick flannel bag, and, if not free from sediment, again strain it until it seems quite clear. When perfectly cold, to be bottled for use.

BEERS (NON-ALCOHOLIC)

964. GINGER BEER (1822)

Ginger beer of a very superior quality may be prepared as follows : Powder of ginger, one ounce, cream of tartar, half an ounce, a large lemon sliced, two pounds of lump sugar and one gallon of water added together, and simmered over the fire for half an hour. Then ferment it in the usual way with a tablespoonful of yeast, and bottle it for use, tightly corked.

965. GINGER BEER (Kent)

Bruise two ounces of the best ginger, two ounces of cream of tartar, four lemons pared and sliced, with the rind of one, and two pounds of loaf sugar. Pour upon them two gallons of boiling water. When nearly cold, strain through flannel, and add two large spoonfuls of yeast. Let it stand till quite cold, and pour off the clear liquor into half-pint bottles, which must be well corked and tied down. It will be fit to drink in three or four days.

966. ANOTHER WAY

Pour one gallon of boiling water over three-quarters of a pound of lump sugar, one and a half ounces of bruised ginger, and the peel of a lemon—when milk-warm add one tablespoonful of yeast. If this be done at night, it will be fit for bottling next night. Put the piece of lemon into the yeast. Not to be used for three days.

967. GINGER BEER (Middlesex)

A very pleasant and wholesome beverage when well made. It was first invented a great many years ago by a Mr. Pitt, a surgeon at Lewes, and rose rapidly into fame. Even when made as it ought to be, it is a cheap beverage, but as it is usually made, it is still cheaper, tartaric acid being used instead of lemon juice. The best way of making ginger beer is as follows :—Pour eleven gallons of boiling water upon fourteen pounds of white sugar, the juice of eighteen lemons, a pound of bruised ginger, and the rind of two lemons. When at the proper temperature, add two or three spoonfuls of yeast and let it ferment for about a day ; then put it into a cask to finish the fermentation, and when that is completed, fine it and bung it down closely. It may be bottled in stone bottles almost immediately. Some persons boil the water and sugar together before it is poured upon the ginger, but this trouble is unnecessary, unless it be intended to add raisins, which are a great improvement. In that case, a pound of good raisins may be boiled with the water and sugar. The quantity

of ginger above ordered is rather larger than would
suit every taste. It may of course be reduced.
In bottling, good corks should be used, and tied
over with twine.

968. GINGER BEER (Staffordshire)

Mix one ounce of powdered ginger, half an ounce
of cream of tartar, one lemon sliced, two pounds of
lump sugar, and one gallon of water together.
Simmer it over the fire for half an hour, and ferment
it in the usual manner with a tablespoonful of yeast.
Then bottle it close for use in half-pint or pint
bottles, such as are used for soda water; in a few
days it will be fit to drink.

969. GINGER BEER (Sussex)

Four gallons of water, two ounces of ground
ginger, two ounces of cream of tartar, two and a
half pounds of moist sugar. Pour half the boiling
water on these ingredients, except the sugar. Let
it stand a day or two, then add the remainder of the
water, boiling also, and the sugar, and a teacupful
of yeast. Bottle it when rather warm.

970. GINGER POP (Ireland)

Take two ounces of cream of tartar, one ounce and
a half of white ginger well beaten (not ground), one
lemon shredded fine, one pound and a half of sugar.
Put them all together in an earthen vessel, and pour
on them ten quarts of boiling water. Let it stand
till nearly cold, then add two tablespoonfuls of
good barm; mix it well; let it stand for thirty

hours, then strain it through a flannel bag, pressing it well through. Bottle it, and confine the corks with twine. It will be fit for use in two days.

971. IMPERIAL POP (Kent, 1809)

To two gallons of boiling hot water add two pounds of loaf sugar, two ounces of white bruised ginger, one ounce of cream of tartar and two table-spoonfuls of yeast. When it is blood warm, put in the yeast. Do not bottle it until quite cold and clear. This quantity will fill ten bottles. Tie down the corks. It will be fit to drink in one week in the summer.

972. NETTLE BEER (Hampshire)

Wash the nettles (which should be young and green), and boil them for about three hours, with a little race ginger. When cool enough, add about one pound of sugar to every two gallons of liquor, and add about a pennyworth of yeast to the same quantity. After it has worked a few hours, skim and bottle it.

973. NETTLE BEER (Surrey)

Boil two quarts of nettle sprouts in one gallon of water. Strain the liquor, and add half a pound of sugar, with a teaspoonful of ginger. When nearly cold, ferment with yeast, and bottle securely while in a state of effervescence. It will be ready for use in a few days.

974. ANOTHER WAY

Into a saucepan or kettle that will hold three gallons, put two gallons of water. When this is boiling, add as many nettles as the saucepan will contain. Boil them for half an hour, and strain into an earthenware pan broader at the top than at the bottom. Make up, with hot water, the quantity of liquor to four gallons. While it is still as hot as possible, add two ounces of best raw ginger, well bruised, one ounce of cream of tartar, the peel of three lemons cut thin, also their squeezed juice, and two pounds of white sugar. Let the liquor stand, stirring it occasionally, until lukewarm, when add two pennyworth of brewer's yeast. While the liquor is hot, a little isinglass may be used to fine it. Stir well, and let it stand in a cool place all night. In the morning, all impurities, etc., will have risen to the top ; skim very carefully and bottle in champagne bottles. The corks cannot be too good ; bad corks will destroy the whole thing. If the corks are boiled in water for a couple of hours before they are used (hot), they will drive much easier and cork much more perfectly. They must be tied down as soon as corked. If the value of this beverage were generally known, no household would be without it.

975. TREACLE BEER (1822)

This is a very pleasant and wholesome beverage. To a quarter of a peck of sweet wheat bran, add three handfuls of hops, and ten gallons of water. Boil the whole together in a copper saucepan, till the bran and hops sink to the bottom. Then strain

it through a hair sieve into a cooler, and when lukewarm add two quarts of treacle (or three pints if
it be very thick). This will be sufficient for a nine-
gallon cask. Before you pour the liquor into the
barrel, which must be done as soon as the treacle
is melted, put two tablespoonfuls of good yeast
into the barrel. When the fermentation has subsided, bung the cask up close, and in four days it
will be fit to use. If you choose to bottle any of
the beer, it will be much improved by so doing,
and will be ready to drink in six or seven days.

LEMONADE, SYRUPS, FRUIT VINEGARS, ETC.

976. BLACKBERRY SYRUP (Essex)

Stew the blackberries with a quarter of a pint
of water to every three pounds, until the juice is
drawn. Strain, and to every pint of juice add six
ounces of sugar. Boil sugar and juice together for
fifteen minutes, and bottle for use when cold.

977. BLACKBERRY VINEGAR (Surrey)

Take three quarts of ripe blackberries, crush
them, and pour over them two quarts of the best
white vinegar. Let it stand twenty-four hours, then
strain it off through a piece of muslin, and pour the
fluid on to three quarts of fresh blackberries. Let
it stand as before ; and if not strong enough when
you strain it off the second time, pour it on to
three quarts of fresh berries again. When rich
enough, put it into a jar, and stand the jar in a

pan of boiling water. Let it boil fast for an hour, then bottle for use. This is very good for colds, etc., diluted with hot or cold water.

978. CHERRY WATER

Take one pound of good cherries, pound them in a mortar till the kernels are broken, put them in a large bowl and add four gills of thick syrup. Put to this the juice of four lemons, and some water, enough to thin the liquid sufficiently. Then strain off through a sieve into glass jugs.

979. COWSLIP SYRUP (Surrey)

Take twelve ounces of fresh cowslip flowers, one pint of boiling water. Infuse twenty-four hours, strain, and then add two pounds of white sugar. Boil it gently until it attains the consistence of a syrup.

980. ELDER ROB (Eighteenth Century)

Gather your elderberries full ripe, pick them clean from the stalks, put them in large stew-jars and tie paper over them. Let them stand two hours in a moderate oven. Then put them in a thin, coarse cloth, and squeeze out all the juice you can get. Put eight quarts into a preserving pan, set it over a slow fire, let it boil till it be reduced to one quart. When it is near done, keep stirring it, to prevent it burning. Then put it into pots, let it stand two or three days in the sun ; then dip a paper, the size of your pot, in sweet oil, lay it on, tie it down with a bladder, and keep it in a very dry place. Black Currant Rob is made the same way, but six quarts

25

of juice will suffice. (These are excellent, diluted with water, for use in feverish colds.)

981. FLUMMERY (Ireland)

To one quart of oatmeal pour one gallon of water and a pint of buttermilk ; let it remain for four days, then strain through a hair sieve. Two quarts more of water may be put on the oatmeal, and let stand four days longer ; it will be sufficiently sour without buttermilk the second time.

982. FRUIT SYRUP (French)

Put the fruit into a pan and let it boil five minutes. Then squeeze out the juice and strain it through a jelly-bag. Add it to a syrup of sugar, in the proportion of half a pound of juice to one pound of sugar. For this purpose your syrup must be very good, the water being evaporated by boiling until the syrup be very thick. When the juice and syrup are thoroughly mixed, strain again through a jelly-bag.

983. GINGERETTE (Sussex)

Three drachms of tincture of cayenne, four drachms of essence of ginger, three-quarters of an ounce of either tartaric or citric acid, four pounds of loaf sugar. Pour three quarts of boiling water on to these ingredients. When cold, add about fifteen drops of essence of lemon, and bottle.

984. GINGER WINE, NON-ALCOHOLIC (Ireland)

Three pounds of lump sugar, four quarts of boiling water, eighteen pepper corns (break nine of them), thirty-six cloves, two pennyworth of citric acid and the same of essence of lemon. Burnt sugar to colour. Put ingredients into a large basin, pour over them the boiling water, and leave till cold, when add the colouring.

985. SYRUP OF GILLIFLOWERS (Yorkshire, 1769)

Take five pints of freshly-gathered clove gilli-flowers, and put to them two pints of boiling water, then put them in an earthen pot to infuse a night and a day. Take a strainer and strain them out ; to a quart of your liquor, put one and a half pounds of loaf sugar; boil it over a slow fire, and skim it while any scum rises. When it is cold, bottle it for use.

986. LEMONADE (Ireland)

One pound of lump sugar, one ounce of citric acid, one teaspoonful of essence of lemon, one quart of boiling water. Put the ingredients into a jug, pour the water over them, leave till cold.

987. LEMONADE (Sussex)

Two pounds of castor sugar, one ounce of citric acid, the grated rind of three oranges, three tumbler-fuls of cold water. Let it stand three or four days, stirring occasionally. Then strain, bottle, and cork tight.

988. LEMONADE SYRUP (Lancashire)

Take two ounces of citric acid, two scruples of essence of lemon ; rub these thoroughly together

in a mortar. Take three pounds of loaf sugar, three
gills of water, boil together and strain it. Pour
into a basin, and when half-cold, add the acid, and
stir it in with a silver spoon. When cold, bottle it.

989. LEMON SYRUP (Essex)

Put twelve ounces of loaf sugar into one quart of
water, and let it boil for fifteen minutes, skimming it
carefully. Take it off and let it get cold, then add
half a pint of strained lemon-juice, and one drachm
of essence of lemon. Mix well and bottle it. Cork
very tightly. To be used with water or soda-water.

990. LEMON SYRUP (Kent, 1809)

To every pint of lemon juice add one pound or
rather more of good loaf sugar, skim it well while
simmering. When all the dross is removed, boil it
briskly for half an hour; when cold, bottle it.
Put into each bottle a very few thin slices of lemon
peel, which must be boiled soft in the syrup.

991. RASPBERRY VINEGAR (1815)

Take six pounds of raspberries, gathered in dry
weather, and six pounds of pounded sugar; put
them in an earthen pan, placing a layer of raspberries, then a layer of sugar, and so on; let them
stand for three days, and stir them once a day
with a wooden spoon; then take three pints of
Burgundy vinegar, put it to them, stir them
well together, put them into a clean preserving
pan, over a charcoal fire, make them boiling
hot, then run them through a jelly bag. Put the

syrup in a clean earthen pot; then put a large
pan of water on the fire, put the pot with the
syrup in the boiling water, and let it boil for two
hours; if not sweet enough, sweeten it to your
palate with fine loaf sugar; let it stand till cold, and
put it into dry pint bottles.

992. RASPBERRY VINEGAR (Surrey)

Bruise two quarts of fresh raspberries, and pour
over them a quart of good white wine vinegar;
cover closely, and let it stand for four days, stirring
it occasionally; strain through a flannel bag without
pressing, and boil the liquor for a quarter of an hour,
with powdered sugar in the proportion of a pound
to a pint, skimming carefully; when cold, bottle
and cork. If it is intended that the vinegar shall
be very acid, less sugar must be used. Some persons add a little brandy when it is bottled; this is
good for keeping, but it injures the flavour.

993. RASPBERRY SHRUB (Surrey)

Take two quarts of good ripe raspberries, pour
one quart of good vinegar over them; cover them
closely and let them stand for two days. Then mash
up the berries in the vinegar, and strain off the
liquid on to two quarts of fresh fruit. Let this
stand another two days, then mash and strain as
before. To every pint of liquid, add two teacupfuls
of white sugar. Let it simmer very gently for
fifteen minutes in a lined saucepan over the fire,
keeping it well skimmed. Then strain it, bottle it,
cork, and cover closely, seal the cork. This should
be taken with cold water.

994. SHERBET (Sussex)

Take half a pound of castor sugar, half a pound of
tartaric acid, quarter of a pound of carbonate of
soda. Put forty drops, or rather more, essence of
lemon in the sugar. Mix well, then add the other
ingredients.

VARIOUS MIXED BEVERAGES (ALCOHOLIC)

995. ALE SYLLABUB (American)

Put a quart of strong ale into a large bowl, add
sugar to taste, and a little nutmeg. Milk the cow
into the bowl, as quickly and strongly as possible
to make a good froth ; let it stand for an hour before
drinking.

996. BISHOP (Middlesex)

Roast four good-sized bitter oranges till they are
of a pale brown colour, lay them in a tureen, and
put over them half a pound of pounded loaf sugar,
and three glasses of claret ; place the cover on the
tureen and let it stand till the next day. When
required for use, put the tureen into a pan of boiling
water, press the oranges with a spoon, and run the
juice through a sieve ; then boil the remainder of
the bottle of claret, taking care that it does not
burn ; add it to the strained juice, and serve it
warm in glasses. Port wine will answer the purpose
as well as claret.

997. BISHOP (Surrey)

Stick twelve cloves into a lemon (not right through
the rind) and put it in the oven for half an hour.

Put a good-sized pinch of mixed spice into half a pint of water, and boil it. Boil separately one and a half pints of sherry, add the lemon and the spiced water to this, stand it in a very warm place for a few minutes. Take another lemon, rub two ounces of lump sugar on the rind, and squeeze out half of the juice ; add these to the rest, and serve up very hot.

998. CLARET CUP (Cheshire)

Two bottles of Bordeaux, one bottle of soda-water, powdered sugar to taste, peel of a lemon cut fine, a wineglassful of rum or curaçao, and a sprig of borage. To be well iced.

999. ANOTHER WAY

Take a large jug, put into it a lemon and half a cucumber (about four inches of it), cut in slices, without paring them ; pour in one bottle of claret, two bottles of soda-water, one gill of sherry. Add a quarter of a pound of loaf sugar, and a sprig of borage. Cover it up for an hour, then strain out the lemon, cucumber, and borage.

1000. EGG FLIP (American)

Put one quart of ale into a lined saucepan ; beat up in a bowl the yolks of four eggs and the whites of two. Mix in four tablespoonfuls of brown sugar, and a little nutmeg. When the ale boils, pour it gently into the egg, so that it shall not curdle. Pour it to and fro and back and forward with the hand raised high, so that it shall look frothy and fleecy.

1001. EGG FLIP (Cheshire)

Heat one quart of ale to boiling point. Beat up
to a froth, separately, the yolks of four eggs, and the
whites of two. Mix them, by degrees, with six
ounces of powdered sugar, and half a nutmeg,
grated. Pour the mixture rapidly from one jug to
another, hot ale and all together, raising the jug to
a height that will froth the liquid and continue till
it is smooth and foaming. Serve hot. Sherry may
be used instead of ale ; in which case, a little lemon
peel is an improvement.

1002. EGG HOT (Middlesex)

A very agreeable posset, taken in many parts of
England after great fatigue, and not infrequently as
a remedy for colds ; in which case, however, it is
not to be recommended, as it increases feverishness
and fails to promote copious perspiration. Beat up
the yolks of three eggs and the white of one in a
teacup of weak ale, with a little nutmeg ; in the
meantime have upon the fire a quart of the same
kind of ale. When it has nearly boiled, add the
eggs thus beaten up, and let the boiling finish
very gently, stirring the whole time ; when it has
thickened, pour it into a jug containing about
a quartern of brandy and three ounces of loaf
sugar. Have another jug handy and pour back-
wards and forwards for three or four minutes before
serving. White French wine mixed with about a
third of water may be substituted for the beer.

1003. MINT JULEP (American)

Put into a tumbler about one dozen sprigs of the tender shoots of mint, put upon them a spoonful of white sugar, and equal proportions of peach brandy and common brandy, so as to fill up the glass one-third, or perhaps a little less. Then take rasped or pounded ice and fill up the tumbler. (The lips of it should be rubbed with a piece of fresh pineapple, but this is not absolutely necessary.) As the ice melts, you drink.

1004. MULLED WINE (Middlesex)

Boil in a quarter of a pint of water, for about ten minutes, three cloves, a bit of cinnamon, a little fresh lemon peel, and one ounce and a half of loaf sugar ; skim, and then add a pint of port wine ; when the whole begins to boil, take it off, strain it, and grate in some nutmeg ; serve with toasted bread. French red wine may be used, but in that case more sugar will be necessary.

1005. MULLED WINE (Surrey)

Break nine eggs, the yolks and whites separately, and beat them separately, adding three or four spoonfuls of sugar. Pour a bottle of good wine into a skillet, with half a pint of water ; and when it boils, put the yolks and whites together, beating them well, with half a pint more water, and pour them to the wine in the skillet, stirring quickly as you pour. When all is thoroughly blended, turn out the liquor into a hot jug (earthenware for

preference) and grate some nutmeg in it. To be
served very hot.

1006. NEGUS (Surrey)

Put half a pint of port (or sherry if preferred) in a
saucepan, and let it heat without boiling. Put
into a jug or basin four thin slices of lemon, a little
nutmeg, and six or seven lumps of sugar. Put
half a pint of boiling water on this, and stir well
with a wooden or silver spoon until the sugar is
melted. Then pour in the hot wine ; cinnamon,
cloves, or allspice may be added at pleasure.

1007. A RESTORATIVE (Sussex)

Put two quite fresh eggs, without breaking the
shells, into a basin ; squeeze over them the juice of
two or three lemons, cover close and leave them,
three or four days, till almost dissolved. Then beat
them well together, strain, put into a bottle, add
one pint of good rum, half a pound of sugar candy,
two tablespoonfuls of best salad oil, and shake well
together. Dose : half a wineglassful in a little cold
water, fasting. The best time to take it is quite
early in the morning, say five o'clock, and then
go to sleep again.

1008. WHITE WINE WHEY (Eighteenth Century)

Put one pint of skimmed milk, and half a pint of
white wine, into a basin ; let it stand a few minutes,
then pour over it one pint of boiling water. Let
it stand a little, and the curd will gather in a lump,
and settle to the bottom. Then pour off your whey

into a china bowl, and put in a lump of sugar, and a sprig of balm or a slice of lemon.

COFFEE AND TEA

1009. COFFEE (Surrey)

To make really good coffee, four things are essential. (1) Let the coffee be freshly ground, and, if possible, freshly roasted. (2) Do not stint the amount : weak coffee is unendurable. (3) Let the water be *boiling* hot, and the utensils *thoroughly heated*. (4) Use only earthenware and wooden utensils : let no metal approach the coffee.

Have ready two earthenware jugs (size at least one and a half pints each), *well heated*. Into the first, measure four *wooden* tablespoonfuls, or not less than two and a half ounces to the quart, of freshly ground coffee. Fill up with boiling water, stir it with the spoon, cover, and leave the jug to stand in a warm place for two or three minutes. Then stir it thoroughly once more, let the grounds settle again, and strain it off through a piece of butter-muslin into the *hot* second jug, and serve at once, with a jug of *boiling* milk. Should any coffee be left over, boil it up along with the milk the second day. This makes it particularly bland and palatable, and for those who prefer " French " coffee, *i.e.* mixed with chicory, it is especially advisable. Any well-known good brand of the latter, such as the " Red, White, and Blue," can be used with success according to above directions. Between the result of the above, and the ordinary wish-wash served as coffee, the difference is too great to be expressed.

1010. TEA FOR A HEADACHE (Surrey)

This is a special remedial tea, an expensive one, and not for ordinary use : but it will cure, or ameliorate, in most cases, the nervous headaches which otherwise yield to nothing.

Take half a pound of a *good* Congou blend, about 2*s*. 2*d*. or 2*s*. 6*d*. per pound, such as Ridgway's, two ounces of a good China Tea, not less than 3*s*. per pound, and one ounce of a good green tea, about 4*s*. 6*d*. per pound. Blend these thoroughly well and keep in a closed tin in a dry place. Do not entrust the making of this (or any other tea) to servants. The " scalding " of the teapot and making of tea with *freshly boiling* water are essential : and this is just what servants usually ignore. Water that has been boiling some time will not " draw " tea properly : much less so, water that " has boiled," which is too frequently made use of.

LIQUEURS, CORDIALS, RATAFIAS

NOTE.—Those quiet days being long since past, when every well-to-do household possessed a still-room or at least a still, the art of making cordials and liqueurs, so precious to our predecessors, is in danger of being lost for ever. Yet these things are so infinitely preferable, both for health's sake and economy's sake, to the foreign manufactured article, that I cannot shut out a few good old recipes. Not all of them, it will be seen, require a process of distillation ; and in some cases mere filtering through a flannel bag suffices. It is particularly difficult to make a hard-and-fast definition of (A) liqueurs, (B) cordials, and (C) ratafias. Roughly speaking, one may say that (A) Liqueurs are mostly prepared by distillation ; the dry ingredients having to be ground to dust, pestled to a paste, or chopped to minute fragments, and then steeped in spirit for a month, before proceeding with the individual formula. (B) Cordials are usually not so strong nor so spirituous as liqueurs : they may be prepared by distillation, but are generally infused. The noyeaus in the following pages may be classed as cordials. As for (C) Ratafias, they are, correctly speaking, non-alcoholic infusions of fruit, sweet and syrupy. But the three terms are more or less interchangeable, so that it is hard to say where one begins and another ends. Some twenty years ago it was declared that " there are very few liqueurs which are not as good when made by infusion as they would be by the more tedious process of distillation." Distillation, indeed, is only necessary where the flavouring substance, in the form of essential oil, has a deteriorated flavour. There is certainly no reason or excuse for paying fancy prices, when these excellent liquids can be produced at home with perfect ease. They are invaluable for flavouring purposes, when not required for beverages.

The *Aqua Vitæ Composita* prescription is given chiefly as a curiosity ; but a modification of it, usin*g* spirit instead of wine, might conceivably result in a cordial of singular efficacy.

1011. ALKERMES (French)

Pound one drachm of cardamom seeds, one drachm of nutmegs, two drachms of cinnamon.

Infuse in spirit for a week, then strain and filter.
Add five drops of attar of rose, and proceed as for
any other liqueur. Colour it rose with cochineal.

1012. ANISEED (1815)

For four bottles of brandy, take half a pound of
aniseeds, a quarter of a pound of fennel, and three
cloves, to be cut in small bits, with a little salt ;
put all in the brandy ; it is to be infused twelve
hours before you distil it ; two pounds of sugar
must be clarified, with the whites of two or three
eggs well beaten together, and two bottles and a
half of water, and added to the rest.

1013. ANISETTE (French)

Take five pints of good spirits of wine, add one
and a half drachms of essence (or oil) of aniseed,
eight drops of oil of cinnamon, and then add syrup
in usual proportion.

1014. ANGELICA RATAFIA (Surrey)

Put half a pound of angelica shoots into two
quarts of brandy, with a pint of water, two pounds
of sugar, a few cloves, and a little cinnamon. Let
the whole infuse for two months in a close vessel,
then strain and bottle. This is a very rich and fine
cordial.

1015. APRICOT RATAFIA (Middlesex)

Cut thirty apricots into small pieces ; crack the
stones and take out the kernels, which must be
peeled and bruised ; then put the whole together

into a jar, with two quarts of good brandy, half a pound of sugar, a little cinnamon, eight cloves, a very small quantity of mace; close the jar well, and let it remain for three weeks, shaking it frequently; then strain it off into bottles, and keep in a cool place.

1016. AQUA VITÆ COMPOSITA (Sixteenth Century)

Take one gallon of strong French wine, and of sage, mints, red roses, thyme, pellitory, rosemary, wild thyme, camomile, lavender, each a handful. These herbs shall be stamped all together in a mortar, and then put in a clean vessel with a pint of rosewater and a quart of Spanish wine, and closely stoppered and let to stand so three or four days. Then put it into a still and distil it once; then take your distilled water and pour it back upon the herbs again into the still, and strew upon it these powders following: Cloves and cinnamon, of each half an ounce; orris, one ounce; a few maces; nutmegs, half an ounce; a little saffron, musk, spikenard, amber; and some put camphor in it. Stir all well together, and distil it clean off, till it come fat like oil, then get away the distilled water and let it be well kept (in bottles). After that make a strong fire and distil oil of what is left, and receive it in a phial. ("It is wonderful good," adds the old writer.)

1017. CARAWAY CORDIAL (Surrey)

Steep one ounce of caraway seeds in one pint of brandy for a fortnight, then strain off, and add one pint of strong syrup; mix well, and bottle. This makes a warm and pleasant cordial.

1018. CHERRY BRANDY (Kent)

To one pound of black cherries—sticks, stones, and all—put one quart of brandy, or good spirit, and a pound of lump sugar. Let it stand for three weeks, stirring now and then. Strain and bottle.

1019. CHERRY BRANDY (Middlesex, 1822)

Stone six pounds of black cherries, pour on them four quarts of the best brandy. Bruise the stones in a mortar, and put the kernels in with the cherries. Cover them close, and let the whole stand for a fortnight ; then squeeze them clean from sediment, through muslin. Boil two pounds of very white sugar to clear syrup ; mix it with the strained liquor, and bottle it into clear dry bottles. It may be used in two months, and should be kept in a cool cellar.

1020. BLACK CHERRY BRANDY (Yorkshire, 1769)

Take eight pounds of black cherries, stone them, and put them in a gallon of the best brandy and cover up all close. Let the cherries steep for a month or six weeks, then drain off and bottle it for use. You may distil the liquor if you please.

1021. LISBON CHERRY BOUNCE (Kent, 1809)

Six pounds of black cherries, four quarts of rum, three pounds of loaf sugar, half a pound of bitter almonds, a quarter of an ounce of cloves, half a drachm of cinnamon. Dissolve the sugar in the spirit, then add the other ingredients, and keep them in a well-corked jar or bottle for six months, occasionally shaking the mixture. The fruit is to be strained, and two ounces of gum arabic dissolved in a little water may be added to give it the consistency of a liqueur.

1022. CHOCOLATE LIQUEUR (1815)

For four bottles of brandy, take one pound of the best chocolate, cut in small bits, a little salt, two cloves, and a little cinnamon ; infuse all in the brandy ; add two pounds of sugar clarified in two and a half pints of water, with whites of eggs, and filter it through a paper.

1023. CINNAMON WATER (Middlesex)

Cinnamon water is made by distillation. The cinnamon must be infused for several days in an equal quantity of water and brandy, with some lemon peel and liquorice, and then distilled, being afterwards sweetened with sugar and filtered. The preparations are : one ounce of cinnamon, two quarts of brandy, a pint of water, the peel of a lemon, and an ounce of fresh liquorice root ; after distillation add a pound of sugar dissolved in a quart of water for each ounce of cinnamon.

1024. CLOVE WATER (Middlesex)

Clove water is a fine stomachic, either taken alone or as a vehicle for medicine ; it may be made by infusing bruised cloves in spirits of wine or brandy for a fortnight, and distilling it, then adding six times its quantity of water.

26

1025. COFFEE LIQUEUR (1815)

For four bottles of brandy, take one pound of the best Turkey ground coffee, a little salt, two cloves, and a little cinnamon ; then mix all together for twelve hours before you distil it ; add two pounds of sugar, two bottles and half a pint of water clarified with whites of eggs, filtered through a paper.

1026. CORIANDER CORDIAL (Surrey)

Take one ounce of coriander seed, a quarter of an ounce of caraway seed, a small piece of cinnamon, and steep them for a fortnight or three weeks in one pint of good brandy. Strain off the liquor and add to it one pint of good syrup ; mix well, and bottle.

1027. CORIANDER WATER (Middlesex)

The best way of using coriander for the kitchen is to bruise two ounces of the seed, and put it into a bottle with four ounces of spirits of wine. This must stand for a fortnight or three weeks, and then be filtered off. A few drops may be used for dishes or pastry, in which coriander seed forms a part of the formula.

1028. CORNELLA OR CINNAMON CORDIAL (1815)

For four bottles of brandy, take four ounces of cinnamon of the best quality, thirty cloves, thirteen coriander seeds, a little salt, mixed all together in brandy, let it infuse for eighteen hours ; take from the still as much as you can ; two pounds of sugar clarified in two bottles and a half of water, with two or three whites of eggs well beaten together, to be mixed with the spirit, and filtered through blotting paper : after you have mixed the spirit, take care to cork your bottles well.

1029. CURAÇAO (Surrey)

Make a very strong syrup, boil in it for five minutes the juice and rind of four large oranges and three bitter ones. Strain and filter it, add six drops of cinnamon and six drops of neroli.

1030. ANOTHER WAY

Infuse the peel of four bitter oranges in some spirit and syrup for a week, flavour with cinnamon, cloves, or mace, strain off, and add to the rest of the spirit and syrup ; i.e. there should be about one-third spirit to nearly two-thirds of syrup.

1031. HAWTHORN BRANDY (Middlesex, 1822)

Put as much full blossom of the white thorn (hawthorn), picked dry and clean from leaves and stalks, as a great bottle will hold lightly, without pressing down. Fill it up with French brandy, let it stand two or three weeks, then decant it off clear, and add as much sugar as may make it of a proper sweetness.

1032. HAWTHORN BRANDY (Surrey)

Take a large bottle, fill it three-parts full with haw-thorn petals, picked when the day is dry and sunny (putting the flowers only, not the stalks), and fill up with brandy. Let them infuse for about five or

six weeks, then strain off the liquid into a clean
bottle, and cork up well. This imparts a delicious
flavouring to puddings, etc.

1033. LOVAGE (Surrey)

Take five drachms each of oil of nutmeg and oil of
cassia, and mix with three drachms oil of caraway
in one quart of the best spirits of wine. It should
be thoroughly well mixed and shaken. Then you
put this to two gallons of spirits of wine, and pour
it into a ten-gallon cask. Take twenty pounds of
lump sugar dissolved in hot water, mix into this
a quarter of a pint of colouring of any kind preferred,
pour all into the cask, fill up with water, and pour
it in while hot ; lastly add one ounce of salts of
tartar, and let the whole be well mixed and stirred.

1034. NOYEAU (1822)

The following recipe will furnish a liqueur in no
way inferior to the veritable Martinique at not half
the cost of the foreign article. (Smaller quantities
may be made in proportionate admixture.) Blanch
and pound one pound of bitter almonds, half a
pound of sweet almonds, and two ounces of cassia
buds, *separately*. Put them with two gallons of
British gin into a barrel, and shake it every day for
a fortnight. Then make a syrup of twelve pounds
of sugar and three quarts of water, and put it into
the barrel milk-warm. Add three quarts of spirits
of wine, one pint ratafia, four ounces of orange-
flower water, the juice of two lemons, and a piece of
calcined alum, about the size of a walnut. Then

add half an ounce of isinglass, dissolved in half a
pint of gin, reserved from the two gallons for that
purpose. Shake the barrel only once afterwards,
let the whole remain three or four days, and then
filter it through an earthenware colander, with
filtering paper laid on it, changing the paper every
time it is empty. In two days and nights, sixteen
clear quarts will be produced. When bottling, dip
the corks in melted resin.

1035. NOYEAU (Kent, 1809)

Put six ounces of bitter almonds, blanched and
cut, into two quarts of English gin ; keep it in a
moderate heat three days, shaking it well. Add two
pounds of good loaf sugar, just melted in boiling
water ; let it stand for twenty-four hours longer,
frequently shaking the bottle. Filter it through
double blotting paper, and it is fit for use.

1036. NOYEAU (Kent)

To a quart of reduced spirits put three-quarters of
a pound of loaf sugar, one and a half ounces bitter,
and the same of sweet, almonds, powdered very
fine, and four tablespoonfuls boiled milk. To be
shaken every day for twenty-one days, then filtered
through blotting paper ; and it will be fit for use.

1037. NOYEAU (Lancashire)

Take two quarts of rum, the juice of three lemons,
three pounds of double-refined sugar, two ounces
of sweet almonds, and two ounces of bitter almonds,
beat fine. Put the above ingredients into a deep
covered pot, pour two quarts of new milk and one

of water boiling hot upon them, let it stand four or
five days, stirring it two or three times a day. Run
it through a flannel and bottle it for use.

1038. NOYEAU (Middlesex)

Collect the kernels of peach, apricot, and plum
stones. Bruise them and put them to steep in
strong spirits of wine, for a fortnight or three weeks.
To, say, three ounces of kernels, use half a pint of
spirit. About half a dozen blanched bitter almonds
may be added, but not more, as they contain so
much prussic acid. Make a syrup of one pound
of sugar with as much water as will yield about one
pint of syrup when boiled ; when this is cold, add a
pint of good white French brandy (or spirits of wine
can be used instead, but brandy is best), using as
much of the kernel tincture (strained off) as will
impart the right flavour. You must add the tincture
very carefully and slowly, and taste it from time to
time. If you want pink noyeau, boil some crushed
cochineal in a little water, and strain it off, and add
it drop by drop to the liqueur.

1039. OIL OF ROSES (Surrey)

This is a very nice liqueur. To three quarts of
white brandy, put three pounds of roses with the
best scent ; add one pint of water, let them infuse
for a week in a jar, and then distil. After distilling,
add a syrup of two pounds of sugar dissolved in three
pints of water, and a little filtered cochineal for
colouring.

1040. ANOTHER WAY

Put a few drops of attar of roses, according to taste, into a quart of good spirits of wine. Add the same quantity of strong syrup, and colour with a little tincture of cochineal.

1041. OIL OF ROSES (French)

Make a syrup of one pound of sugar, with as much water only as will, when boiled, yield about one pint of syrup. When this is quite cold, add one pint of good white French brandy, and about ten drops of attar of roses, colouring it a rich pink by a tincture which may be made by boiling some crushed cochineal in a little water, and straining it off.

1042. PERFETTO AMORE (1815)

For four bottles of brandy, peel six large and fresh lemons ; the peels are to be very thin, cut in small bits, and put in the brandy with a little salt, half a handful of currants, five coriander seeds, five cloves, and a little cinnamon ; the whole to be infused together for twelve hours, from which draw off only two bottles of spirit ; then add two pounds of sugar, boiled and clarified in two bottles of water with three eggs ; take a little rock alum, which you must mix in a little boiling water, and a little cream of tartar, mix them in a small mortar, and add to the liquor ; (but first you are to strain it); then mix them all together, and filter it through blotting-paper.

1043.   PERSICO (1815)

For four bottles of brandy, take four handfuls of
bitter almonds of the best quality, and very fresh ;
they are to be cut in small bits, with a little salt,
two cloves, and a little cinnamon ; put all in the
brandy, and infuse them for twenty hours ; add
two bottles of spirit, two pounds of sugar, with two
bottles of water, without clarifying it, as this liquor
will clarify itself.

1044. PINEAPPLE LIQUEUR

Scrape one and a half pounds of pineapple into
the spirit which is to be used, let it infuse for a
week ; then drain it off and add the syrup.

1045.   MILK PUNCH (1815)

Take two gallons and a half of French brandy,
and infuse in it for one night the outer rind of fifteen
lemons, and as many oranges pared very thin ; add
to it the juice of the before-mentioned quantity of
fruit, and fifteen quarts of cold water that has been
boiled, seven pounds and a half of fine loaf sugar,
and half a pint of milk ; let them be well mixed
and stand till cold ; then add a bottle of Jamaica
rum, put it into a cask the proper size, and stop it
up close for a month or six weeks.   *N.B.*—Take
out the lemon and orange peel before you add the
juice of the fruit and the water.

1046. TO MAKE ANY KIND OF LIQUEUR (Surrey)

All cloves, cinnamon, mace, or other dry ingredients must be finely ground or grated.   All leaves,

flowers, peels, or rinds, must be cut or shredded as small as possible. All kernels or almonds must be pounded into a paste in a mortar, a very small quantity of spirits being added at the time. The ingredients, whatever they are, should then be soaked in the spirit (spirits of wine or brandy) for a month in a warm place, shaking up the mixture every day. The spirit is then poured off, and water added (when directed in a recipe). After a few days more, the liquid is pressed out and mixed with the spirits ; sugar and colouring matter is added (see "Syrup," No. 1050), and the liquid is strained through a flannel bag. Good French brandy is always preferable even to the best spirits of wine.

1047. TO MAKE ANY KIND OF RATAFIA (Surrey)

The best fruits to use are red currants, black currants, raspberries, mulberries, or cherries. Press out two quarts of juice of the fruit, let it stand for twenty-four hours in a cold place, then skim it, and add two quarts of good brandy, two pounds of sugar, a few cloves, and a little cinnamon. Mix it well, and put it into a stone bottle, where it must stand, well corked, for a month. Then pour off and bottle it.

1048. RASPBERRY RATAFIA (Middlesex)

Stand two quarts of raspberry juice in a cold place for twenty-four hours. Then skim it, and mix in two quarts of good brandy, two pounds of sugar, and a little cinnamon and cloves. Put it in a stone bottle, and keep it well corked for a month, then pour off and bottle it.

1049. ANOTHER WAY

Take the juice of three pounds of raspberries (or strawberries) strain and filter it : boil it for a few minutes with one and half pounds of sugar.

1050. RATAFIA OF ROSES (Middlesex)

Infuse a quarter of a pound of rose leaves in a pint of lukewarm water ; let them lie for two days and then press them through a cloth ; add as much brandy as there may be infusion, and a thick syrup, made in the proportion of half a pound of sugar to a quart of the above liquid, and a little coriander seed, mace, and cinnamon ; let them infuse for a fortnight, and then filter.

1051. SYRUP FOR RATAFIAS, ETC. (Surrey)

To make a strong syrup, you merely add just as much water as will cover your sugar in the pan, and boil it gently for a long time, removing the scum as long as it rises. The stronger the syrup is to be, the longer it must simmer. When cool, put it by in bottles for use. When it is wanted to be very clear, you add beaten whites of eggs to the syrup while it is hot, and mix them well in, and strain through a jelly-bag. The straining is not absolutely necessary : a quicker method is used in France, as follows :

For ten bottles of any syrup, take seven pounds of sugar, break it into small bits, dissolve it in six pints of cold water, then filter it carefully. Meanwhile, mix your essences and colouring with five pints of good spirits of wine, and add the syrup by

small quantities at a time, stirring all the while ;
then filter the whole. This method does not give,
however, the oily appearance which is desirable in
liqueurs.

1052. RATAFIA (1822)

Boil equal quantities of gooseberries and sugar
into a thick jelly, over which a sufficient quantity of
white wine must be poured, and suffered to remain
for some time. Press out and filter the mixture, and
add half the quantity of brandy, with any spices
that may be agreeable.

1053. ROSOLIO (French)

Put one drachm of vanilla into about half a pint
of the spirit to be used. Let it stand a week, then
strain and filter it. Use this liquor with six drops
of neroli and five drops of attar of roses. Boil the
syrup before mixing, with the juice of six oranges
and one ounce of syrup of capillaire. Then filter
and mix with the spirit.

(The rosolio specially prepared for Louis XIV.,
said to be called thus from *ros solis*, dew of the sun,
was made with equal quantities of brandy and
Spanish wine, in which were infused angelica, anise,
fennel, citron, coriander, and sugar-candy, boiled
to a syrup in camomile water. Ed.)

1054. SLOE GIN (Essex)

Into one quart of best gin put one and a half
pints of ripe sloes (some of them bruised), three-
quarters of a pound of loaf sugar, and half an ounce
of bitter almonds (blanched and split). Cover the

vessel containing the cordial closely, and leave it six months, stirring the contents occasionally, then strain off the liquor and bottle for use.

1055. VESPETRO (French)

Take equal quantities of angelica seed, aniseed, fennel seed, and coriander seed. Put them in to steep in white brandy or spirits of wine for about a month. Shake the bottle from time to time. Then filter the infusion and add a mixture of strong syrup (about two-thirds) and spirit (about half), but do not drown the flavour with syrup, as this is a stomachic and medicinal cordial.

1056. ANOTHER WAY

Three ounces of angelica seed, two ounces of coriander seed, half an ounce each of aniseed and fennel seed, six ounces each of sliced oranges and lemons. Proceed as above.

1057. HUILE DE VIOLETTES (French)

Boil three ounces of dried violets for two minutes with water and sugar ; strain and filter, and add to the spirits and syrup.

CHAPTER XXI

INVALID AND CONVALESCENT COOKERY

NOTE.—For the fastidious invalid, if the truth be told, our robust predecessors did not take much care to cater. If an unhappy wight should suffer loss of appetite and turn with disgust from ordinary palatable food—well, it was unfortunate, but unavoidable. There were certain "possets" and broths and gruels provided for such unfit folk; but the real regard to sick fare is of comparatively recent growth; and hence the recipes under this heading are not numerous; some, indeed, are quite of modern date. Such as they are, they are peculiarly good, and the "Jaunemange" and "Salisbury Minced Beef" are worth their weight in gold, as countless convalescents can bear witness.

1058. ARROWROOT BLANCMANGE (Kent)

One pint of milk, sugar, cinnamon, and vanilla to taste, all boiled together; blend a tablespoonful of arrowroot with some cold milk, then pour it into the milk that is boiling, give it a few minutes' boil, and pour it into a shape.

1059. ARROWROOT JELLY (Middlesex)

Pound three bitter almonds, and put them with
the peel of a lemon into a large wineglassful of water,
and let them steep therein for four or five hours ;
then strain the liquid, and mix it with four tablespoonfuls of arrowroot, an equal quantity of lemon-
juice, and two tablespoonfuls of brandy; sweeten to
taste, and stir it over the fire until it becomes quite
thick. When cold, put it in jelly-glasses, and set by
in a cool place.

1060. "SALISBURY" MINCED BEEF FOR IN-
VALIDS OR CONVALESCENTS

One pound of lean rump steak (this will make
two meals). Remove all fat, skin, and gristle. Put
it three times through a mincer, and then into a
small saucepan, with just enough water to cover it,
and a little salt. When it turns from red to brown
(simmering very slowly and *never coming anywhere
near boiling*), it is done enough. Serve some in a
hot soup-dish, with bread or bread and butter.
The remainder can be reheated once, but not twice ;
if any is left the second time, it must be eaten cold.
To beat it with a fork while cooking, improves it.

1061. CHICKEN PANADA (Cheshire)

Cut up the meat from which chicken broth has
been made, pound it in a mortar if obtainable, or
roll it with a rolling-pin. Put it in a pan on the fire
with a little milk and salt ; stir it, but do not let it
boil. Add a few bread crumbs to thicken it; stir
in one whole egg to each quarter of a fowl. It may

be used either as spoon-meat when hot, or made into little balls and served in the chicken broth. It will keep good for some days.

1062. WHITE-OF-EGG FLIP (Surrey)

This is a doctor's recipe for a nourishing pick-me-up, of which a spoonful or two can be taken at odd moments. It has the advantage of utilising the whites of eggs left over from the Jaunemange. Beat three whites to a stiff froth ; add (for colour and flavour) a teaspoonful of good strawberry jam, and beat it well in ; lastly, beat in one dessert-spoonful of brandy. Brandy, by the way, should here be regarded purely as medicine, and as you would not willingly administer cheap medicine to an invalid, procure the best cognac that your means will allow. It pays in the long run.

1063. JAUNEMANGE (Hampshire)

Take one ounce of Swinborne's isinglass, put it into a jar or basin, pour half a pint of cold water over it, add the rind of a large lemon cut very thinly. Let it stand for at least ten minutes. Then add to it a quarter of a pound of loaf sugar, the juice of one and a half lemons, a tablespoonful of brandy, and a wine-glassful of sherry. If no sherry is added, put a little more water, the yolks of four fresh eggs well-beaten, and half a pint of boiling water. The whole to be very well mixed, care being taken that the eggs do not " break." Now stand the jar in a pan of boiling water, and let the jaunemange just *nearly* come to the boil ; it needs careful attention and stirring.

When the ingredients are quite melted, take out the lemon-peel. Lift the jaunemange out and stand it in a bowl of cold water to set, or in a cool place. Or pour it off, when a little cool, into a mould. This is an exceedingly nourishing and strengthening preparation, and can be taken at any time, a few teaspoonfuls being sufficient. It is so pleasant to the taste, and so unlike anything else, that the most fastidious invalid will hardly refuse it. In cases involving diarrhœa, the lemon-juice had better be omitted.

1064. BEEF JELLY (Surrey)

Take a small knuckle of veal, break it into small pieces, and let it soak two hours in two pints of cold water. Then boil it till reduced to a pint. Strain it. Take one pound of lean beef, remove all skin and fat, and scrape or finely mince it. Let it stand in a jar in one pint of cold water for one hour. Then cover the jar and put it in a saucepan of cold water, and let it warm very slowly till it simmers. Then strain it, add the veal stock and a little pepper and salt, and pour off into a mould to cool.

1065. BREAD JELLY (Kent, 1809)

Take a penny French roll, cut it in thin slices, and toast it a pale brown, boil it in a quart of water till it comes to a pint, then strain it, and add wine and sugar to your taste.

1066. CLARET JELLY (Kent)

Take one bottle of claret, ten ounces of loaf sugar, a one pound pot of red currant jelly, the peel and juice of one lemon, and a quarter of an ounce of best isinglass. Let this simmer for a few minutes, and add half a wineglassful of brandy, and strain through muslin into a mould.

1067. PORT WINE JELLY (Sussex)

One ounce of isinglass, one ounce of gum arabic, three ounces of sugar-candy, one pint of port wine. Soak the dry ingredients in the wine all night, then let all simmer for half an hour.

1068. PORT WINE JELLY (Kent, 1809)

One ounce of gum arabic, one ounce of isinglass, a little spice, boiled half an hour in a pint of cold water, then add a pint and a quarter of old port wine and sugar to your taste. Let it simmer a quarter of an hour, strain it off, and keep it for use. It may be taken cold or hot.

1069. RESTORATIVE JELLY (Kent, 1809)

Dissolve an ounce of isinglass in a quart of water, let it simmer gently till reduced to a pint, then add half a pound of fine loaf sugar. When dissolved, strain it off, and put it into a pudding-dish in the cellar till cold. To be taken in the quantity necessary to sweeten any liquid such as tea, etc.

1070. STRENGTHENING JELLY (Kent, 1809)

One ounce of best isinglass, one ounce of gum arabic, infused together in half a pint of (either) Tent, Mountain, or Calcavella, for twenty-four hours, then add one ounce of brown sugar-candy pulverised ;

27

these are to be simmered and (to prevent burning) must be constantly stirred, until the whole is dissolved. Strain it through a fine hair sieve, and when cold it becomes a stiff jelly. A piece the size of a large nutmeg to be taken two or three times a day, or at night, according as it agrees.

1071. PORT WINE LOZENGES (Kent, 1809)

Take two ounces of isinglass and half an ounce of gum arabic. Steep them all night in a pint of port wine ; then put them in a saucepan, with two ounces of brown sugar-candy and half a nutmeg grated. Simmer them together till quite dissolved, strain through a hair sieve, and pour on clean plates to harden. Cut it in pieces, and take a piece the size of a nutmeg three times a day.

INVALID BEVERAGES

1072. APPLE BARLEY-WATER (Cheshire)

Add to one pint of the above half a pound of apples, cut in slices, with the skin on, removing only the pips ; cut a lemon in slices, boil gently till the apples are done, and pass through a colander.

1073. APPLE TOAST-AND-WATER (Cheshire)

Bake an apple with a little brown sugar over it, and add to the toast-and-water. It will be ready in an hour. A little lemon or orange-peel is an improvement.

1074. AROMATIC BARLEY-WATER (Cheshire)

Take one quart of barley-water, boil it down to one-third. Add to it, while it is hot, a pint of sherry, one drachm of tincture of cinnamon, and one ounce of sugar. Three ounces of this can be taken two or three times a day. A good cordial.

1075. PEARL BARLEY-WATER (Cheshire)

Wash two ounces of pearl-barley well in cold water. Add about one and a half pints of water, a little lemon peel, and sugar to taste. Let it simmer, stirring it often till it is of a nice thickness. Strain and add lemon juice. A few sweet almonds beaten to a paste will give a pleasant flavour.

1076. BEEF TEA (Lancashire)

One pound of gravy beef, one pint of cold water, half a teaspoonful of salt. Shred meat finely, place in an earthenware jar, add the water and salt. Cover closely. Place jar in a saucepan of boiling water, or in the oven, and cook for three hours. Stir occasionally.

1077. GOOD COOLING DRINK (Cheshire)

Take half an ounce of cream of tartar, the strained juice of one lemon, two tablespoonfuls of honey, one quart of boiling water. Cover up till cold.

1078. IMPERIAL (Surrey)

Put two drachms of cream of tartar, the juice of one lemon, and a little peel, into a jug ; pour on them one quart of boiling water ; sweeten to taste. Stir, and cover close till cold.

1079. LIVELY IMPERIAL (Kent, 1809)

Two ounces of cream of tartar, two pounds of lump sugar, four lemons sliced. Put them in a pan. Two gallons of boiling water must be poured over the above. When near cold, add two dessert-spoonfuls of yeast. Let it stand two days, and then strain and bottle it. Cork it close, and in three days it will be fit for use.

1080. QUIET IMPERIAL (Kent, 1809)

Seven quarts of water, two ounces of cream of tartar, the peel of two or three lemons. Boil it just to simmer, then take it off, and pour it on a pound of sugar and let it stand till the next day.

1081. SAGO POSSET (Cheshire)

Boil three ounces of sago in a quart of water, till a mucilage is formed. Rub half an ounce of loaf sugar on the rind of a lemon, and put it, with a tea-spoonful of ginger tincture, into half a pint of sherry. Add to this the sago mucilage, and boil the whole for five minutes. This is an excellent cordial, where acute diseases (not of an inflammatory kind) have left the patient in a state of debility. A little may be taken at a time, every four or five hours

CHAPTER XXII

VARIOUS

THIS final section includes such recipes as do not fall with accuracy under any of the previous headings, but are too useful to leave out.

1082. BREAD CRUMBS FOR ROAST GAME (Surrey)

Put some stale white bread through a coarse sieve, and fry the crumbs in *fresh* butter, enough to saturate them well. Turn and stir them in the pan till they are a nice light brown, but not too brown ; drain them on a sieve before the fire.

1083. TO PRESERVE BUTTER (Ireland)

Take two parts of the best common salt, one part sugar, and one part saltpetre. Beat them up together, and blend the whole completely. Take one ounce of this composition for every sixteen ounces of butter. Work it well into the mass, and close it up for use. Butter thus cured requires to stand a month before it is begun to be used ; it will then be delicious.

1084. TO PRESERVE BUTTER FIRM IN SUMMER (Kent)

Get a large bowl, and fill it with silver sand, leaving a hole in the centre, in which stand a smaller bowl with your butter in. Keep the sand just moist with cold water, and your butter will remain firm in the hottest weather.

1085. RICE FOR CURRY (Middlesex)

The rice to be served with curry should be of the best quality, and should be washed perfectly clean ; it may be then boiled in a bag, or as follows :— Boil half a pound of rice for about twenty minutes in one quart of cold water, then put it to drain in a sieve, after which dry it before the fire to get rid of all superfluous moisture, stirring from time to time, and serve very hot.

1086. CURRY POWDER (Kent, 1809)

Coriander seed, six ounces ; cummin seed, one and half ounces ; fenugreek seed, one and a half ounces ; turmeric root, three ounces. To be made into a fine powder, with the addition of cayenne to your taste.

1087. CURRY POWDER (Middlesex)

Pound six ounces of coriander seed, three ounces of black pepper, and one and a half ounces of fenugreek seed, one ounce of cummin seed, three ounces of turmeric, and three-quarters of an ounce of cayenne : sift through muslin, and dry it thoroughly for several hours before the fire, stirring repeatedly ;

then bottle, and cork very tightly. If the powder be made for the use of persons who have lived much in India, and been accustomed to eat curry there, the quantity of cayenne should be increased to an ounce, or even one and a quarter ounces. Another preparation of curry is made by omitting the coriander seed, doubling the quantity of turmeric, and substituting for the coriander two ounces of ginger : in fact, if turmeric and cayenne be made the basis of the powder, the other ingredients may be varied according to taste.

1088. IRISH FADGE

Mix a quarter of a pint of milk and three ounces of butter together over the fire. Then take four ounces of whole brown meal—(wheaten meal) and pour in the milk and butter to a hole in the middle of the meal. *Knead it well* and roll it out to about three-quarters of an inch thick. Bake on a griddle, turning it often to prevent burning. Time, one hour.

1089. MOCK ICE (Middlesex)

You can make a sort of mock ice, by mixing half a pint of water, in which rather more than a quarter of an ounce of isinglass has been boiled, with a pint of cream and a sufficient quantity of sugar, and the juice of any fruit ; the mixture must be made before the solution of isinglass is quite cold. If you have any ice at hand, this mixture can be set in a mould in some vessel, and surrounded with ice ; or if there be none, put it in the coldest situation possible. The solid appearance given to the mixture, when cold, by the isinglass, causes this to be a pretty good imitation of an ice, if it can be made quite cold.

1090. LIME WATER FOR PRESERVING EGGS
(Yorkshire)

Take one pound of stone lime, two handfuls of salt, two gallons of water. The water to be boiling, and poured upon the lime and salt, and to be stirred every day. In a fortnight it is ready for use. Be careful the eggs are not cracked.

1091. MUSTARD (Seventeenth Century)

Dry your mustard seed very well, then beat it by little and little at a time in a mortar, and sift it. Then put the powder in a gallipot, and wet it very well with vinegar ; put in a whole onion peeled but not cut, a little pepper and salt, and a lump of sugar.

1092. ANOTHER WAY

Take horseradish roots and make them very dry in an oven, then beat them to powder. And when you would use any, wet it with wine vinegar, and so it will rather be better than the other.

1093. MUSTARD (Surrey)

If mustard be mixed, first with the merest drop of water, and then with tarragon vinegar, it will have a pleasant pungency and piquancy which gives a relish to every dish. This is half the secret of French mustard—which is also much milder than ours, and occasionally, I believe, has a dash of flour put in, beside other ingredients.

1094. PORRIDGE (Ireland)

Irish porridge is particularly good, being made of specially fragrant oatmeal. Boil a quart of water with a large teaspoonful of salt in it. When boiling, pour in one and a half teacupfuls of meal (more or less according to taste), *without stirring at all*, and keep it gently boiling twenty to thirty minutes ; then stir well, and serve in bowl or porridge plate (like small soup plate), very hot. It should be taken with cold milk, and, if liked, a small piece of butter in the middle of the plate. A double saucepan should be used. In England, sugar is used, and stirring. There is no need for the latter, as, if not stirred at first, the porridge will not burn, just like rice.

1095. POT-POURRI (1822)

Take one pound each of orange flowers and of common rose leaves, half a pound of the flowers of red pinks, leaves and flowers of myrtle ; flowers of musk roses, leaves of thyme, lavender, rosemary, sage, camomile, melilot, hyssop, sweet basil, and balm, two ounces of each ; two or three handfuls of jessamine flowers, a large handful of lemon rinds, cut as thin as possible ; the same quantity of rinds of small green oranges (tangerines), and fifteen or twenty laurel leaves. Put them all into a well-headed earthen jar, with half a pound of bay salt, and stir the whole carefully with a wooden spatula, or spoon, twice a day for a month. Then add Florentine white orris and benzoin, of each twelve ounces ; powdered cloves and cinnamon, two ounces, of each ; mace, storax, calamus aromaticus, and cypress, of each one ounce; lemon-coloured sandal, and long sweet cypress, of each six drachms. Stir all together, and if the proportions be carefully attended to, according to the above directions, a most delightful compound of fine odours will be obtained, in which no one scent will predominate, while the fragrance of the whole will remain unimpaired for a great number of years.

1096. ROSE-WATER (Surrey)

Gather the rose-leaves very dry, add a quart of water to every four pounds of petals, and place them with a handful of salt, in a closely stoppered vessel. Leave them so for three days, stirring them well at least once a day : at the end of that time, distil the mixture, take care to line the bottom of the still with a sufficient amount of clean straw to keep the flowers from burning, and leave a space of at least one-third in the still. For every twelve pounds of flowers you put in, add six quarts of water ; and when, for every twelve pounds, three quarts have been drawn off, stop distilling. A very much stronger rose-water is made thus : Take thirty pounds of rose-leaves, gathered before sunrise, crush them in a large mortar, and put them into a jar, with four pounds of common salt, in alternate layers of roses and sprinkled salt. Press them down well, and cover the jar so that no perfume can escape. When they have macerated for twelve days, distil them with a sharp heat, protecting them carefully as described above. The result of this distillation will be small in quantity, but rich in quality.

1097. HINTS ON STORAGE (Surrey)

It is advisable to keep all groceries in closed tins
or jars, not in paper or cardboard : the drier articles
in tins ; the moister, such as raisins, etc., in jars.
It is essential that all store-provisions should be
kept covered, otherwise they accumulate dust and
germs, and become really unfit for use, even though
they may not appear so. This is a fact which no
servant can get into her head, and which requires
constant attention.

Stock should be boiled (not merely warmed up)
every day. Dripping should be examined and
clarified at least twice a week in warm weather.
Pieces of bread should be utilised, so far as possible,
day by day ; the crumb can be sieved, dried in the
oven, and kept in a closed tin for use in frying fish,
etc., but it will not keep too long. The crust can be
soaked overnight, when sufficient has been collected, for use in a bread pudding. Those who keep
fowls, or pigs, have no need of instruction in the
disposal of their odds and ends.

MADE GRAVIES AND SAUCES

A few drops of Lea & Perrins' Sauce make an
excellent flavouring for soups, stews, gravies, minced
meat, etc., and harmonise well with any other flavouring agent that may be used.

FISH SAUCES

A good proprietory sauce should always be kept in
the house. One that goes well with any kind of fish
is Lea & Perrins', which has the advantage of being an
all-round sauce, suitable for hot and cold meats, soups,
stews, etc.

PRINTED IN GREAT BRITAIN BY
HAZELL, WATSON AND VINEY, LD.,
LONDON AND AYLESBURY.

Lightning Source UK Ltd.
Milton Keynes UK
UKHW010207250220
359245UK00001B/87